HTML
Manual of Style

HTML
MANUAL OF STYLE

A Clear, Concise Reference for Hypertext
Markup Language (Including HTML5)

Fourth Edition

Larry Aronson

✦✦Addison-Wesley

Upper Saddle River, NJ • Boston • Indianapolis • San Francisco
New York • Toronto • Montreal • London • Munich • Paris • Madrid
Cape Town • Sydney • Tokyo • Singapore • Mexico City

Many of the designations used by manufacturers and sellers to distinguish their products are claimed as trademarks. Where those designations appear in this book, and the publisher was aware of a trademark claim, the designations have been printed with initial capital letters or in all capitals.

The author and publisher have taken care in the preparation of this book, but make no expressed or implied warranty of any kind and assume no responsibility for errors or omissions. No liability is assumed for incidental or consequential damages in connection with or arising out of the use of the information or programs contained herein.

The publisher offers excellent discounts on this book when ordered in quantity for bulk purchases or special sales, which may include electronic versions and/or custom covers and content particular to your business, training goals, marketing focus, and branding interests. For more information, please contact:

U.S. Corporate and Government Sales
800-382-3419
corpsales@pearsontechgroup.com

For sales outside the United States, please contact:

International Sales
international@pearson.com

Visit us on the Web: informit.com/aw

Library of Congress Cataloging-in-Publication Data:

Aronson, Larry.
  HTML manual of style : a clear, concise reference for hypertext markup language (including HTML5) / Larry Aronson.
      p. cm.
  ISBN 978-0-321-71208-0 (pbk. : alk. paper)
  1. Hypertext systems. 2. HTML (Document markup language) I. Title.
  QA76.76.H94A7624 2010
  006.7'4--dc22
10 9 8 7 6 5 4 3 2   2010031013

ISBN-13: 978-0-321-71208-0
ISBN-10: 0-321-71208-0
Text printed in the United States on recycled paper at RR Donnelley in Crawfordsville, IN.

Editor-in-Chief
Mark Taub

Acquisitions Editor
Trina MacDonald

Development Editor
Songlin Qiu

Managing Editor
Kristy Hart

Project Editor
Anne Goebel

Copy Editor
Gayle Johnson

Indexer
Erika Millen

Proofreader
Apostrophe Editing Services

Technical Reviewers
Elliotte Rusty Harold
Benjamin Schupak

Publishing Coordinator
Olivia Basegio

Interior Designer
Bumpy Design

Cover Designer
Anne Jones

*This book is dedicated to my wife, Heidi Cohen,
a much better writer than I am, who provided encouragement
and inspiration throughout the project.*

*It was also written in fond memory of people who were
major forces in my life, especially my parents,
Manny and Dorothy Aronson, and my
friends Andy Cohen, Bobo Lewis, Milan Stitt, and
Lynne Thigpen.*

CONTENTS AT A GLANCE

TABLE OF CONTENTS

ACKNOWLEDGMENTS

I would like to acknowledge and express my gratitude to my acquisitions editor, Trina MacDonald, whose patient guidance and understanding made it possible for me to have fun working on the project despite the pressures of deadlines. I would also like to thank my development editor, Songlin Qiu, who caught my errors and turned around chapters with lightning speed, and Elliotte Rusty Harold, who checked my facts and, as mentioned in the preface, started the whole process. Finally, I am deeply grateful to my wife, Heidi Cohen, who helped me find my writing voice and contributed significantly to my knowledge of online marketing and search engine optimization.

ABOUT THE AUTHOR

Larry Aronson grew up in Evanston, Illinois, graduated with honors from Evanston Township High School, and attended the University of Illinois in Champaign-Urbana. Before graduating with a BA in computer science and a BS in psychology, he worked two summers as an assistant systems engineer with IBM's Chicago manufacturing branch office.

After graduation, Aronson visited New York City, fell in love, and decided to live there. He worked at a number of jobs in New York's radio, theater, and recording industries before returning to computers working for the user services department of Columbia University's Center for Computing Activities. Four years later, with faculty status and postgraduate work in electrical engineering and computer science, but little money, he left academia to work for Boeing Computer Services, starting as a technical sales representative and working his way up to tech manager of BCS's New York office.

Aronson left Boeing to start his own business as an independent consultant after seeing his first personal computer. His first client was the CBS News election unit, where he wrote the House Race Analysis Model and other components of their election system. His other major client was the Product Safety Information Systems division of Mobil Oil Company. Aronson was the principal programmer responsible for migrating Mobil's safety data publishing systems to a relational database management system and to graphical, full-screen, data-entry and display technology.

In late 1993, Aronson downloaded Mosaic from his alma mater and discovered the World Wide Web. He became active in the newsgroups and discussion lists devoted to Web authoring and publishing, and in mid-1994, wrote the first book on Web publishing, *HTML Manual of Style*, for Ziff-Davis Press. The first edition went through five printings and seven foreign languages, and the second edition, *HTML3 Manual of Style*, was equally successful. By 1995, he was teaching HTML around the country and online, conducting the inaugural classes for Ziff-Davis University on CompuServe.

Aronson lives in a Manhattan loft in the heart of "Silicon Alley." He devotes his time to building Web applications for individuals and small businesses, helping people work and live on the World Wide Web. He was a founder of the World Wide Web Artists' Consortium, a board member of the New York Software Industries Association, and a founding member of the Social Media Club.

PREFACE

WHAT THIS BOOK IS ABOUT AND WHY YOU'LL FIND IT USEFUL

This book is about using HTML to put your stuff on the Web. HTML (Hyper-Text Markup Language) is the language that tells a web browser what to do with the text, images, and other media—the stuff—you want others to see. There are good ways to use these tools, and there are bad ways. Web browsers are smart application programs. They can take badly written HTML and still present a respectable-looking web page. However, there are still very good reasons for learning how to write good markup. This book is about creating web pages that

▸ Are pleasing to look at and fun to play with

▸ Are friendly to search engine robots

▸ Are easy to update and maintain over time

The Web can be understood through a number of metaphors that allow us to think of a website as a place within a realm we explore. We even socialize within its "spaces." But that is just a useful illusion. Under the hood, the Web is not like that at all. Chapter 1 introduces the client/server technology that web authors and developers use to create the illusion. Even if you consider yourself an experienced web user, Chapter 1 is worth skimming.

Chapter 2 is all about the elements of HTML, including some of the more interesting HTML5 additions. It has many examples illustrating how to mark up documents semantically so that the resulting web page provides all the right information to readers, both human and robot, and that it is easy to update.

Our first obligation in design is to please ourselves. With good document structure, a website can be easily styled in a consistent manner across all pages. Chapter 3 explains, with many examples, how to use Cascading Style Sheet (CSS) statements to apply styling to document elements and create people-pleasing web pages.

Chapter 4 is about using HTML as a contributor to other websites that accept marked-up content. Five examples are given: blogging, Google Docs, eBay selling, Wikipedia editing, and HTML email.

Despite the many options for putting content online, sometimes your organization's objectives or your personal goals dictate building and running your own website. Chapter 5 explores many of the issues involved, including website structure, organization and navigation, and search engine optimization.

At the end of this book you'll find quick-reference guides to HTML elements and CSS properties, including the new elements and properties in the HTML5 and CSS3 draft specifications. There is no list of references to resources. The W3C's website at w3.org and Wikipedia's articles on HTML and CSS should cover anything from a technical perspective. You know how to search the Web for other guides, tutorials, and examples.

Finally, this book is about you, because you are changing from a person who uses the Web for information and services to one who contributes to the Web. People are discovering that the joys of online shopping pale in comparison to the pleasures of creative collaboration. There is a place on this new Web for your stuff, and this book is about how to create content with style. I hope you will find it useful.

What's Not Covered in This Book and Why Not

This book is not intended to be a complete reference guide to HTML5. Such a book would be at least three times larger than this one and would be out of date shortly after publication. Web technologies are changing fast. The information in this book is based on the World Wide Web Consortium's (W3C) draft recommendation for a proposed HTML5 standard. Although that might sound a bit tenuous, much of the draft specification has already been adopted by our favorite browsers (even though certainly much will change by the time the standard is officially approved). That being the case, I don't claim to be an authority on HTML5, only an author of a book on HTML5.

Along with HTML and CSS, JavaScript plays a part in some of this book's examples. Teaching JavaScript is way beyond the scope of this book, but it is included for two reasons. First, the HTML5 specification formalizes the behavior of document elements in response to user actions using JavaScript syntax and methods. Second, JavaScript libraries, such as jQuery, provide rich new vocabularies of element behaviors that previously were unavailable to web authors and developers.

Other technologies play an important part in the operation of some websites, but they are not really discussed in this book. If you want to learn about using Microsoft's Silverlight technology or Adobe's Flash platform to develop web pages, you've reading the wrong book. As a freelance developer, I tend to favor tools that are free and community-supported. It is not that I think the tools I use are superior to these other technologies; I just have never used them, and I don't have a basis of comparison.

How This Book Happened and What's to Come

The World Wide Web was born more than 20 years ago on the border of Switzerland. When I first became aware of the Web, I was working as a consultant for one of those large Wall Street investment firms that no longer exist. It was the fall of 1993, and I was converting a mainframe-based system for modeling mortgage-backed derivatives to run on a minicomputer. I was in the office of the network administrator, whom I had become friends with, and he was showing off a cool application he had recently downloaded from the University of Illinois' FTP site. It was called Mosaic. My life was about to change, and I was ready for it.

At the time, I was already into the world of hypertext applications as an avid fan and user of Apple Computer's HyperCard application. I had created a number of "stacks" (which is what HyperCard programs were called) for myself and others. I kept up with the field by participating in the Usenet news-group, alt.hypertext, and local discussion groups on Panix, an early Internet service provider (ISP) based in New York City.

I immediately saw the potential of Mosaic and the Web in its seamless integration of anonymous File Transfer Protocol (FTP) and hypertext navigation. Prior to the availability of Mosaic, to read a particular document, first you had to know where that document was on the Internet. Then you logged in to that FTP server, downloaded the file, and opened it for reading. Not only did Mosaic automate these intermediate steps, it also helped you find the next document you were interested in.

It was an exciting time. Dozens of new websites were appearing every week. Updated versions of the web browsers available then—Mosaic, MacWeb, WinWeb, and Arena—were released frequently, supporting more HTML markup elements and new authoring abilities, such as centered text and inline images. Every day, new techniques were discovered and shared in newsgroup discussions and at usergroup meetings.

In the early summer of 1994, shortly after the U.S. government allowed the Internet to go commercial, I was contacted by another frequent newsgroup contributor, Clay Shirky. He asked if I would be interested in meeting his publisher, who was looking for a knowledgeable author to write a book about HTML. Clay had other commitments, so I became the author of the first book on Web publishing. Clay is an excellent writer. His books *Voices from the Net*, *Here Comes Everybody*, and *Cognitive Surplus* are must-reads for anyone looking to explore the cultural impact of new technologies.

The first edition of this book came out at the end of 1994, and a second edition, *HTML3 Manual of Style*, was published a year later.[1] Fast-forward 14 years to the fall of 2009, and I'm attending meetups and blogging about HTML5. Another author of programming books, Elliotte Rusty Harold, emails me, wondering if I would be interested in talking to his publisher about redoing *HTML Manual of Style*. Talks led to a formal book proposal and a contract, and now I'm an author again.

In reviewing the second edition, I came across this paragraph in the Preface:

> This is a book in the middle. The first edition was written just before HTML2 was finalized. Today, HTML is in the middle of the transition to level 3. The Web itself is moving from an academic to a commercial focus, and yours truly is in the middle of a career change from programmer/analyst to author/lecturer. Some of the topics covered herein are illustrated using products that were still in beta testing, which means that my best guess today may not accurately describe where the Web will be tomorrow. This book will get you started in Web publishing; the rest of your education will come online.

The sense of that paragraph is true again today. The Web is undergoing a major technological upgrade as it expands from its commercial focus to encompass and shape our social activities. Support for the emerging HTML5 and CSS3 specifications by the principal browser makers are making it possible for Web authors and developers to create exciting new websites and applications. It is safe to say that the Web will change over the next couple of years more than it has in the last decade. That excitement is also what this book is about.

---

1. A third edition, *HTML3.2 Manual of Style*, was published in 1997 without my participation after ZD Press was acquired by a larger publishing company. So technically, this book is the fourth edition of *HTML Manual of Style*.

HTML and the Web

HTML is the framework of the Web. This chapter describes how the Web works and provides a bit of Web history for context. You will learn about the client/server architecture of the Web and how it is hyperlinked. I'll present the Web Bestiary of acronyms and definitions and discuss the philosophy and implications of HTML5.

Although this chapter is about the Web and HTML, it actually contains very little HTML. If you want to get right into learning the HTML language, skip this chapter and go to the next. You can come back here later to help consolidate what you have learned.

HTML: THE LANGUAGE OF THE WEB

HyperText Markup Language (HTML) is the language of the Web. If you could listen to the conversation between your computer and the websites you visit, you would hear HTML spoken. **Web servers** accept requests from your browser as you visit and interact with the sites they host. In reply, the servers return marked-up content that your browser formats into the web page you see. Web servers also send requests to each other, gathering and exchanging data that power search engines and make a rich variety of social and commercial transactions possible.

HTML is not a programming language like C, Perl, or Ruby. HTML is a semantic language for marking up text. The markup provides a description of the content that Web browsers use to construct the corresponding web page.

Links are defined in HTML. This ability to have active references in a document to other documents, no matter where they are physically located, is very powerful. All of the Web's resources are addressable using a Uniform Resource Locator (URL). Any information can be easily located and linked with related content, creating frictionless connectivity.

The Web hosts many protocols and practices, but HTML is the foundation, providing the basic language to mark up text content into a structured document by describing the roles and attributes of its various elements. A companion technology, **Cascading Style Sheets (CSS)**, lets you select document elements and apply styling rules for presentation. CSS rules can be mixed into the HTML code or can reside in external files that can be employed across an entire website. This keeps content creators and site designers from stepping all over each other's work. HTML describes the page's content elements, and CSS tells the browser how they should look (or sound.) The browser can override the CSS instructions or ignore them.

Example 1.1 creates a very simple web page. You can copy this HTML code into a plain text file on your computer and open it in any browser. Give it a filename ending in the extension .html.

Example 1.1: HTML for a very simple web page

```
<!DOCTYPE html>
<html>
<head>
  <title>Example 1.1</title>
  <style type="text/css">
    h1 { text-align: center; }
  </style>
</head>

<body>
  <h1>Hello World Wide Web</h1>
  <p>
    Welcome to the first of many webpages.
    I promise they will get more interesting than this.
  </p>
</body>
</html>
```

The code in Example 1.1 (shown in boldface) consists of two parts: a document *body* containing the page's content, preceded by a head section that contains information about the document. In this example, the head section contains the document's title and a CSS style rule to center the page's heading. The body consists of a level 1 heading followed by a paragraph. The result should look something like Figure 1.1.

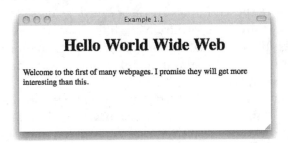

Figure 1.1: A simple web page

This brings up a fundamental principle about how the Web works: Web authors should not make assumptions about their readers, the characteristics of their display devices, or their formatting preferences. This is especially important with mobile Web users and people with visual disabilities. A Web author or developer shouldn't even assume that a site visitor is human! Websites are constantly visited by automated programs that gather and catalog information about the Web. The general term user agent is used to describe any software application or program that can talk to a web server. A modern website regards visits from all user agents with the same importance as human visitors using Web browsers. The best approach is to keep the HTML simple so that it provides a semantic description of the various content elements and leaves the presentation details to the reader.

The other major player on the Web programming team is **JavaScript**, a programming language that runs inside a browser and manipulates HTML page elements in response to user actions and other events. There are other scripting languages besides JavaScript, but it is the most popular. Also, JavaScript syntax and terms are used in the HTML5 specification. Like CSS, JavaScript code can be embedded within the HTML source code of a web page or can be imported from a separate file. User agents other than browsers generally ignore JavaScript and other embedded executable code. It can be dangerous for robots.

Robots?!

 **Robots** are a very important class of Web user. They are automated computer programs that run on Internet servers and visit web pages the same way people do using a browser. But instead of presenting the page, the robot analyzes it, stores information about the page in a database, and decides what page to visit next using that information. This is how Google, Yahoo!, Bing, and other search engines work. Other robots perform similar data collection for marketing and academic purposes. Robots are often called "spiders" because of how they seem to "crawl" over the Web from one link to the next. Also, there are malicious robots. These automatic programs leave spam comments on blogs or look for security loopholes to gain control of resources with which they should not be messing. *Bad robots!*

When creating content for the Web, you generally are not concerned with any of this. Most of the HTML structure that deals with browsers, robots, and widgets is supplied by the Web editing software you use or by server-side scripts and template systems. If you are editing content directly online, all you need to understand is how to mark up the content with simple HTML elements. Web developers—that is, programmers as opposed to authors—need to fully understand how these three principal components—HTML, CSS, and scripting—work together to form the framework of the Web (see Figure 1.2).

Figure 1.2: The three components of a web page

By the way, did I mention that all of this is essentially *free*? It is free in two senses of the word. It's free because there is no acquisition cost, and free because you can use it for your own purposes. With only minor limitations, all the HTML, CSS, and scripting that go into a Web page are available for you to examine, copy, and reuse. **Tim Berners-Lee**, the inventor of HTML, the URL, and the HTTP protocol that web servers and user agents use to talk to each other, put all these components into the public domain. Working at CERN, the European Center for Nuclear Research, he was trying to find a better way for large teams of researchers, working in different countries with different word processors, to quickly publish research papers. Patent rights and Nobel Prizes were at stake. In a post to the alt.hypertext newsgroup on August 6, 1991, which was effectively the Web's birth announcement, Berners-Lee wrote:

> The WWW project was started to allow high energy physicists to share data, news, and documentation. We are very interested in spreading the web to other areas, and having gateway servers for other data. Collaborators welcome!

Twenty years later, Berners-Lee is still very much involved in the evolution of the Web as head of the **World Wide Web Consortium (W3C)**. I stress "evolution" here to point out that, while the Web has transformed society, freeing us to work and play in a global sea of information, a lot of that happened by accident. HTML is still a work in progress.

A BIT OF WEB HISTORY

The early Web was text only—without images or colors—and browsers worked in line mode. In other words, you cursor-keyed your way through page links sequentially, like browsing on a low-end cell phone. It was not until 1993 that a graphical browser called **Mosaic** was made available from the University of Illinois National Center for Supercomputing Applications (NCSA) in Champaign-Urbana, Illinois. Mosaic was easy enough to install and use on Windows, Macintosh, and UNIX computers.

Mosaic was written by a group of graduate students—principally, Marc Andreessen and Eric Bina. They built Mosaic because they were excited by the possibilities of hypertext and were dissatisfied by the browsers available at the time. They were supposed to be working on their master's projects.

Mosaic was the progenitor of all modern browsers. It displayed inline images, multiple font families, weights, and styles, and it supported a pointing device (a mouse). Distribution of the technology and Mosaic trademarks was managed for the NCSA by the Spyglass Corporation and was licensed by Microsoft, which rewrote the source code and called it **Internet Explorer**.

After graduating from the University of Illinois, Andreessen teamed up with Dr. Jim Clark to form Netscape Corporation. Dr. Clark was the former CEO of Silicon Graphics, Inc., whose sexy, powerful graphics computers/workstations revolutionized Hollywood moviemaking. The **Netscape Navigator** browser introduced major innovations and became extremely popular because Netscape Corp. did something quite astounding for the software industry at the time—it gave away Navigator! At its peak, Netscape had captured close to 90% of the browser market.

In 1994, something wonderful happened. Vice President **Al Gore**, as chairman of the Clinton administration's Reinventing Government program, arranged for the National Science Foundation (NSF) to sell the Internet to a consortium of telecommunications companies. This ended the NSF's strict "no commercial use" policy and gave birth to the dotcom era and jokes about Al Gore inventing the Internet. In mid-1994 there were 2,738 websites. By the end of that year there were more than 10,000.[1]

From the beginning, competition to commercialize the Internet was fierce. In the mid-1990s, the tech community was abuzz about the "browser wars" as browser makers threw dozens of extra features into their software, adding many new elements to HTML that appealed to their respective markets. Netscape added features that appealed to graphic designers, including support for jpeg images, page background colors, and a controversial FONT tag that allowed Web designers to specify text sizes and colors. Microsoft bundled Internet Explorer into its Windows operating system and tied Web publishing into its Microsoft Office product line. These moves resulted in considerable legal troubles for Microsoft. These problems lasted until 2001, when the U.S. government suddenly dropped its antimonopoly suit against the corporation in the first days of George W. Bush's presidency.

 HOTJAVA Other companies introduced browsers with interesting ideas but never captured any significant market share from Netscape and Microsoft. Arena, an HTML3 test bed browser written by Dave Raggett of Hewlett-Packard (HP), introduced support for tables, text flow around images, and inline mathematical expressions. Sun Microsystems came out with a browser named **HotJava** that generated a lot of interest. It was written in **Java**, a programming language that Sun developed originally for the purpose of controlling TV set-top boxes. Sun repurposed the language for the Internet with the dream of turning the browser into a platform for small, interactive applications called applets that would run in a virtual Java machine in your PC. Sun put Java into the public domain to encourage its adoption. This allowed Microsoft to make and market its own version of the language. Microsoft's Java was sufficiently different from Sun's version to make using applets (not to mention writing them) difficult. Although the Java language eventually gained widespread use in building in-house corporate applications, HotJava died along with Sun's Internet dreams.

---

1. Wikipedia: http://en.wikipedia.org/wiki/List_of_websites_founded_before_1995

On a related note, a company called **WebTV Networks** produced a low-cost Internet appliance and service for consumers to browse the Web and do email on their TV sets using a wireless keyboard and remote control. Despite funding difficulties and an on-again/off-again relationship with Sony Corporation that almost killed the project, WebTV succeeded in bringing the Web and email to nearly a million customers seeking to avoid the cost and complexity of personal computer ownership.

To illustrate how weird Web-related events can get, according to Wikipedia, WebTV was for a brief time classified as a military weapon by the U.S. government and was banned from export because it used strong encryption. In 1997, Microsoft bought WebTV and rebranded it as MSN TV to expand its Web offering. Without marketing the service or servicing its customers, MSN TV died a few years later. But the WebTV technology survived, eventually resurfacing in Microsoft's **Xbox** gaming console.

One of my favorite Web browsers was **Virtual Places**, created by an Israeli company, Ubique. Virtual Places combined Web browsing with Internet chat software and enabled collaborative Web surfing. It turned any web page into a virtual chat room where you and other visitors were represented by avatars—small personal icons that you could move around the page. Whatever you typed in a floating window would appear in a cartoon balloon over your avatar's head. It had a "tour bus" feature that allowed a teacher, for example, to take a group of students to websites around the world and back.

Unfortunately, the server overhead in keeping open connections and tracking avatar positions kept Virtual Places from expanding as the number of websites exploded. At the time, Netscape was updating Navigator every few weeks. Because Ubique couldn't keep up, nobody used Virtual Places as their default Web browser. AOL bought Ubique for no apparent reason and sold it to IBM a few years later. IBM used some of the technology in its software for corporate communications and collaboration. Virtual Places died during the **dotcom crash** at the start of the twenty-first century, but the avatars survived.

While Java was hot, Netscape developed JavaScript, a scripting language that ran in the Netscape Navigator browser and allowed Web developers to add dynamic behaviors to the HTML elements of a web page. Despite having the same first four letters, JavaScript and the Java programming language are quite different. It is suspected that Netscape changed the name from LiveScript just because of the buzz around Java. Superficially, the code looks similar because both are object-oriented programming (OOP) systems and have similar syntax.

America Online (AOL) acquired Netscape in 1998, and the browser's source code was made public. Eventually, this became the foundation on which the Mozilla organization built the Firefox browser. Other companies followed suit, and over the ensuing years, a variety of graphical browsers based on Netscape came to market. Microsoft's **Internet Explorer (IE)** browser improved with each new version and eventually became the most popular browser due to its bundling with the Windows operating system.

The browser wars ended with the dotcom crash, and manufacturers began to bring their browsers into compliance with emerging standards. Under the W3C's guidance, HTML language development slowed and stabilized on an HTML4 specification. The use of CSS was promoted to give Web developers finer control over typography and page layout over a much wider selection of devices. HTML attributes and actions (more about these later) were generalized. The HTML syntax was modified slightly to conform to **XML (eXtensible Markup Language)**, and a transition path was provided to the merging of the two in the **XHTML** specification.

The way HTML source code looks has changed. Currently, most websites are written to the HTML4 and/or XHTML standards, in which valid markup element and attribute names are written using lowercase letters. By contrast, a web page written to the HTML3 standard is filled with names written in all uppercase letters. This convention emerged from early website developers, who had to write HTML without the benefit of text editors that provided color syntax highlighting. Using uppercase names provided contrast that distinguished the markup from the content.

More importantly, the ways in which content creators, software developers, and people in general use the Web has evolved dramatically. This change is encapsulated in the term **Web 2.0**. Although this suggests a new version of the World Wide Web, it does not refer to any new technical specifications. Instead, it refers to the changing nature of web pages. The features and functionality that characterize a Web 2.0 site are a matter of debate. Web 2.0 is better understood as simply a recognition that today's websites do new things with newer technology than yesterday's websites.

Many of these changes have come about due to the embrace of **open source** as a philosophy of design and development by the tech community. Much of the software that powers the Web is nonproprietary. It is freely available for people to use, copy, modify, and redistribute as they please. Open-source development has greatly reduced the cost of software development while increasing its availability, stability, and ease of use. Equally interesting is that the Web is self-documenting. Information about what is on the Web, how it is organized, and how it can be used is everywhere on the Web.

HYPERTEXT CONTENT AND ONLINE MEDIA

Content is everything. Online, it is HTML markup that tells your browser what that content means and how to present it to you. The concept of markup comes from traditional print publishing, in which a writer supplies the content, which an editor then marks up with instructions for the printer, specifying the layout and typography of the work. The printer, following the markup, type-sets the pages and reproduces copies for distribution.

With the Web and HTML, the author and the editor are often the same person. The work, or content, lives in a linked set of HTML files on a web server. The content is not distributed in discrete copies, as in the print publication model. Instead, copies of web pages are served in response to user requests. The information returned by the web server is processed by the user's browser to display a web page in a window or tab.

Often the content of a web page does not reside in an HTML file but is generated dynamically by the web server from information stored in a database, using templates to produce **web pages**. It is common for web page to encompass resources from other servers. That is, a request a browser sends to a web server may result in that web server making requests of other servers. These distinctions, however, are immaterial to the user's browser. It just downloads whatever the web server provides without caring how that content was created or who marked it up.

The technological concepts are simple: an open exchange of data and information about that data (metadata), including content and markup. As a connected world of places to visit, the Web is more than a metaphor. The language of the Web, including verbs such as *surf, browse, visit, search, explore*, and *navigate*, and nouns such as *site, home page, destination, gateway*, and *forum*, creates a very real experience of being someplace.

UNIFORM RESOURCE LOCATORS (URLs)

How does a browser know what to request of a web server? How does your browser know which web server, of the millions in the world, to ask? The answer, as you've probably guessed, is links! A **link** is a reference, embedded in the content of a document, to another resource on the Web. This is the essence of hypertext media.

The destination of a link is given by a string of characters called a **Uniform Resource Locator (URL)**. A special bit of HTML markup, called the anchor element, makes this portion of text, or that image or those buttons, "active." When you click one, your browser requests a new document from the web server indentified in the URL.

In addition to links, URLs are used in HTML to load images, video, and other online media into a page; to apply stylesheets and create pop-up windows; and to specify where form input should be sent. In HTML a URL can be in partial form, often called a relative URL. A browser fills in any missing parts of the URL from the corresponding parts of the current page's URL to create a full URL. This neat trick makes it easy to relocate a website. A full URL starts with the protocol to use for the transfer. The URL design is universal and can reference other Internet things besides Web resources. We will go into more detail later. For now, suffice it to say that the Web's protocol is HyperText Transport Protocol, abbreviated as "http" or "https" when used in a URL. The "s" means that a secure (that is, encrypted) connection is made to the web server so that nobody eavesdropping on the conversation between your browser and the web server can steal anything important, such as a credit card number. Otherwise, the https protocol works the same way as http. By having secure transactions at the protocol level, web page authors and developers can write HTML that works in either environment.

The web server address comes after the protocol designation. Following that, the path to the file or resource is given. (There's more, but this will do for now.) Thus, when you click a link whose defining anchor element[2] contains a URL, such as http://www.google.com/about.html, your browser understands this as a request to open a connection to the Internet server, *www.google.com*, using the HTTP protocol and to get the resource, *about.html*.

Of course, you do not always have to click a link or button to get somewhere on the Web. You can just type a portion of a URL into the location window at the top of your browser, and you are taken there. Alternatively, you can open an HTML file from your local computer. (Web developers commonly do this when working on a website.)

Web Browsers and Servers

As intelligent as Web browsers currently are, web servers are smarter still. A single web server can host hundreds of different websites, manage many different types of content, read/write information from/to databases, and speak

---

2. `<a href="http://www.google.com/about.html">About Google</a>`

multiple languages, both human and artificial. A web server knows who you are (to be precise, it knows the Internet address of your computer and what browser is being used), it keeps track of each request you make, and it logs whether it was able to comply with the request.

The Web has a **client/server** architecture, as illustrated in Figure 1.3. Most Internet protocols are client/server, including File Transfer Protocol (FTP), email, and many online games. A web server is a computer that resides on a rack somewhere, or is tucked into a back closet, patiently waiting for a client program to send it a request it can fulfill. As far as the web server is concerned, anything that sends it a request is considered an important client. In Web-speak, the client programs are called user agents. Web browsers are the most important user agents. Robots, or "bots" as they are sometimes called, are another kind.

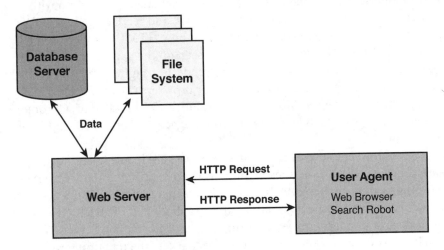

Figure 1.3: The Web's client/server architecture

Widgets can also be user agents. Loosely defined, a widget is a small computer program. It is packaged so that it can be easily installed as an extension of a larger computer program, such as a web browser or mobile device, and it runs in its user interface. A widget can, in response to a mouse click or other user action, send requests to web servers just like browsers and robots do. Unlike robots running on large servers, organizing large masses of information, a widget typically uses the returned information to update the content in a specific page element.

Widgets come in many varieties and are rarely harmful. They run within the browser's security setup and are generally isolated from your computer's file system. However, they can cause trouble if they are not well written. The problems include messing up the display of a web page, using up too much of the browser resources, or even causing a browser to crash.

Any stand-alone computer application or software program that exchanges information over the Web (Twitter clients, for example) is a user agent. So are the automatic software update programs that come with computer operating systems. So is the online Help feature of Microsoft Word or, for that matter, an Xbox, Nintendo, or PlayStation game console. Many of the apps on a modern smartphone are user agents, sending requests to web servers and using the returned information to do something useful or keep you informed.

Every web browser must provide three basic functions: 1) It must provide a control interface for human users; 2) it must exchange information with other computers; and 3) it must interpret HTML and render a web page. We are primarily interested in this last function—how HTML is understood by a browser and how that determines what is seen on the page. Many browser makers use the same open source, HTML rendering engines and differ mostly in their user interfaces. As a result, only four browser types cover most Web surfing: Internet Explorer, Mozilla (Firefox, Flock), Webkit (Safari, Chrome), and everything else (mobile phone browsers, legacy versions of IE, and Internet appliances).

As with browsers, several different web servers are in use today, hosting nearly a quarter billion websites in total. By far the most popular web server, according to a November 2009 survey by Netcraft, is **Apache**, an open-source product from the Apache Foundation. It hosts about half of all sites worldwide. The next most popular web server is the Internet Information Server (IIS) from Microsoft, with about one-third of the market. The remaining web servers are Google Web Server (GWS), which the company uses internally to host its massive search engine and user sites; nginx (pronounced "engine X"), a free, lightweight, high-performance server written by Igor Sysoev; and Qzone, a Chinese web server used by QQ.com to host upward of 20 million blogs under its domain.

When a web server receives a request from a user agent, all it has to do is figure out which file to return. Actually, it is a bit more complicated than that. Apache, for example, has a modular structure with "hooks" that allow a systems administrator to include custom components. Apache analyzes the incoming request, applying defaults and rewriting rules. It determines whether to satisfy the request by returning the contents of a file or by executing a program and returning the output. If the requested resource requires authentication, Apache returns a status code instructing the browser to resubmit the request after prompting for a username/password combination. The HTTP request contains additional information such as the name of the browser or user agent and the preferred language. This enables Apache to provide a different page for mobile users or to substitute a translation of the requested page if one is available.

Web browsers and servers speak many other Internet protocols. Browsers are, in a sense, the Swiss army knives of Internet clients. Web servers have plug-in interfaces to email, database, FTP, streaming video players, and other services. Web servers can also make requests to each other and serve as mirrors or proxies for each other.

THE WEB BESTIARY

This section contains a lot of acronyms and definitions. Much of the descriptive material is taken from Wikipedia. In a very real sense, Wikipedia represents the current usage and understanding of these terms by the Web community. I've listed them in order of decreasing importance, or their likelihood of ever coming up in casual conversation. This list is by no means complete.

- ▸ **HTML (HyperText Markup Language)** The predominant markup language for web pages. It provides a means to create structured documents using semantic tags for such things as headings, paragraphs, lists, links, quotes, and other items. It lets you embed images and other media objects and can be used to create interactive forms.

- ▸ **CSS (Cascading Style Sheets)** The language for describing the presentation (that is, the formatting and layout) of an HTML document. CSS is designed to enable the separation of document content from the details of how it should be presented, including the typography, positioning, colors, and margins. This separation improves content accessibility and provides more flexibility in controlling presentation characteristics.

- ▸ **JavaScript** An object-oriented scripting language. Although JavaScript has other uses, we are concerned here about client-side JavaScript—the version that runs inside a user's browser and manipulates HTML page elements. JavaScript code can be embedded within the HTML elements of a web page or imported from a separate file. Not all web pages have JavaScript components, and users can turn off their browsers' JavaScript engine if they want to. Robots generally ignore JavaScript code as they examine web pages.

▸ **HTTP (HyperText Transport Protocol)**   The set of rules governing how user agents, web browsers, and the like send requests to a web server and how the web server responds to the request. The web server returns a status code and data, or sometimes just the status code, when something goes wrong. The familiar 404 error code is returned when the web server cannot find what you are looking for. There are two primary HTTP request methods. A *Get* request is typically sent by your browser when you click a link with the intention of going to another web page. A *Post* request is typically sent when you click a form's submit button, essentially asking that the web server do something with your input.

▸ **CGI (Common Gateway Interface)**   A protocol for dynamically generating web pages in response to a get request or form submission. The term is typically used as an adjective to indicate a server-side process, such as CGI script. CGI programs are typically written using a scripting language such as Perl, Ruby, C, vBasic, or Python. Many websites are entirely driven by CGI processes, although the relative number of such sites has probably been declining as newer technologies, such as AJAX and PHP, have become popular.

▸ **AJAX (Asynchronous JavaScript and XML)**   The most recent versions of JavaScript and other client-side scripting languages contain features that a developer can use to create web pages that can make independent HTTP requests to the server while the page is loading or anytime thereafter. AJAX is the set of techniques used to create web pages with elements that can be independently updated with new content in response to a user's mouse click or some other event without having to reload the entire page. This is how many widgets work.

▸ **XML (eXtensible Markup Language)**   A set of rules for marking up documents that emphasizes generality and global usability. It is widely used to transmit arbitrarily structured data in mixed client/server environments. XML and HTML are compatible members of a family of markup languages called Standard Generalized Markup Language (SGML). HTML is an SGML language with a specific Document Object

Model (DOM) focused on describing hypertext documents. The two technologies are combined in the XHTML specification.

▶ **JSON (JavaScript Object Notation)**   Although based on JavaScript, JSON is a language-independent system for representing data objects. It is simpler than XML and is often used as an alternative to XML in AJAX applications to transfer data objects between a server and a script running in a user's browser.

▶ **CMS (Content Management System)**   An application program or a package of software tools that facilitates the creation of web pages and automates their maintenance using a Web-based interface for authoring, editing, and administration. The term has broader use beyond the Web. For our purposes, it refers to any site or software that generates web pages from content stored in a database and provides a means of creating, editing, and managing that content without requiring knowledge of HTML, CSS, or FTP. A good CMS permits you to directly enter HTML with the content for finer control of web page presentation. **Blogs** are a form of content management system.

▶ **Flash (Adobe Flash, formerly Macromedia Flash)**   A popular multimedia platform for adding animation and interactivity to web pages. Flash is commonly used to create animations, advertisements, and various interactive components, to integrate video into web pages and to develop rich Internet applications. Some websites are done entirely in Flash. However, this is now considered a poor practice, partly because the content of a Flash site is generally inaccessible to robots.

▶ **PHP (PHP Hypertext Preprocessor)**   PHP originally stood for Personal Home Page. The PHP Group, the informal organization that currently oversees the development of the language, decided to expand the meaning of PHP a few years ago and gave us the current recursive acronym. PHP is a server-side technology for dynamically generating websites. It is powerful and easy to write but often difficult to read. A PHP file intermixes program logic—PHP statements enclosed in special tags—with HTML markup. When a request is sent to a web server for a file ending with the .php extension, the web server preprocesses the coded file, executes the PHP instructions, and returns an HTML document to the user's browser. Many modern Web applications, such as the popular blogging software WordPress, are written in PHP.

▸ **FTP (File Transfer Protocol)**   An Internet protocol for transferring files from one computer to another, usually using a stand-alone application. Web browsers and page editors also use FTP to upload and download files. Dozens of FTP clients are available. One of the most popular is FileZilla, a free, open-source program that runs on Windows, Macintosh, and UNIX computers.

▸ **jQuery (JavaScript Query Language)**   A library of JavaScript functions (often called a framework) that simplifies the development of dynamic, interactive web pages. It provides a language for selecting DOM elements and giving them complex behaviors. jQuery takes care of cross-browser differences in the DOM and facilitates the use of AJAX. In much the same way that CSS does with web page presentation, jQuery encourages the separation of semantic HTML markup from the descriptions of how HTML elements should respond to events. jQuery makes Web programming fun.

▸ **RSS (Real Simple Syndication)**   An XML protocol for distributing content. Such distributed content from a website is called a *feed* and provides an alternative means for users to access the content. Users can subscribe to feeds using a number of stand-alone newsreaders or by using the feed-reading facilities incorporated into their browsers and email clients. Feeds from one website can also be embedded into web pages on another site in a syndicated publishing model. RSS is quite popular but evolved in an ad hoc way and is not a recognized standard. A newer feed protocol called Atom is more robust and follows the applicable standards.

▸ **DNS (Domain Name System)**   A system for assigning names to computers connected to the Internet or a private network. It translates domain names meaningful to humans into the numerical addresses associated with networking equipment for the purpose of locating these devices worldwide. The Domain Name System can be thought of as the "phone book" for the Internet.

▸ **DOM (Document Object Model)**   A dictionary and grammar for interpreting HTML. A DOM describes HTML elements and their attributes and properties and how they are used to create web pages. DOMs are published in a form that can be read by both humans and machines. Every web browser has at least one DOM, and most modern browsers conform to DOMs published by the W3C. Yet there are still some differences in browser behavior arising from coding bugs, DOM misinterpretation, and edge conditions where browser behavior is not fully defined.

In this book, whenever you encounter the term DOM, it means the *W3C's draft specification for HTML5* as interpreted by your favorite browser. Your browser may or may not support this or that new HTML5 element when you experiment with the examples given. The same is true of any particular editing tool or environment you like to use. My aim is to present HTML that works reliably across all modern browsers and is pleasing to all user agents.

HTML5 and Web Standards

Over the past two decades, HTML has evolved through several iterations—HTML, HTML2, HTML3, HTML3.2, HTML4, HTML4.1, XHTML. These changes have been driven by both standards-setting organizations, such as the W3C, and individual software companies, such as Netscape and Microsoft. HTML5 is the next iteration. Technically, it is not yet a standard, and it will not be for several years. It is the W3C's working draft for the standard that it will eventually recommend to official standards organizations around the world. Still, browser manufacturers are already adopting HTML5 features.

For now, HTML5 is best thought of as a directional guide to good standards of practice in Web design. New HTML5 elements and attributes provide a richer description of online documents as interactive multimedia spaces. Prior HTML versions (HTML4 and XHTML) are tied to a print metaphor of a page to which interactive capabilities and media support have been added ad hoc. Many pages on the Web are the online equivalent of printed pages. In contrast, HTML5 encourages a broader conception of the Web as a unified, intelligent, interactive, hyperlinked medium.

For online document authors, HTML5 adds **new elements** to define document sections (the section element) and new section subelements to define page headers (header) and footers (footer). Section headings can be composed of heading groups (hgroup) and can contain the new navigation (nav) element. HTML4 provided only a single division element (div) for these purposes, and coders used id and class attributes to make the distinction in usage. There is a new article element (article) and a means (the aside element) to designate text that's tangential to the main topic. There is even an element for indicating sarcastic remarks (sarcasm) in the W3C draft specification, but I think this is an inside joke.

For Web developers, the HTML5 draft specification for the first time describes how the browser should expose HTML elements to scripts. Using JavaScript syntax, it describes the methods that scripts may call on document objects. In other words, it describes what commands a given HTML element understands and obeys. Previous HTML specification referred generally to ECMAScript, a standardized family of languages that includes JavaScript, JScript (Microsoft's version of JavaScript), and ActionScript (Adobe's scripting language for Flash). The use of JavaScript in this book is not meant to imply the exclusion of other scripting languages.

Equally exciting is the new HTML5 canvas element. It provides a bitmap canvas area that scripts can draw on or load images and video into. A canvas element can be used to render graphs, game graphics, or other visual images on-the-fly. There are also new elements for creating meters (meter) and progress bars (progress). There are also new element attributes that allow parts of a document to be moved around the page or edited in place and saved across sessions.

Even with all these new features, HTML5 emphasizes simplicity. This is achieved by segregating the description of document content from the descriptions of presentation and interactive behavior. Web authors are encouraged to code the minimal HTML necessary to provide a semantic description of a document. This is what **Web Standards** is all about: the standards of practice that create web pages that display well on all devices and that are pleasing to everyone and everything that reads them.

Allow me to expand on this last point. **Search** has changed how we use the Web. Although a work must be read and understood by people, it is just as important that the information to help people find that work be properly constructed. In other words, a web page must be both robot-friendly and people-friendly.

This dictum of being friendly to everything (within reason) goes beyond just being browser- and robot-friendly. The Web embraces all kinds of devices, including phones, tablets, netbooks, computers, game consoles, and large public video displays, as well as devices for the visually handicapped. The Web also embraces all languages and writing systems, including right-to-left languages such as Hebrew and Farsi and ideographic character sets such as Japanese and Chinese.

We are entering the age of the collaborative Web. It is important to think about pleasing the coauthors, contributors, curators, archivists, and translators who will work with your documents long after you write them.

Do We All Have to Learn HTML5 Now?

The short answer is no. First of all, new versions of the HTML specification do not make older versions obsolete. For example, the first home page I ever created looks the same in Firefox and Chrome today as it did in Mosaic and Arena in 1994. What's important is the assurance that the web pages we build today will look and function the same in another 15 years. We may update those pages for marketing and aesthetic reasons, but we will not be forced to edit them for technical reasons. Second, if you already know some HTML, it is not a matter of learning a new language or dialect, but simply incorporating new elements into your HTML vocabulary.

If you are a content creator/editor using Web-based tools to update web pages and post articles, you need to know that any HTML markup you use in a blog post, press release, or email newsletter will be the same in all your readers' browsers. It is best for you to stick with the elements and attributes of HTML4 until HTML5 has been more widely adopted and more guidance is forthcoming on how to use the new features.

If you design websites and keep up with tech trends on a regular basis, you will learn from your online resources about browser support for new HTML5 elements, which you can incorporate into your work with appropriate fall-backs and cross-browser testing. Now is the time to play with HTML5, while you reexamine your Web design and development methods. The HTML5 Web is collaborative.

If you manage a Web design company or development shop, your websites are probably sophisticated enough that you already do browser detection. My suggestion is to let one of your programmers become your HTML5 specialist, creating HTML5-aware versions of some of your in-development and existing websites.

Summary

Here are the important points to remember from this chapter:

- ▶ HTML is a semantic markup language for online, hypertext-linked documents.
- ▶ The Web has a client/server architecture. Web servers respond to requests from user agents such as web browsers, search robots, and web page editors.

▶ HTML is supported by many other technologies, the most important of which are Cascading Style Sheets (CSS) for describing the presentation aspects of page elements, and JavaScript for describing element behaviors.

▶ The Web is global and collaborative. Observing Web standards in creating documents will help others build upon your work.

▶ HTML5 provides new elements and attributes for Web designers to work with. However, it is still a draft specification and thus should be seen as a guide for future projects, when more support is available.

The HTML Language

This chapter presents the various elements of the HTML language. This includes the syntax of character entities and markup tags and how a browser or other user agent interprets the markup to display a page. This description follows the draft specification for HTML5 developed by the World Wide Web Consortium's (W3C) HTML Working Group. In general, the term "HTML" is used to describe elements of the language in general use that are currently supported by modern browsers. The term "HTML5" is used to describe elements that are new in the HTML5 draft specification and that may or may not be supported by a specific browser.

LANGUAGE OVERVIEW

A page on the World Wide Web is composed of a set of files stored somewhere on a device accessible to a web server. The exact location of a page is known by its URL (Uniform Resource Locator). A web page has content consisting of text, inline images, and embedded media objects. The page's marked-up text is in one file, and the individual images and media objects are in separate files. Images and media objects are also referenced by their URLs, so the same objects can be used more than once on a page or on many different pages. Video and audio objects are supported directly by HTML5. Other multimedia is accessed through plug-ins or external helper applications that the browser associates with the content type of the media object. The documentation or online help for a specific browser lists the recommended helper applications appropriate to a specific operating system.

Authoring web pages is different in many respects from using word processing programs. A web page has no fixed size. It can be as long as it needs to be without page breaks. The default browser behavior is to word-wrap text to fit the available width of a containing element or, in the trivial case, to fit within the margins of the display window. If there is more content than fits in the window, the browser enables scrolling to accommodate the length. Furthermore, the properties of pages elements can change in response to user actions, and a web author's preferences can be overridden by the reader.

In desktop publishing, the focus is on the printed page. Authors and editors specify the document's layout, typography, colors, and other properties and have complete control over the document's final appearance. Web authors and developers, on the other hand, relinquish some measure of this control so that their content can be consumed on a wide variety of devices. For example, an author might design a web page so that it is pleasing when viewed in a modern browser such as Safari, Firefox, Internet Explorer, or Google Chrome, running on a typical desktop computer with a standard color monitor. However, the readers of that page might include people on the go using cell phones or people with visual impairments using text-to-speech readers. A new class of tablet devices from companies such as Apple and Google is changing how people use the Web, and website authors must increasingly take this into account.

Moreover, we are long past the days when a web developer had to consider only how a page looked to able-bodied people. Today, it is critical that a web page makes good reading for search robots. In addition, it must be able to be read and worked on by editing applications and content-management systems.

Creating a web page is the process of inserting HTML markup tags into the content that describe the elements of the page semantically. Web authors have a wide range of tools for editing HTML, ranging from simple text editors to powerful integrated development environments. Because HTML has elements to define input forms, it is not very difficult to write web pages that create and modify other web pages. Web pages displayed in HTML5 browsers can be editable and even self-modifying.

Web pages are living documents that require ongoing care and maintenance. Web spaces in particular tend to grow like weeds. Existing pages are cloned and adapted to new uses continually. Unlike desktop publishing pages, which are finished works rushed out the door to meet a deadline, web pages are perpetually "under construction," and the tools to work on them keep getting better.

You will learn that when it comes to coding web pages, there are often several ways to accomplish the same thing and that every rule has an exception.

Like a living language, HTML has dialects and slang expressions. Let's begin by looking again at the simple "Hello World" page from Chapter 1, "HTML and the Web." It is reproduced as Example 2.1.

Example 2.1: HTML for a simple "Hello World" web page

```
<!DOCTYPE html>
<html>
<head>
  <title>Example 2.1</title>
  <style type="text/css">
    h1 { text-align: center; }
  </style>
</head>

<body>
  <h1>Hello World Wide Web</h1>
  <p>
    Welcome to the first of many webpages.
    I promise they will get more interesting than this.
  </p>
</body>
</html>
```

The HTML markup is shown in bold. This code can be saved in a text file and opened in a browser. The filename should end with the extension .html or .htm. Figure 2.1 shows how it looks in my browser (Firefox on Mac OSX) with all the extra toolbars and status bars removed.

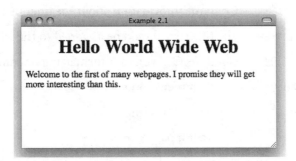

Figure 2.1: The "Hello World" page as displayed by a browser

HTML markup uses only the familiar keyboard characters and is enclosed in angle brackets (<>). These characters, especially the left angle bracket, are reserved for HTML use and must not appear in the content. If a left angle bracket appears in the content somewhere (for example, as a less-than sign), the browser parsing your code assumes that it marks the beginning of a new HTML element. Because browsers are free to ignore any markup they cannot understand, some of the content following the angle bracket may fail to appear on the displayed web page.

As a result, HTML has syntax for defining single **character entities** in the content. You refer to the character's codename, preceded by an ampersand (&) and ending with a semicolon (;). For example, the less-than sign (<) must be entered as <. The greater-than sign (>) may be entered as >, although most browsers should recognize it if the context is clear. This scheme requires the congenial ampersand to be entered in the content using its character entity, &. Character entities are the method for inserting special symbols such as quotation marks that are not standardized across languages.

In reading the code in Example 2.1, note that the spacing and indentations exist only to make the code pretty to read and easier to explain. Web browsers and other user agents are instructed to replace all extraneous white-space characters with single spaces. This includes tabs, carriage returns, line feeds, and leading and redundant blanks. All of Example 2.1 could be written on a single line, and it would still look the same in a browser.

In Example 2.1, notice how the HTML elements appear as paired sets of start and end tags. The start tag of each pair has a name identifying what kind of HTML element it is, and the end tag of each pair repeats the name preceded by a slash (/). The following HTML elements can be found in Example 2.1:

`<html></html>`	The HTML part of the document
`<head></head>`	Contains information about the document
`<title></title>`	The title that should be assigned to the window
`<style></style>`	Contains CSS rules for formatting document elements
`<body></body>`	The document content and HTML markup
`<h1></h1>`	A level-one heading
`<p></p>`	A paragraph

The HTML elements of Example 2.1 are nested inside one another. The document is defined by the outer html element, which contains two child elements: head and body. Every web page must have exactly one head element and one body element. Each of those elements has its own child elements. The title and style elements are the children of the head element, and the heading and paragraph elements (h1 and p) are children of the body element.

HTML has sensible rules for which elements can be nested inside other elements. Headings, for example, cannot be nested inside paragraphs. HTML elements are not allowed to overlap. For instance, if we had the following two elements inside the body element in the preceding example

```
<h1>Welcome Page
<p>Hello World Wide Web</p>
</h1>
```

the web page would be considered invalid. It might still display correctly in a chosen browser, because the browser might be smart enough to fix things when it finds an error. However, it is still bad HTML because some amount of semantic meaning is lost and because such uncorrected errors will cause problems for people who work with the code going forward.

Example 2.2 adds a little more complexity to the Hello World code. It also introduces some additional HTML concepts before we get into the specifics of the language. Figure 2.2 shows how this code appears in a typical web browser.

Example 2.2: A slightly more complex "Hello World" page

```
<!DOCTYPE html>
<html>
<head>
  <title>Example 2.2</title>
  <style>
    h1 { text-align: center; }
    .intro-text { font: 12pt sans-serif; }
  </style>
</head>

<body>
  <h1> Hello World Wide Web</h1>
  <p class="intro-text">
    Welcome to first of many webpages.<br/>
    <em>I promise</em> they will get more interesting than this.
  </p>
</body>
</html>
```

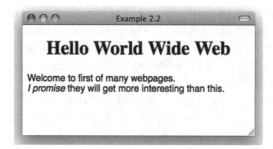

Figure 2.2: A web page with a heading and paragraph

In this example, another CSS rule has been added to the `style` element in the head of the document, and some additional markup has been added to the elements in the document body. The `class` attribute added to the paragraph element (`class="intro-text"`) is one of three attributes that can be used to associate an HTML element with a set of CSS rules. One of the places CSS rules can appear is in a `style` element in the document head. In Example 2.2, the second style rule says that any element having a `class` attribute with the value `"intro-text"` should be rendered in a 12-point sans serif font. By default, this is usually the Arial or Helvetica typeface, but the readers of the page can set their browser's preferences to other fonts.

Inside the paragraph element are two other HTML elements. The first looks rather strange because it appears to be a start tag for an element, but it is not paired with an end tag. That's exactly what it is. The break element, `<br/>`, inserts a line break into the text, which is like pressing Shift-Enter in Microsoft Word. The break element is an example of a self-closing HTML element. Because a line break, unlike a heading or paragraph, cannot contain any content, there's not much point in having a corresponding end tag to create a container. The image tag is another important self-closing HTML element.

In the second line of the paragraph element, the words "I promise" are emphasized by being enclosed in the emphasis element, `<em></em>`. The default behavior is to render the enclosed text in italics. Unlike the heading and paragraph elements, the emphasis element is an **inline element**. It does not change the flow of text. Headings and paragraphs are **block elements** and have box properties that inline elements do not have, such as height, width, margins, and padding.

The HTML5 specification is structured so that the HTML elements of any web page can be described in a hierarchical tree diagram with the `html` element as the root, the `head` and `body` elements as the main trunks, and the rest sprouting as branches to leaves of content. A browser—or for that matter, any software parsing a web page—builds this tree structure in its memory. This in-memory representation is called the Document Object Model (DOM).

PAGE STRUCTURE AND THE DOM

In HTML5, the DOM is central to the interpretation of an HTML document and its presentation as a web page. The DOM provides a map of the structure of an HTML document and describes how its various parts work together. The DOM also provides interfaces for assigning CSS styles to various page elements and methods that can be called to dynamically manipulate those elements using JavaScript or some other scripting language.

The language of the DOM is different from the language of HTML. It is like a marriage of two people with different family backgrounds. HTML comes from the family of markup languages, whereas the DOM family background is object-oriented programming. In HTML, the web page is composed of elements, and elements can have attributes. In working with the DOM, each HTML element and attribute becomes a DOM *object*, and the HTML attribute values become properties of those objects.

Your favorite browser has a DOM built in—probably more than one. Most browsers use the W3C's DOM, but HTML is still evolving. "Edge" conditions exist in which browsers differ in their interpretation of a given bit of HTML. This is like a natural language such as English, where the word "knickers" means something different in the United Kingdom than it does in the United States. Fortunately, browsers are allowed to gracefully ignore any markup they can't understand and not be embarrassed by the encounter. Humans are not so lucky. We have an obligation to write code that makes sense to all web user agents—browsers, robots, and authoring tools.

On a web page, every HTML element corresponds to a DOM object, and the HTML attributes of the elements are properties of their DOM objects. If an HTML element is contained inside another HTML element, the nested, inner object is considered a property of the outer, containing object. It is referred to as a child of the containing object, and the containing object is referred to as the parent object. The text content inside any HTML element is also considered a property of its parent DOM object. Each object has one and only one parent object, except for the window object corresponding to the outermost HTML element.

The window object is the window or tab that is currently active in your browser. The web page loaded into the window corresponds to a document object. All the various elements of the web page defined by the HTML markup are objects and can be accessed by scripts and styled by CSS.

Example 2.3 expands on the previous versions of the Hello World page by adding a script that adds a simple behavior to the page when the user clicks in the body of the page. The paragraph text has been changed to keep things interesting. Only the relevant parts of the coding are highlighted in boldface type. Figure 2.3 shows the result of this code.

Example 2.3: An HTML page with CSS rules and HTML attributes

```
<!DOCTYPE html>
<html>
<head>
<title>Example 2.3</title>
<style>
  h1 {
    text-align: center;
    color: darkblue;
  }
  .intro-text { font: 12pt sans-serif; }
</style>
</head>

<body>
<h1>Hello World Wide Web</h1>
<p class="intro-text">
  Welcome to this webpage,<br/>
  It's <em>so</em> nice to see you.
</p>
<hr/>  <!-- horizontal rule -->
</body>

<!-- function to make the text red when clicked -->
<script type="text/javascript">
  document.body.onclick = function () {
    document.body.style.color = 'red';
  }
</script>
</html>
```

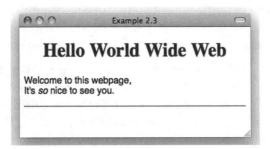

Figure 2.3: A web page that responds to a mouse click

First, note that another rule has been added to the CSS style container in the document head section for the h1 element:

color: darkblue;

This CSS rule renders any of the page's level-one headings in a dark blue color. Also, a horizontal rule has been added below the paragraph using the self-closing element <hr/>. You can't miss it. It is next to the comment <!-- horizontal rule -->. Comments are an important part of any web page and should be used frequently to help other people understand what the code is supposed to do. Browsers ignore comments, which do not affect the display of the page in any way. Robots are free to ignore comments or to make of them what they will.

At the end of Example 2.3, a script container has been added after the closing body tag, following a comment describing what the JavaScript is supposed to do:

```
<script type="text/javascript">
  document.body.onclick = function () {
    document.body.style.color = 'red';
  }
</script>
```

The script consists of a single statement that adds a behavior to the document's body element. When the reader clicks the document, the text turns red. Try this out in your favorite browser, and you will notice some behavior that you might not have expected:

▶ First, the mouse must be clicked on or above the horizontal rule that marks the end of the document body. Clicking below the horizontal rule will not have any effect. It is just extra space the browser put there because the document is shorter than the browser window.

▶ The window's width does not matter. The document will always occupy the window's full width. A click will work anywhere above the rule, except at the very edges of the page. This is because there is space between the document's window and the body content. This space is called *padding*.

▶ The heading text does not change color when you click in the body. This is due to the cascading nature of CSS. Child objects inherit properties from their parents but can override and add to them. So, even though the level-one heading is inside the document body, the heading text does not change to red because a more specific CSS rule takes precedence.

▶ After the paragraph text changes to red, there's no going back for the user, short of reloading the page. It is not that the change is permanent. It is just because no behavior has been defined to allow users to go back to the initial state.

The JavaScript code does not in any sense "live" in the space after the document body. Script elements can appear anywhere in an HTML document. In Example 2.3, the script code must be placed after the body element because the browser executes scripts as they are encountered in the source code. It would be an error to reference an object before it is fully defined. There are other ways to accomplish this, including calling JavaScript functions within the HTML code using special HTML event-handling attributes. Also, external JavaScript libraries, such as jQuery, provide a means to execute functions when the document is "ready"—that is, when all the DOM objects are fully defined. This allows code to be placed apart from the HTML source. Without going into the details of jQuery syntax, the equivalent jQuery code to define the body behavior of Example 2.3 would look like this:

```
<script type="text/javascript">
  jQuery(document).ready( function () {
    jQuery('body').click( function () {
      jQuery('body').css('color', 'red');
    });
  });
</script>
```

This code could be placed in the document's head section or in an external file linked from the document's head. The function to assign the body's click behavior is not defined until the document is ready. jQuery gives the web developer a simple way to access DOM objects using the same syntax that CSS uses to select elements for the application of presentation rules. It is one of many tools that make web programming fun! See Chapter 5, "Building Websites," for more information on using JavaScript, jQuery, and other scripting resources to add dynamic behaviors to your web page elements.

HTML5 Syntax

You must learn a few general syntax rules to work with HTML documents. First, an HTML document consists of text content along with HTML **comments, character entities**, and **markup elements**. HTML markup elements are further classified into a few categories, depending on what kind of content can be inside the element.

COMMENTS

Comments are the easiest markup element to understand. HTML authors are encouraged to use comments to annotate HTML source code so that other people can understand what the code should do. A comment is a string of characters beginning with <!-- and ending with -->. Comments can extend over several lines, making them useful for temporarily disabling and enabling alternative code segments. However, you should be careful not to overlap comments, because that usually results in unexpected content appearing on a page. Also, avoid using a double dash (--) inside a comment. It is technically invalid in HTML5, and some older browsers have difficulty processing that sequence of characters.

Although user agents are supposed to ignore comments, and most do, there are instances where comments do matter. For example, Microsoft's Internet Explorer browser pays attention to comments containing conditional tests for certain browser features. In the following code, placed in the head section of the document, the link element inside the comment loads in the special CSS style sheet file ie6.css only when read by version 6 of Internet Explorer or earlier releases:

```
<link rel="stylesheet" type="text/css" href="/css/style.css"/>
<!--[if lte ie 6]>
<link rel="stylesheet" type="text/css" href="/css/ie6.css"/>
<![endif]-->
```

All other browsers will ignore everything between the double dashes. Due to the cascading nature of CSS, element styles in the ie6.css style sheet overwrite previous styles for the same elements set in the style.css style sheet. This is a common way to deal with the CSS problems Internet Explorer 6 causes due to its incomplete and buggy implementation of CSS.

HTML comments are not effective inside a script or style element. JavaScript and CSS have their own syntax for comments. Both use a slash-asterisk, asterisk-slash sequence to denote comments in the code:

```
/* this is a CSS or JavaScript comment */
```

However, when both scripting and CSS were new, page authors enclosed everything inside a script or style element in HTML comment tags. They did this so that older browsers would not stumble over the JavaScript statements or CSS rules and include them as page content. When you look at the HTML source of some of these older pages, you might see something like this:[1]

```
<STYLE TYPE="text/css">
<--
   /* a bunch of CSS statements in between HTML comment tags */
-->
</STYLE>
```

CHARACTER ENTITIES

A character entity is an escape sequence that defines a single letter or symbol that normally cannot be entered in the text content. A character entity begins with an ampersand (&) and is followed by either the name of a predefined entity or a pound sign (#) and by the character's decimal number. A semicolon is used to terminate the character entity. The tilde (~), for example, can be generated by either ˜ or ~. Using the named entity is preferable because different language encodings have different numberings.

Character entities are predefined for the symbols that are needed to mark the beginnings and ends of HTML elements. A complete list of predefined character entities can be found in the HTML5 specification. Most good HTML editors provide a table to assist in editing documents. Three character entities

---

1. Before the HTML4 specification, many Web authors used uppercase type for HTML element and attribute names to visually distinguish them from mixed-case content. Beginning with HTML4, authors were encouraged to use lowercase names for compatibility with XML syntax rules. In strict XHTML and HTML5, lowercase names are required.

are particularly important. They must be used to show the symbols that would ordinarily be taken as the beginning (or end) of an HTML markup tag or character entity:

&lt;	<	Left-angle bracket or less-than sign
&gt;	>	Right-angle bracket or greater-than sign
&amp;	&	Ampersand

The following are also useful:

&quot;	"	Double quote mark
&ldquo;	"	Left smart (curly) double quote
&rdquo;	"	Right smart (curly) double quote
&ndash;	–	Medium-length dash (en dash)
&mdash;	—	Long dash (em dash)
		Nonbreaking space
&copy;	©	Copyright symbol

MARKUP ELEMENTS

Every HTML markup element begins with a start tag consisting of an opening angle bracket (<) followed by the element name, followed by zero or more attributes separated by spaces, followed by the closing angle bracket (>). Markup tags are either self-closing or paired with a closing tag to create a container. Inside the container is content with possibly its own markup code. Containers can be nested as deeply as needed. Self-closing tags have a slash (/) immediately before the closing angle bracket. Ending tags have a slash immediately after the opening angle bracket, followed by the element name, followed by the closing angle bracket. Ending tags do not contain attributes, nor should they contain any blanks or other white space.

A markup container can also be empty, as is common in the HTML elements for creating tables or just for creating an entry in the DOM that will be filled later by a script function, triggered by a mouse action.

In general, containers segregate and modify content, and self-closing tags, which are sometimes called empty tags, insert objects into the content. Here are a couple examples of self-closing tags:

```
<br/> <!-- Line break. Following text begins at the left margin.
-->
<hr/> <!-- Horizontal rule. Draws a line across the page. -->
```

Attributes are written in name and value pairs with an equals sign (=) between and with the value enclosed in double quote marks. There should not be any spaces around the equals sign, because spaces are used to separate attribute-value pairs from each other. The ordering of attributes in a list does not matter.

Although it is usually clear whether a number or a character string is needed, the value of an attribute should always be appropriate to the domain of that attribute. Unexpected values can have unexpected results. HTML character entities are recognized inside attribute values, but other HTML markup is not. Single quote marks and apostrophes are allowed inside attribute values, but double quotes are unwelcome troublemakers. The double-quote character entity, ", should be used instead.

> **Note:** The HTML5 specification does not require quotation marks around attribute values if the meaning is unambiguous, however other versions of HTML do require them. I think it is a good practice to always enclose attribute values in quotes.

The following tag specifies that an inline image should be inserted into the page. It has two attributes: src, whose value is the name (source) of the file containing the image data, and alt, which provides alternative information for user agents that do not know how to present an image (or do not have anyone to present it to):

```
<img src="corplogo.gif" alt="Logocorp Inc."/>
```

Here are a few more examples of container elements:

```
<title>Don Quixote's Home Page</title>
<strong>Strong emphasis, usually bold</strong>
<a href="catalog.html">Our New Catalog</a>
```

The title element provides the title that appears in the top of the window. It is valid only inside the head element. Like most head elements, it cannot contain any nested elements. The other two markup examples can appear only in the document body. The strong element tells a user agent that the contained content should be given strong emphasis. Visually, this defaults to boldface type. The strong element and the anchor (a) element on the last line are both **inline elements**. They only change the appearance of the type; they do not change the flow of the content.

Anchor elements define the nodes of hypertext links. In the preceding HTML, the browser highlights the phrase Our New Catalog to indicate that clicking this text will take the reader somewhere else on the Web. The href attribute provides the link's destination. In this case, the file catalog.html, which is assumed to be in the same directory as the current page, becomes the new page—if it exists. Otherwise, the server returns an error code, and the browser displays a File Not Found error message.

Example 2.4 illustrates the use of comments, character entities, and markup elements.

Example 2.4: A web page with a heading and two paragraphs

```
<!DOCTYPE html>
<html>
<head>
<title>Example 2.4</title>
</head>

<body>
<h1>The Title Of A Page</h1> <!-- Show the page title -->

<p><strong>Window Titles</strong> should have some relation
to the outside world, Level 1 Headings should introduce the
major sections of a work.</p>

<p>This is a second paragraph of text that exists only to show
how <em>paragraph elements</em> are used to separate text. It
also
points out the use of the &lt;strong&gt;&lt;/strong&gt; tags in
the first paragraph.</p>
</body>
</html>
```

Figure 2.4 shows what this example looks like in a browser. The body of this page consists of a level 1 heading (<h1>...</h1>) and two paragraphs of text enclosed by paragraph tags (<p>...</p>). To get the string <strong></strong> to appear in the second paragraph without being interpreted as a tag, character entities are used for the angle brackets.

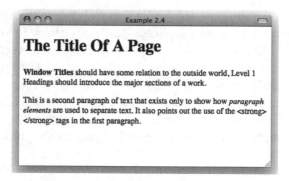

Figure 2.4: An example of the use of a level-one heading

Although the HTML source code in Example 2.4 is neatly formatted, it does not matter where the tags are placed with respect to the content. Browsers are supposed to ignore any leading, trailing, or redundant white space. The following HTML segments all produce the exact same heading as the one shown in Figure 2.4:

```
<h1> The Title Of A Page</h1>
<h1> The          Title Of    A Page  </h1>


<h1> <!-- show the page title -->
     The Title Of A Page
</h1>
```

HTML5 SEMANTICS

HTML elements are divided into two classes: **block elements**, which change the content flow, and **inline elements**, which do not change the content flow. Content flow describes how the document's elements appear as a page displayed in the browser's window. Block elements are normally separated from each other by line breaks and an amount of vertical white space that varies by the type of element. By default, most block elements occupy the full width available and just enough height to accommodate the content. Within that area, text and other inline elements are normally wrapped into lines that fit nicely inside the block element.

Block elements have *box properties* that include margins, height and width, padding, and borders. Inline elements do not have box properties and are not separated from each other. They flow together into lines of word-wrapped text with other inline elements. The HTML elements that are only allowed inside the head element are neither block nor inline elements, because these elements are not involved in content flow. Collectively, these elements provide *metadata* about the page and its relation to other web resources.

Some HTML elements can be nested inside other block elements. Inline elements are always found inside block elements, but a block element should not be, in most circumstances, inside an inline element. For example, paragraphs and lists can be inside sections and divisions, but a heading cannot be nested in another heading. The distinction between block and inline elements is "loose" because it is subject to the CSS display property. Example 2.5 illustrates how this works and introduces an important new HTML block element, the division.

Example 2.5: Using a division element with margins

```
<!DOCTYPE html>
<html>
<head>
  <title>Example 2.5</title>
  <style type="text/css">
    #preamble { margin: 36px; }  /* set margins */
  </style>
</head>

<body>                   <!-- No Page Title -->
<div id="preamble">
Whereas recognition of the inherent dignity and of the equal and
inalienable rights of <em>all members</em> of the human family
is the foundation of freedom, justice and peace in the world,
&hellip;
</div>

<p style="font-style: italic;">Emphasis, mine.</p>
</body>
</html>
```

There are two block elements inside the body element in Example 2.5: a division element, div, with an id attribute, and a paragraph element, p, with a style attribute. The id attribute provides a unique identifier for the division for use in the style element in the document head. The style attribute provides a means of specifying CSS rules directly within the HTML element. Inside the division element, an inline emphasis element, em, emphasizes the phrase "all members."

Figure 2.5 shows how this appears in a browser. Note that the division has a margin of 36 pixels separating it from the rest of the content on all four sides. The paragraph following the division has default margins. Also, even though the phrase "all members" in the division and the words "Emphasis, mine." in the paragraph both appear in italics, a search engine robot reading this page will regard the former as having some importance, but not the latter. This is because the italic styling of the paragraph is done with CSS, which robots generally ignore, whereas the styling of the words "all members" comes as a result of the semantic markup applied to the phrase.

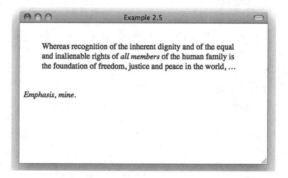

Figure 2.5: A web page with a division element to control margins

The emphasis element in the preamble division can be changed from an inline element to a block element by adding the CSS rule display: block;. We can do this by adding a style attribute to the starting em tag, as was done with the paragraph:

```
<em style="display: block;">
```

or by adding a selector followed by the rule to the `style` element in the document's head element:

```
#preamble em { display: block; }
```

This applies only to the emphasis element inside the preamble division. When opened in a browser, the emphasized words will appear on a line by themselves, breaking the flow of the division's content.

The HTML5 elements for marking up sections, divisions, headings, paragraphs, lists, tables, block quotes, address blocks, and code examples—to name a few—are all block elements. All block elements have box properties: margins, borders, padding, height, and width (and depth, too!). Box properties can be visualized as a set of nested boxes, as shown in Figure 2.5a.

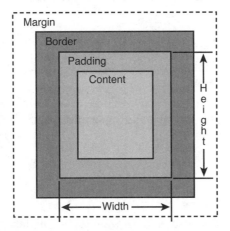

Figure 2.5a: Box properties of block elements

Imagine a cardboard shipping box. The cardboard shell is the "border" of the box, and it has a certain margin of space between it and the other boxes on the shelf. The inside of the box will accommodate an object of a certain height and width, plus whatever padding is desired to protect the object.

Normally, block elements appear on a web page in the same order as they are defined in the HTML source code: from top to bottom. Unless otherwise changed by an attribute or CSS rule, a block element is as wide as it needs to be to accommodate its contents and padding. If there is sufficient content, the element occupies the full width of its container minus whatever is needed for the element's margins, borders, and the padding of the containing element.

Block elements also have a float property: They are allowed to float alongside other elements if there is sufficient room. The float property can take the values left, right, or none, which is the default. left means that the element adheres to the left margin of the containing element and that other HTML elements following the floated element wrap around it on the right. right does the opposite. The element sticks to the right margin, and the HTML elements following it wrap around to the left. Example 2.6 illustrates a common use of floating elements to create a page with a leading thumbnail image. The contents are from a Wikipedia article on the America's Cup regatta.

Example 2.6: Flowing text around an image

```
<!DOCTYPE html>
<html>
<head>
<title>Example 2.6</title>
<style type="text/css">
  body { padding: 2em; }
  .image-left { float: left; padding-right: 1em; }
</style>
</head>

<body>
<div class="image-left">
  <img src="images/Americas_Cup.jpg" alt="The America's Cup
trophy">
</div>

<p>
The America's Cup is a trophy awarded to the winner of the
America's Cup sailing regatta match. It is the oldest active
trophy in international sport, predating the Modern Olympics
by 45 years. Originally named the Royal Yacht Squadron Cup, it
became known as the "America's Cup" after the first yacht to
win the trophy, the schooner America. The trophy remained in
the hands of the New York Yacht Club (NYYC) from 1857 (when the
syndicate that won the Cup donated the trophy to the club) until
```

```
1983 when the Cup was won by the Royal Perth Yacht Club, with
their yacht, Australia II, ending the longest winning streak in
the history of sport.
</p>

<p>
The America's Cup regatta is a challenge-driven series of match
races between two yachts which is governed by the Deed of Gift
which was the instrument used to convey the cup to the New York
Yacht Club. Any yacht club that meets the requirements specified
in the Deed of Gift has the right to challenge the yacht club
that holds the Cup. If the challenging yacht club wins the match,
the cup's ownership is transferred to that yacht club.
</p>
</body>
</html>
```

The body of Example 2.6 consists of a division element, with an image tag inside it, followed by two paragraphs of text. The division has a class attribute with the value "image-left". There is nothing special about that name. "Garfield" would have worked as well, but image-left is more helpful. In the style element in the document's head, two CSS rules, in curly braces, are assigned to the division with the image-left class attribute value:

float: left;

padding-right: 1em;

The first rule assigns the value "left" to the float property, which forces the following paragraph elements to wrap around the division. The second rule provides one em^2 of padding on the right of the image to give the page a professional, typeset look. The image is 120 pixels wide. That plus the one em of padding leaves plenty of room for the text.

Figure 2.6 shows the page in a browser window. Notice how the paragraph text returns to the left margin once it extends below the image.

---

2. An em is a typographic unit equal to the width of the letter M.

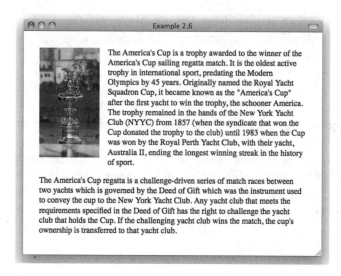

Figure 2.6: A page with a floating image

Left and right floating elements can be used together to create a two-column page. Example 2.7 uses CSS classes named floatleft and floatright.

Example 2.7: Using floating elements to create columns

```
<!DOCTYPE html>
<html>
<head>
<title>Example 2.7</title>
<style type="text/css">  <!-- styles for two columns -->
  h2 { text-align: center; }
  p  { text-align: justify; padding: 2%;}
  p.floatleft  { float: left;  width: 46%; }
  p.floatright { float: right; width: 46%; }
</style>
</head>

<body>
<h2>Points Of Interest</h2>

<p class="floatleft">Notable buildings in the district include
the Flatiron Building, one of the oldest of the original New York
skyscrapers, and just to east at One Madison Avenue is the Met Life
```

```
Tower, built in 1909 and the tallest building in the world until 1913.
</p>

<p class="floatright">Nearby, on Madison Avenue between 26th and
27th Streets, on the site of the old Madison Square Garden, is
the New York Life Building, built in 1928 and designed by Cass
Gilbert, with a square tower topped by a striking gilded pyramid.
</p>
</body>
</html>
```

The content of the body element in Example 2.7 is simple—one level-two heading followed by two paragraphs. All the magic happens in the CSS style element in the document head. The first statement in the style element centers the text of the level-two heading. The second statement says to block-justify all paragraphs, reserving 2 percent of the available width (and height) for padding. The final two statements apply only to paragraph elements having the class attribute with values of floatleft and floatright, respectively. Because each paragraph has enough content to fill the full width of the page, each floated paragraph must be constrained to a width small enough to provide enough room for the other. Instead of giving these paragraphs a fixed width, they are each allowed to occupy 46 percent of the document body's width. Thus, with the 2 percent padding, the two columns occupy the full width of readers' browsers, neatly dividing the page. Figure 2.7 shows the result.

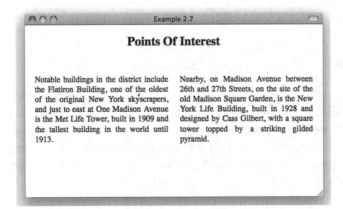

Figure 2.7: A web page with two columns and block-justified text

Inline elements provide the content with the semantic meaning that makes for interesting reading. Browsers interpret inline markup by changing the typography of the text. Browsers for the visually impaired respond to inline markup with changes in tone or volume. Inline HTML elements include markup for explicit semantic purposes:

`<em></em>`	Emphasis; the content has some importance.
`<strong></strong>`	Strong emphasis; the content is very important.
`<abbr></abbr>`	Abbreviation of a term in the content.
`<cite></cite>`	Citation—the title of another work.
`<code></code>`	The content is an example of computer code.
`<var></var>`	The content is a computer variable.
`<q>...</q>`	Inline quotation.
`<sup>...</sup>`	Superscript; reduce the size and raise the content.
`<sub>...</sub>`	Subscript; reduce the size and lower the content.

The strikeout text element, `<strike>...</strike>`, used to designate deleted text in edited documents, may be recognized by many browsers for backward compatibility with earlier versions of HTML. But it is not in the HTML5 specification.

There is a set of inline markup elements for typographic styles that are inherited from earlier versions of HTML:

`<b></b>`	Bold text; increase the font weight.
`<i></i>`	Italics; change the font style to italic.
`<u></u>`	Underline the content.

These typographic elements say nothing about the content they enclose, other than that the author wants the text underlined or displayed with a bold or italic font. No special importance or emphasis should be given to the content, although it may look that way to a human reader. The strong emphasis and/or emphasis elements should always be used when the content to be marked up is important or needs emphasis.

The big and small elements are also from early versions of HTML and are supported by most browsers for backward compatibility:

`<big></big>`	Increases the font size somewhat.
`<small></small>`	Decreases the font size somewhat.

The big element is not in the HTML5 specification. The small element has a semantic purpose in HTML5: It is the element for marking up the "fine print" of a document—the disclaimers, legal terms, and conditions that nobody ever reads.

The time element is new with HTML5. Its purpose is to provide machine-readable publication dates and times of articles and indexes of articles, as found on the front pages of online magazines and blogs. If a document has multiple article elements, there should be no more than one time element per article. If a document has no article elements, there should be only one time element. It provides the publication date and time of the document itself. The time element's datetime attribute holds the machine-readable value, and the element's content can hold the human-readable version. For example:

`<time datetime="2003-03-13">``March 13th`**`</time>`**

The mark element is also new in HTML5. Its purpose is to highlight words or phrases in a quotation that were not given emphasis by the quote's author but that have significance in the current context. You would use the mark element to highlight an important point in quoted text, for example:

`<blockquote>``...nor be deprived of life, liberty, or property, without`
`<mark>``due process`**`</mark>`** `of law;`**`</blockquote>`**

Or you would use the mark element in a passage copied from a historic or religious text to indicate phrases where the translation is in dispute among scholars. The emphasis element used in Example 2.5 could be replaced with the mark element; however, consideration should be given to readers with older browsers that do not recognize this HTML5 element. You could do this by using both elements, for example:

`...<mark><em>due process</em><mark>...`

The span element is a general-purpose inline element that is semantically neutral. It is very useful when given a class or style attribute:

`... wishing you a `**`<span style="color:red">`**`Happy Valentine's Day`**`</span>`**

This is particularly useful when you need to post some temporary content quickly and do not want to bother editing the CSS style sheet.

> **Note:** Netscape introduced a special inline element for text formatting before its Navigator browser supported CSS. Known as the **font** element, it takes three attributes: **size**, which is required, and **face** and **color**. The **blink** element was another Netscape innovation. Guess what that does? Both elements are now deprecated, although they are still supported by many browsers for backward compatibility. The **blink** element is especially annoying and almost universally hated.

Two inline HTML elements are especially important. The anchor element, <a></a>, creates hyperlinks to other pages on the Web, and the image element, <img/>, inserts images into the content.

To give the links on a page a consistent look, the anchor element should be the innermost nested element. It can contain other inline elements, such as images, but it should not contain any elements that change the color or typographic styles of the linked text in a way that suggests that some links are different from others. If a heading is to be hyperlinked to another web page, the anchor element should be nested inside the heading:

```
<h3><a href="chapter_5.html">Chapter 5, Building A Website</a></h3>
```

However, the HTML5 specification allows the anchor element to enclose any other content as long as that content does not itself contain interactive items— links or buttons that are sensitive to the actions of mice and fingers.

The image element is self-closing. It has two required attributes specifying the image's source file and the alternative text to be used if the image itself cannot be displayed. Here's a typical image element:

```
<img src="logo.png" alt="The Logo Corporation"/>
```

Although the alt attribute is required, it can be left empty for image elements that are solely decorative. Not every image needs to have a tooltip window pop up when you hover over it.

```
<img src="blue_square.gif" alt=""/>
```

It is important to remember that images are not block elements. Even though each image has its own height and width, it is still an inline element, and there is no implied white space before, after, above, or below an image. Unless otherwise specified, the bottom of the image is aligned with the baseline of the text it is embedded in. Unless it is floated, it wraps with the words immediately before and after the image tag.

You'll read more about images, anchors, and links later in this chapter.

HTML ATTRIBUTES

A number of HTML attributes can be used with any HTML element. The class and style attributes, used earlier in this chapter, belong to this set of global attributes. Here are a few global attributes recognized by most HTML4 and HTML5 browsers:

id	Specifies a unique identifier that references the element in CSS and scripts
class	Specifies a semantic class that the element should be considered a member of
style	Specifies CSS style rules that should be applied to the element
title	Specifies a title for the element
lang	Specifies the natural language of the element's text content
dir	Specifies the direction, left-to-right or right-to-left, of the element's text content
hidden	Specifies whether the user agent should hide the element's content

The language attribute, lang, affects how punctuation is applied to an element's content, including hyphenation and the choice of ligatures and quotation marks. Content enclosed in the quote element shows a different pair of quotation marks, depending on the value of the language attribute set for that element or inherited from one of its enclosing containers. An element's language is a concept separate from the character set that is used to display the page's text.

The title attribute's original purpose was to provide a window title for links created by anchor and area elements that would display non-HTML data such as images, text files, and directory listings. Internet Explorer was the first browser to display the title attribute's value in a Windows tooltip when the user's mouse hovered over the linked element. Users seemed to like tooltips, and web developers provided them by enclosing elements in anchor tags with null links just so that the tooltip would appear. Seeing the usefulness of the title attribute to search engine robots, the HTML4 specification extended its application to all HTML elements.

The next two global attributes can be added to any element, but they are most useful when used in user input fields and controls:

accesskey — Specifies a shortcut key to be assigned to the element to give it focus

tabindex — Specifies the ordering of elements when tabbing through a document

These four HTML attributes are new with HTML5 and are designed to be used with editable web page content:

contenteditable — Specifies that the content may be editable if the host permits such operation

contextmenu — Specifies a menu that may be presented when the user Alt-clicks the element

draggable — Specifies whether the user may reposition the element

spellcheck — Specifies whether the browser can spell-check the element's content

These last three HTML5 global attributes provide a means for HTML elements to be related to each other across the DOM in scripting applications:

subject — Specifies that the element is the subject of an element with a corresponding item attribute

item — Specifies that the element is an item of an element with a corresponding subject attribute

itemprop — Specifies the properties of an element with an item attribute

A number of HTML attributes existed before CSS. These attributes are supported for backward compatibility even though web authors are encouraged to use CSS in their place.

The align attribute when used in block elements specifies whether the text of the element should be aligned with the left or right margin, or centered within the containing element. This is similar to how the CSS text-align property is used. However, when the align attribute is used in an image (img) or table (table) element with a value of left or right, it acts like the CSS float property. It causes the content following the image or table to wrap around the element on the right or left, respectively.

Sometimes, it is necessary to stop wrapping content around a floated element before all of the available space is used. The clear attribute does this. The valid values for the clear attribute are left, right, and both. Adding this attribute to an HTML element causes the browser to add enough vertical white space before rendering the element to clear it from any floating element. It aligns normally with the left or right margin of the containing element. The clear attribute works the same way as the clear CSS property. The following two statements have the same effect:

```
<h3 clear="left">A heading for this section</h3>
```

```
<h3 style="clear:left">A heading for this section</h3>
```

The second level-three heading is the preferred usage because CSS is more flexible. For example, if a page had many such level-three heading elements, instead of adding the clear attribute to each, the web author could just add a class attribute to accomplish the same thing using CSS. An example would be <h3 class="clearfloat">...</h3>. The CSS statement to clear all h3 elements in the clearfloat class would go in a style element in the document head, along with any other styling needed for the headings:

```
<style type="text/css">
h3.clearfloat {
  clear: left;
  margin-top: 1.5em; /* provide extra space before each heading
*/
}
</style>
```

HTML block elements can have width and height attributes. If the value of one of these attributes is a positive integer, it specifies the element's width or height in pixels. A number followed by the percent sign (%) specifies a width or height that is a percentage of what is available to the element. Example 2.8 shows a floated table with a width attribute. The tr element defines a table row, and the th and td elements define table cells. Tables are discussed in more detail later in this chapter.

Example 2.8: An HTML table with width and float attributes

```
<!DOCTYPE html>
<html>
<head>
<title>Example 2.8</title>
<style type="text/css">
  body { padding: 30px; line-height: 1.5em; }
  td { text-align: right; padding: 5px; }
  th { text-align: left;  padding: 5px; }
</style>
</head>

<body>
<h2 align="center">Final Exam Results</h2>

<table width="33%" align="right" hspace="12" border="1">
  <tr><th></th><th>Points</th><th>Grade</th></tr>
  <tr><th>Larry</th><td>86</td><td>B+</td></tr>
  <tr><th>Heidi</th><td>91</td><td>A</td></tr>
</table>

<p>The final exam required students to create an HTML page
containing a floating table. Larry lost a number of points
because he used <em>align</em> and <em>hspace</em> attributes in
the table statement instead of using the CSS <em>float</em> and
<em>padding</em> properties in his entry entitled, <cite>Example
2.8</cite>.</p>
</body>
</html>
```

Note the use of the cite element to mark up a title. Figure 2.8 shows how this HTML appears in a browser.

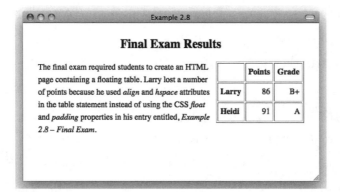

Figure 2.8: HTML page with a floating table element

EVENT HANDLERS

Another class of HTML global attributes is used to specify what actions browsers should take when the user interacts with an element. These event handlers take as their values one or more JavaScript statements. Typically, the value consists of a call to a JavaScript function defined in the document's head or in an external file, and this function does all the work. For example, if you had an input form on a web page that requested the user's email address, you might add the onchange attribute to call a function that checks that the input represents a valid email address. The HTML element would look like this:

```
<input type="text" onchange="check_email_address(this.value);"/>
```

In the late twentieth century, web developers built dynamic web pages using these event handlers and a lot of JavaScript code. These techniques were referred to as dynamic HTML or *dhtml*, although that term had no official standing. Modern web development practice discourages the addition of event handler attributes to HTML elements and encourages the practice of writing functions to handle events on DOM objects separately from the HTML source. Because the use of these attributes is discouraged, they are listed without any description, but the explanation of each is generally obvious from the attribute name. Although these attributes can be used in any HTML element, they do not make sense with every element. Here are the more commonly used attributes:

onabort	onblur	oncanplay
oncanplaythrough	onchange	onclick
oncontextmenu	ondblclick	ondrag
ondragend	ondragenter	ondragleave
ondragover	ondragstart	ondrop
ondurationchange	onemptied	onended
onerror	onfocus	onformchange
onforminput	oninput	oninvalid
onkeydown	onkeypress	onkeyup
onload	onloadeddata	onloadedmetadata
onloadstart	onmousedown	onmousemove
onmouseout	onmouseover	onmouseup
onmousewheel	onpause	onplay
onplaying	onprogress	onratechange
onreadystatechange	onscroll	onseeked
onseeking	onselect	onshow
onstalled	onsubmit	onsuspend
ontimeupdate	onvolumechange	onwaiting

In HTML5, a web developer can create his own attributes to add to any HTML element as long as the attribute name begins with the characters "data-" and has at least one more letter or number following the dash. As many data attributes as needed can be added to an HTML element, provided that there are no duplicate attribute names in any single element. The value of a data attribute follows the same restrictions as other attributes: Character entities are needed for special symbols, but other markup is not parsed as HTML. For example, the following HTML element (a list item) has extra data attributes that can be used by a client-side script to sort a listing or highlight specific items in response to a user action.

```
<li class="book-title"
    data-borrower="Vonnegut, K."
    data-status="overdue">Venus On The Half-Shell</li>
```

The purpose of data attributes is to provide extra information about the contents of an element that can be accessed by client-side scripts. When the HTML source code is itself generated by scripts running on a server, it becomes a powerful tool, because it allows information in database records to be directly incorporated into HTML elements. This was possible in earlier versions of HTML because any attribute attached to an HTML element became a property of the DOM object representing that element. However, in HTML5, this technique is formalized so that pages can have HTML elements containing data attributes and still pass syntax checkers and validation services.

BLOCK ELEMENTS

A web page is given structure by the block elements that comprise it. Headings and paragraphs in a document are block elements, as is the document body itself. There are many different kinds of block elements: block quotes, lists, and tables, to name a few. Some block elements can be nested inside other block elements, and some cannot be. Except in very special cases, a block element should never be inside an inline element.

Every block element occupies a rectangular area on the web page, separated from the content before and after by some amount of white space. The default behavior for browsers is to give each block element as much width as is available. Block elements that are first-level children of the document's body element take up the full width of the browser's window minus any padding assigned to the body element. Block elements that are children of other block elements are as wide as allowed by the width of their parent element.

A big change in HTML5 is the addition of several block elements for marking up new types of content. HTML3 introduced the division element, <div></div>, as an all-purpose container for organizing and referencing collections of other document elements. The HTML5 specification has new block elements for specific types of divisions, such as the section, header, and footer elements. These are discussed later.

HEADINGS

Major segments of a document are introduced and separated by headings. HTML supports six levels of headings, h1 through h6. This is sufficient for most web pages, because most of the structure of a hypertext work is in the links that bind the pages into a website. Additional structure can be generated by using list and table elements. All heading tags are containers and require a corresponding end tag.

The level-one heading h1 is the highest or most significant level heading, and h6 is the least significant. It is customary to put a level 1 heading as the first element in the body of the home page to serve as the page's internal title. Headings should be used in their natural hierarchical order, as in an outline. However, it is perfectly all right to skip heading levels, following an h1 element with an h3, for example.

There another good reason why every web page should have one and only one level-one heading somewhere near the top of the page: It is the most important element that search robots look for after the window title. Try not to break this rule. Even though it might seem that having a level-one heading would hurt your page design, you can still have one at the top of the page by making it invisible to humans with the CSS display property:

<h1 style="display: none;"> ... </h1>

Example 2.9 is an HTML page illustrating the six different heading levels. Figure 2.9 shows how this looks in a browser.

Example 2.9: HTML heading elements

```
<!DOCTYPE html>
<html>
<head>
<title>Example 2.9</title>
<style type="text/css">
  body { text-align: center; }
</style>
</head>

<body>
<h1>Level 1 Heading</h1>
<h2>Level 2 Heading</h2>
<h3>Level 3 Heading</h3>
<h4>Level 4 Heading</h4>
<h5>Level 5 Heading</h5>
<h6>Level 6 Heading</h6>
</body>
<html>
```

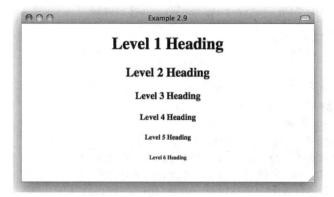

Figure 2.9: HTML heading elements

Figure 2.9 is essentially what a search robot sees when it looks at a page. Speaking of robots, there is an HTML element that groups headings for their benefit. The heading group element, <hgroup></hgroup>, can contain only headings and other heading groups. It implies that those contained headings are related to each other. A browser may or may not visually indicate the group. However, using CSS, you can make the headings and heading groups look how you want them to look. This is illustrated in Figure 2.10. It uses the same body content as Example 2.9 but adds the selectors and rules to the style element in the document's head that are shown in Example 2.10.

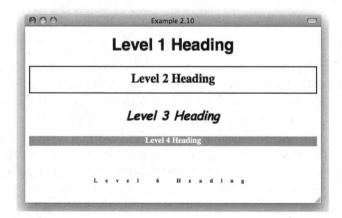

Figure 2.10: HTML headings with CSS styles

Example 2.10: CSS statements for heading styles

```
<!DOCTYPE html>
<html>
<head>
<title>Example 2.10</title>
<style type="text/css">
  body { text-align: center; }
  h1 { font-family: sans-serif; }
  h2 { border: 2px solid black; padding: 10px; }
  h3 { font: bold italic 18pt Comic Sans MS; }
  h4 { color: white; background-color: darkgrey }
  h5 { visibility: hidden; }
  h6 { letter-spacing: 1.5em; }
</style>
</head>

<body>
<h1>Level 1 Heading</h1>
<h2>Level 2 Heading</h2>
<h3>Level 3 Heading</h3>
<h4>Level 4 Heading</h4>
<h5>Level 5 Heading</h5>
<h6>Level 6 Heading</h6>
</body>
<html>
```

Notice that the space formerly occupied by the level-five heading is present in Figure 2.10, but the text is invisible. This is different from giving the element's display property the value none, which effectively sets the height, width, and element margins to 0. Although Example 2.10 has only one heading of each level, the styles used would apply to all headings if there were more on the page. Every level-two heading on the page, for example, would have a black border. If a unique style is needed for one and only one heading, either an id attribute should be added to that heading, or a style attribute should be used to set the element's CSS properties directly within the start tag. For example, this code:

```
<h1 style="font-family: sans-serif;">Level 1 Heading</h1>
```

sets that level-one heading's font the same way as putting the rule in the `style` element in the document's head. However, CSS style information in an element's start tag overrides previously set rules for the same properties. This is useful if you do not have access to the document's head in your editor, such as when editing a blog post. Chapter 3, "Elements of Style," goes into more detail on the syntax and use of CSS.

PARAGRAPHS, BLOCK QUOTES, AND ADDRESS BLOCKS

The **paragraph** is the most commonly used HTML element for representing content. The **block quote** and **address block** are similar. The blockquote element is used to mark up a quotation taken from another source. Block quotes are usually displayed by the browser with wider left and right margins. The address element is intended for designating the contact information associated with a document and is often rendered in an italic font by browsers. Address and paragraph elements are not allowed to contain other block elements.

In HTML2, the paragraph element could be used with or without an end tag. In HTML3 and later versions, the paragraph element is a container, and it is an error to omit the end tag. Web authors should avoid inserting empty paragraph elements or break tags into a page just to achieve vertical spacing of the content elements. If the page design requires more or less space before a paragraph, the top margin of that paragraph should be increased or decreased.

A `blockquote` element can contain any other block and inline elements, but these elements should be related if they are part of the same block quote. A search engine robot finding a `blockquote` element can reasonably conclude that the surrounding content might be related to the quotation and contain links to sources. It is improper to use a block quote as an alternative paragraph style, such as in a list of questions and answers. Likewise, an `address` element on any web page should be used only for the contact information of the page's author or the organization responsible for the page's content. Although it is a common practice, the `address` element should not be used to mark up postal addresses in a business directory. Example 2.11 demonstrates the correct use of these three block elements. Figure 2.11 shows how this HTML appears in most browsers.

Example 2.11: Paragraphs, block quotes, and address blocks in HTML

```
<!DOCTYPE html>
<html>
<head>
```

continues

Example 2.11: Paragraphs, block quotes, and address blocks in HTML *(continued)*

```
    <title>Example 2.11</title>
</head>
<body>
<p>I was recently reminded of one my favorite quotes when it appeared
on the back of a business card given to me at a meeting:</p>

<blockquote>The bitterness of poor quality remains long after the
sweetness of a low price is forgotten.</blockquote>

<p>My associate thought that the quote originated with the
designer, Aldo Gucci. I thought it came from Benjamin Franklin.
If you have a direct reference source, please contact me at:</p>

<address>
Author Dent<br/>
hitchhiker@gmail.com
</address>
</body>
</html>
```

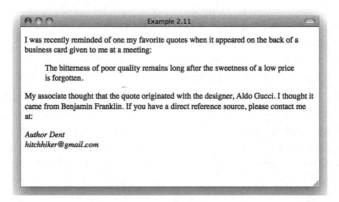

Figure 2.11: Paragraphs, block quotes, and address blocks

Web designers who design page templates for blogs and instant-website generators often style block quotes distinctively by changing the typography and adding backgrounds and borders. Example 2.12 adds a few CSS statements in a style element to the code of Example 2.11, giving the page an entirely different feel, as shown in Figure 2.12.

Example 2.12: CSS styles for paragraphs, block quotes, and address blocks

```
<!DOCTYPE html>
<html>
<head>
<title>Example 2.12</title>
<style type="text/css">
  body {
    font-family: sans-serif;
    padding: 24px;
  }
  p {
    text-align: justify;
    line-height: 1.5em;
  }
  blockquote {
    font: 15pt cursive;
    background-color: #cccccc;
    padding: .5em;
    border: 2px dotted;
  }
  address {
    margin-left: 50%;
    font-family: courier,monospace;
  }
</style>
</head>

<body>
<p>I was recently reminded of one my favorite quotes when it appeared on the back of a business card given to me at a meeting:</p>

<blockquote>The bitterness of poor quality remains long after the sweetness of a low price is forgotten.</blockquote>
```

continues

Example 2.12: CSS styles for paragraphs, block quotes, and address blocks *(continued)*

<p>My associate thought that the quote originated with the designer, Aldo Gucci. I thought it came from Benjamin Franklin. If you have a direct reference source, please contact me at:**</p>**

<address>
Author Dent**
**
hitchhiker@gmail.com
</address>
</body>
</html>

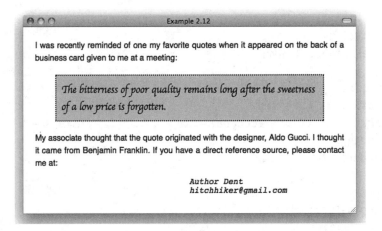

Figure 2.12: Styling block quotes and address blocks with CSS

The break element, <br/>, is used in the address block in Example 2.12, where an explicit line break is needed in the text content. It is a self-closing element often used to clear a floating element by including either a clear or style attribute:

<br clear="both"/>

<br style="clear:both"/>

Two line breaks in a row does not mean twice the vertical space on the page. A break element calls for a line break to be present in the content flow. The browser is free to ignore the tag if a line break already exists at that point. Also, when working with many WYSIWYG and online content editors, the software strips extra line breaks from the HTML or adds its own. It is better to control vertical space using CSS than to try to position things with extra line breaks or empty paragraphs. Example 2.13 shows how to use line breaks in formatting lines of a poem.

Example 2.13: Paragraphs and line breaks

```
<!DOCTYPE html>
<html>
<head>
    <title>Example 2.13</title>
</head>

<body>
<h1>Twelve</h1>

<hr/>

<p>The five colors blind the eye.<br/>
The five tones deafen the ear.<br/>
The five flavors dull the taste.<br/>
Racing and hunting madden the mind.<br/>
Precious things lead one astray.</p>

<p>Therefore the sage is guided by what
he feels and not by what he sees.<br/>
He lets go of that and chooses this.</p>

<hr/>
</body>
</html>
```

The content is from a translation of Lao-Tsu's *Tao Te Ching* by Gai Fu Feng and Jane English. Figure 2.13 shows how it appears in a browser.

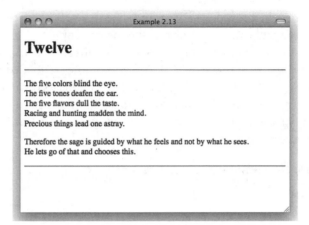

Figure 2.13: Using line breaks

The preformatted text element provides another means to control the spacing of text content. It is sort of an anti-paragraph. Any text between the starting and ending tags, <pre></pre>, is left essentially as is. Preformatted text retains all line breaks and redundant blanks. Horizontal tabs are recognized and expanded as if there were tab stops every eight characters across the page. This is ideal for text copied from another source, such as an email message, which needs to keep its line breaks and spacing intact. It can be pasted inside a preformatted text element. The text is rendered in a monospace font by default, although this can easily be changed with CSS.

Within the preformatted block no other block elements should be used. Inline elements, including anchor and image elements, are appropriate. Example 2.14 shows a simple example of preformatted text that creates the display shown in Figure 2.14.

Example 2.14: Preformatted text in HTML

```
<!DOCTYPE html>
<html>
<head>
 <title>Example 2.14</title>
</head>

<body>
<h2>Puzzle</h2>
<pre>
```

```
|\   /        Here's one way to
o o o         connect all 9
|   X         dots using only 4
o o o         straight lines:
|/   \
o-o-o-
</pre>
</body>
</html>
```

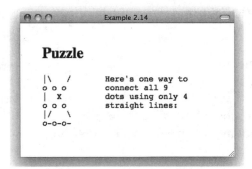

Figure 2.14: A web page with a preformatted element

LISTS

A list is a block element containing a sequence of list items. HTML provides several types of lists, including **ordered lists**, **unordered lists**, **definition lists**, and **menus**. Ordered lists have sequenced items, whereas unordered lists have bulleted items. The **list item** element, which is where the content goes, is also a block element. A list element may have only list items as its direct descendents.

Ordered lists use the tags <ol></ol> to enclose and mark the entire list structure. Unordered lists use <ul></ul> tags. List items are enclosed in the tags <li></li>. When rendered by the browser, list items are usually indented from the left margin. Although ordered and unordered lists can contain only list items as their immediate child elements, list item elements can contain any content and markup, including other lists. Example 2.15 shows the HTML markup for nesting an unordered list inside an ordered list. This might be used in an outline or table of contents, for example.

Example 2.15: Nested ordered and unordered lists

```html
<!DOCTYPE html>
<html>
<head>
<title>Example 2.15</title>
</head>

<body style="margin: 36px">
<h1>The Autobiography Of A Biographer</h1>
<hr/>
<h2>Table of Contents</h2>     <!-- use headings for major sections -->

<ol>
    <li>Introduction</li>
    <li>Early Years
        <ul>                     <!-- use bullets for this level -->
          <li>The Joy of Writing</li>
          <li>Meeting Interesting People</li>
        </ul>
    </li>
    <li>The Major Biographical Works</li>
</ol>

</body>
</html>
```

Figure 2.15 shows how this example appears in a browser.

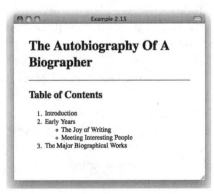

Figure 2.15: Nested lists

Ordered lists have two attributes that let you control the appearance of list items. The `start` attribute can be used to set the number for the first item of the list to a value other than 1. The `type` attribute controls how the list is sequenced. `type` can have any of the following values:

`type="1"`	Normal numeric numbering; the default
`type="A"`	Uppercase letters: A, B, C, D, …
`type="a"`	Lowercase letters: a, b, c, d, …
`type="I"`	Uppercase Roman numerals: I, II, III, IV, …
`type="i"`	Lowercase Roman numerals: i, ii, iii, iv, …

For unordered lists, the `type` attribute can take the values `circle`, `square`, `disc`, or `none` to indicate the type of bullet used. The `start` attribute is ignored in unordered lists.

The items of a definition list are enclosed in `<dl></dl>` tags. Each item of a definition list is a pair of objects called the **definition term** and **definition description**. The definition term's HTML tags are `<dt></dt>`, and the definition descriptions are `<dd></dd>`. The default behavior of most browsers is to treat both the definition terms and descriptions as normal paragraphs, with the definition element indented from the left margin. No bullets or list numbers are added. Definition lists are intended to be used by authors to mark up content that has a topic-comment structure. This is useful for lists of frequently asked questions and answers (FAQs), as well as for glossaries and indexes.

A definition list has no restrictions regarding the use of other HTML elements within either the defining term or description part. It is common to nest a heading inside the term part of the element to provide emphasis and spacing. Authors are encouraged to stick to the semantic use of the element to mark up short phrases as topics followed by longer comment terms. Definition lists should not be used just to provide alternating paragraph styles, because this is what CSS classes do. Example 2.16 shows the HTML for a simple definition list.

Example 2.16: HTML for a definition list

```
<!DOCTYPE html>
<html>
<head>
```

continues

Example 2.16: HTML for a definition list *(continued)*

```
<title>Example 2.16</title>
</head>

<body>
<dl>
    <dt><h3>Bucky Balls</h3></dt>
    <dd>Technically, Buckminster Fullerene, a family of all carbon
molecules named after the great designer-architect-engineer,
Buckminster Fuller. The most stable member, C60, is a hollow
sphere with the same architecture as the geodesic structures
Fuller pioneered a half century ago.</dd>

    <dt><h3>Penrose Tiling</h3></dt>
    <dd>A method of tiling a plane thought impossible until
discovered by Roger Penrose. Combining two differently shaped
rhomboids, the tiling has five-fold symmetry, yet <em>the pattern
is not periodic!</em>. A mathematical curiosity until it was found
in some natural minerals with rather strange properties.</dd>
</dl>
</body>
</html>
```

Figure 2.16 shows how this definition list appears in a typical browser.

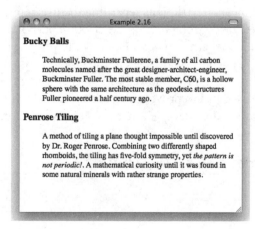

Figure 2.16: A definition list

Without any attributes, the menu list element, <menu></menu>, has the same effect as an unordered list element. It should be used where the content consists of a list of commands, links, or similar navigation or control elements. Using menu elements in place of unordered lists allows for better styling control of page navigational elements.

In HTML5, the menu element has an optional type attribute. The default value is list, which preserves the behavior of existing code. However, if the type attribute has a value of context, the element can provide a context menu for a form input field or other control on the page. In other words, the menu list is hidden until the user Alt-clicks the associated control. Context menus are associated with a control through the use of the contextmenu attribute, whose value should be the ID of the menu list element. For example, in the following code snippet

```
Player Name: <input type="text" contextmenu="namemenu"/>

<menu type="context" id="namemenu">
  <command label="Pick random name" onclick="getRandomName();"/>
  <command label="Use your real name" onclick="getRealName();"/>
</menu>
```

the menu element provides a context menu for the input field defined above it. The value of the input element's contextmenu attribute is the value of the menu's id attribute. The command element, two of which appear inside the menu element just shown, is a new HTML5 element that provides a generalized means of generating controls that can respond to user actions. In the preceding code, when the user clicks the input element while holding down the Alt or Ctrl key, the browser can display a submenu of the two commands. Clicking either context menu item calls a function (not defined in this example) to fill in the value of the input field.

The other permissible value of the menu element's type attribute is toolbar. It is intended to provide web authors and developers with a means of specifying a list of items, possibly icons, that HTML5-level browsers can display as a horizontal toolbar. However, until browsers add support for the toolbar and context states of a menu element, web authors should continue to use the CSS float property to create horizontal toolbars and menus. Example 2.17 shows how the same list can be made to display either vertically or horizontally.

Example 2.17: HTML and CSS for vertical and horizontal lists

```
<!DOCTYPE html>
<html>
<head>
<title>Example 2.17</title>
<style type="text/css">
  body { padding: 36px; }
  menu li {
    float: left;
    list-style: none;
    margin-right: 8px;
    border: 2px solid;
    padding: 4px;
}
</style>
</head>

<body>
<h2>Vertical and Horizontal lists</h2>

<ul>
    <li>Gold</li>
    <li>Silver</li>
    <li>Bronze</li>
</ul>

<menu>
    <li>Gold</li>
    <li>Silver</li>
    <li>Bronze</li>
</menu>

</body>
</html>
```

In this example, it is not the menu element that creates the horizontal toolbar. The CSS rules in the style element operate on each list item in the menu element, causing it to float up on the right of the previous list item. The

CSS statements setting the margin, border, and padding style the list items as separated buttons. The CSS statement list-style: none; is needed to suppress the bullets. Figure 2.17 shows how the preceding HTML code appears in a browser.

Figure 2.17: Vertical and horizontal lists

DIVISION AND SECTION ELEMENTS

Divisions are general-purpose block elements that can contain any other content and markup, including other divisions. Content marked up with division tags, <div></div>, has no special semantic meaning other than that the separate elements of that content belong together. Divisions are most useful as containers for CSS properties providing a means of grouping headings, paragraphs, and other elements for visual styling with backgrounds and borders. Divisions are also useful as targets of scripting actions. It is common practice to use a division for content that is hidden or shown by a script responding to a user's mouseover or click actions.

In contrast to the division element, the **section** element, new in HTML5, is intended for marking up major sections of a larger work, such as the chapters of a book. For example, a publisher may choose to publish a work online in two different formats: the book as a set of linked pages, one per chapter, and the entire book as a single web page. Assume that the content is provided by a content management system that provides all the content and markup to create a single chapter page. For the all-on-one-page version, each chapter's content can be placed in a section element without having to reduce all the headings by one level. Remember, there should be only one level-one heading on a page. The exception to this rule is when a page is composed of multiple sections. In that case, each section is allowed to retain the level-one heading it would have when published on its own. Although a section element may contain other sections, a section's parent element should only be another section or the body element. It would be incorrect to have a section inside a division.

Also in HTML5, a number of elements behave as divisions but actually provide specific semantic meaning for robots and other HTML processors.

The article element, <article></article>, should be used when marking up content that is article-like, such as the posts on a blog or the articles in an online magazine. Like the section element, an article element can contain all markup that would be appropriate if the article was published on a page by itself, including a single address element with authorship information. Unlike the section element, an article should not be nested inside another article.

Similarly, the navigation (<nav></nav>), header (<header></header>), and footer (<footer></footer>) elements are semantic markup intended to provide more information for search robots and other nonhuman readers than can be gleaned from division elements. To illustrate, consider a web page using division elements with id and class attributes to define the various parts of the page. Example 2.18 shows the HTML. Figure 2.18 shows how this page appears in a browser.

Example 2.18: HTML divisions

```
<!DOCTYPE html>
<html>
<head>
   <title>Example 2.18</title>
<style type="text/css">
   body        { padding: 0 36px; }
   h1          { font-family: sans-serif; padding-top: 60px; }

   #header     { margin-bottom: 36px; }
   #header img { float: left; }
   #header a   { text-decoration: none; }

   #top-menu,
   #bottom-menu  { margin-left: -36px; }
```

```css
#top-menu li   { float: left;
                 padding: 5px;
                 border: 1px solid;
                 list-style: none;
                 margin-right: 5px; }

#bottom-menu li { float: left;
                  padding: 0 10px;
                  border-right: 1px solid;
                  list-style: none; }

div.navigation  { clear: left; font-family: arial,sans-serif;}

address         { clear: left; text-align: right; padding-top: 36px;}
</style>
</head>

<body>
<div id="header">               <!-- Logo and main menu -->
  <div id="logo">
    <img src="../images/logo.gif" alt="Logocorp Inc."/>
    <h1>Welcome to Logocorp</h1>
  </div>
  <div class="navigation">
    <ul id="top-menu">
      <li><a href="home.html">Home</a></li>
      <li><a href="about.html">About</a></li>
      <li><a href="what.html">...</a></li>
    </ul>
  </div>
</div>

<hr/>

<div id="content">            <!-- content division -->
  <h2>Logocorp News</h2>
  <p>We are doing good things... </p>
  <p>Logos are everywhere... </p>
```

continues

Example 2.18: HTML divisions *(continued)*

```
</div>

<hr />

<div id="footer">            <!-- page footer -->
  <div class="navigation">
    <ul id="bottom-menu">
      <li><a href="home.html">Home</a></li>
      <li><a href="about.html">About</a></li>
      <li><a href="what.html">...</a></li>
    </ul>
  </div>
  <address>copyright &copy; 2010, Logocorp, Inc.</address>
</div>
</body>
<html>
```

Figure 2.18: Using division elements

The id and class attributes used in Example 2.18 may be useful to the next web developer who works with the code, but they do not provide any useful information to search robots, because they are arbitrary names. If the division elements are replaced with appropriate header, footer, and nav elements, an HTML5-aware browser would display the page similarly to the page shown in Figure 2.18. An HTML5-aware robot, on the other hand, would be able to make greater sense of the page. Note that if you experiment with the preceding code, clicking the links gives you File Not Found errors unless you also have files named home.html, about.html, and what.html.

TABLES

Often you need to present information in a more structured fashion than that provided by lists. Tables allow information to be displayed in rows and columns. Tables are defined by table tags, <table></table>, enclosing one or more table row elements, <tr></tr>, each of which encloses one or more table cells. There are two different kinds of table cells: table header cells (<th></th>), and table data cells (<td></td>). The default for browsers is to use the default font for data cell text and bold, centered text for header cell content.

Tables are intended for the layout of tabular data such as the contents of a spreadsheet. However, tables are used extensively on the Web to position and lay out page elements. Tables give web designers and developers a powerful tool to precisely position page elements on a fixed grid. As a bonus, developers can set the background color of a table cell by adding the BGCOLOR attribute to that element. Before this change, designers could only set the background color of the entire page.

Example 2.19 generates a simple three-row-by-three-column table, and Figure 2.19 shows the result.

Example 2.19: HTML markup for a simple table

```
<!DOCTYPE html>
<html>
<head><title>Example 2.19</title></head>
<body>
<table>
<caption>total table items</caption>
    <tr>
        <th></th> <th>lunch</th> <th>dinner</th>
```

continues

Example 2.19: HTML markup for a simple table *(continued)*

```
    </tr>
    <tr>
        <th>kitchen</th> <td>23</td> <td>30</td>
    </tr>
    <tr>
        <th>dining room</th> <td>31</td> <td>45</td>
    </tr>
</table>
</body>
</html>
```

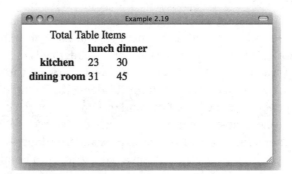

Figure 2.19: A simple table

For the table displayed in Figure 2.19, it is important to note the following. First, the table is only as wide as it needs to be. Second, the caption is centered above the table because that is where table captions are placed by default, not because the caption element appears before the table rows. To place the caption below the table, add the attribute align with the value bottom to the caption element. Finally, no grid lines indicate the table's borders and cells. Grid lines are a function of the border attribute specified in the table tag and any CSS border properties assigned to the table's elements.

The table element has optional subelements for marking up logical groups of rows. The table head element (<thead></thead>), table foot element (<tfoot></tfoot>), and table body element (<tbody></tbody>), can each contain zero or more table row elements. A table can have many table body elements but no more than one table head and one table foot element. Combining these factors, the model for a table follows this form:

```
<table>
    <caption>    <!-- title text for this table -->    </caption>
    <thead>
        <tr>
            <th>row 1, col 1 head</th>
            <th>row 1, col 2 head</th>
        </tr>
    </thead>

    <tbody>        <!-- first table body section -->
        <tr>
            <td>row 2, col 1</td>
            <td>row 2, col 2</td>
        </tr>
        <tr>
            <td>row 3, col 1</td>
            <td>row 3, col 2</td>
        </tr>
    </tbody>

    <tbody>        <!-- second table body section -->
        <tr>
            <td>row 4, col 1</td>
            <td>row 4, col 2</td>
        </tr>
        <tr>
            <td>row 5, col 1</td>
            <td>row 5, col 2</td>
        </tr>
    </tbody>

    <tfoot>        <!-- table footer section -->
        <tr>
            <td>row 6, col 1</td>
            <td>row 6, col 2</td>
        </tr>
    </tfoot>
</table>
```

A number of attributes can be used with table elements, although the functions of many of them have been replaced by CSS properties. Here are some of the more useful attributes that can be added to the table tag:

align	Valid values are left, right, and center. left and right are equivalent to the CSS float property.
width	The table's width, specified as either an absolute number of pixels or a percentage
height	The table's height, specified as either an absolute number of pixels or a percentage
border	The pixel width of the table's border and grid lines
cellspacing	The number of pixels between the "walls" of adjacent cells
cellpadding	The number of pixels between the "walls" of a cell and its contents. Similar to the CSS padding property.
bgcolor	The table's background color, expressed as an RGB value

The align attribute can also be added to table row and cell elements. But the values control the text alignment property of the cell contents, not the floating properties of the element, as with the table element. This inconsistency is due to the need for browsers to be backward-compatible with earlier versions of HTML. In addition to the values left, right, and center, the align attribute can have the value justify when used in table row or cell elements. The valign attribute (vertical alignment) controls the vertical positioning of the content within a cell. It can have the values top, bottom, or middle (the default).

Alignment specified at the table cell level has precedence over row alignment, which has precedence over table body, head, or foot alignment. Conversely, alignment is inherited from the head/body/foot level if not specified at the row level, and cell alignment is inherited from the row level if not specified at the cell level.

The width attribute sets an initial maximum width for the table to occupy. A browser attempts to adjust the cell sizes and word-wrap the contents of the cells to fit within this value. However, content always has a minimum width that is determined by the number of letters in the longest word or the width of the widest image. Therefore, it is possible for a table to be wider than the value of the width attribute's value. By contrast, the height attribute sets an initial minimum height for the table. A browser just adds extra space above and/or below cell contents, depending on the value of the `align` attribute. In general, it is better to specify table widths and heights using CSS properties.

Adding a `border` attribute with a positive integer to the table tag turns on the table's grid lines and draws a border around the entire table, excluding any caption. The table border is always that number of pixels thick. The grid lines, however, are that size only if there is enough spacing between the cells. The spacing between cells is controlled by the cellspacing attribute, which can have any nonnegative integer value. The default value is about 2 pixels (depending on the browser). Specifying a `table` element with 0 cell spacing and a border of 1 pixel causes the browser to draw a hairline (1-pixel) grid.

Cell padding is the number of pixels that separate the contents of table cells from the cell walls, and it applies to all cells within a table. This attribute is of less importance than the cellspacing attribute because web developers have much more control using the CSS `padding` property, which can be used to add different amounts of padding on each side of the content.

To make it look better, we will add some attributes to the table defined in Example 2.19, along with some CSS styles. Example 2.20 shows the HTML that generates the page shown in Figure 2.20.

Example 2.20: Providing table alignment and spacing

```
<!DOCTYPE html>
<html>
<head>
  <title>Example 2.20</title>
  <style type="text/css">
    body     { padding-top: 36px;  }
    th, td   { padding: 3px 6px;   }
    thead th { text-align: right;  }
    th       { text-align: left;   }
    td       { text-align: right;  }
    caption  { font-style: italic; }
  </style>
</head>

<body>
<table cellspacing="0" border="1" align="center" width="80%">
<caption>Total Table Items</caption>
```

continues

Example 2.20: Providing table alignment and spacing *(continued)*

```
<thead>
  <tr>
      <th></th> <th>lunch</th> <th>dinner</th>
  </tr>
</thead>
  <tr>
      <th>kitchen</th> <td>23</td> <td>30</td>
  </tr>
  <tr>
      <th>dining room</th> <td>31</td> <td>45</td>
  </tr>
</table>
</body>
</html>
```

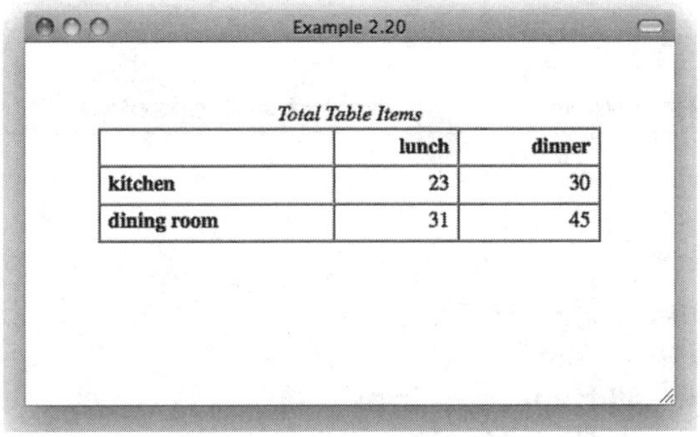

Figure 2.20: A table with good alignment and spacing

Numeric data in a table looks better when aligned on the right. This CSS statement

```
thead th { text-align: right; }
```

specifies right alignment for table head cells with the thead element. The statement following that specifies left alignment for the th elements used as row labels. The padding property for both th and td elements is given the value 3px 6px, which is a shorthand way of saying 3 pixels for the top and bottom padding and 6 pixels for the left and right padding. The table shown in

Figure 2.20 has additional padding in the table cells because the width attribute sets a minimum width of 80 percent of the available space for the table, causing the cells to be stretched horizontally.

To make even fancier tables, web developers use the rowspan and colspan attributes. Example 2.21 illustrates these techniques.

Example 2.21: A table with spanned rows and columns

```html
<!DOCTYPE html>
<html>
<head>
  <title>Example 2.21</title>
  <style type="text/css">
    body    { padding: 36px;        }
    th, td  { padding: 3px 6px;     }
    th      { text-align: left;     }
    td      { text-align: right;    }
    caption { font-style: italic;   }
  </style>
</head>

<body>
<table border="2">
<caption align="bottom">The Inner Planets</caption>
  <tr>
    <th rowspan="2"></th>
    <th colspan="2">Distance from sun</th>
    <th rowspan="2">Year<br/>Length</th>
    <th rowspan="2">Day<br/>Length</th>
  </tr>
  <tr>
    <th>Kilometers</th><th>AUs</th>
  </tr>
  <tr>
    <th>Mercury</th>
    <td>57,900,000</td><td>.38</td><td>88 days</td><td>59 days</td>
  </tr>
  <tr>
```

continues

Example 2.21: A table with spanned rows and columns *(continued)*

```
    <th>Venus</th>
    <td>108,200,000</td><td>.72</td><td>225 days</td><td>243 days</td>
  </tr>
  <tr>
    <th>Earth</th>
    <td>149,600,000</td><td>1.0</td><td>365 days</td><td>24 hrs</td>
  </tr>
  <tr>
    <th>Mars</th>
    <td>227,900,000</td><td>1.5</td><td>687 days</td><td>24.6 hrs</td>
  </tr>
</table>
</body>
</html>
```

Figure 2.21 shows how the code in Example 2.21 appears in a browser.

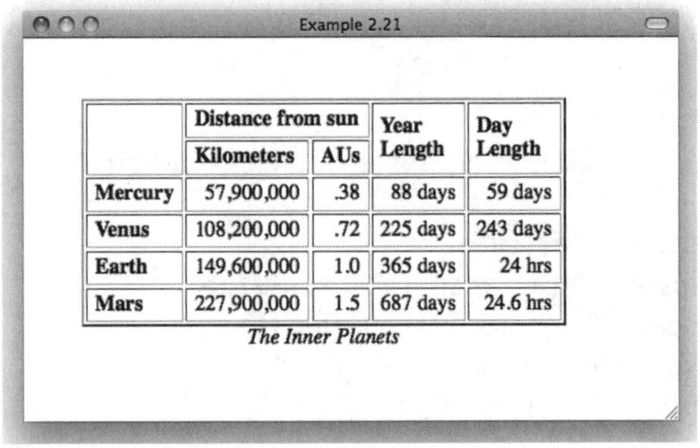

	Distance from sun		Year Length	Day Length
	Kilometers	AUs		
Mercury	57,900,000	.38	88 days	59 days
Venus	108,200,000	.72	225 days	243 days
Earth	149,600,000	1.0	365 days	24 hrs
Mars	227,900,000	1.5	687 days	24.6 hrs

The Inner Planets

Figure 2.21: A table with spanned rows and columns

It goes without saying that web developers must be careful when using the rowspan and colspan attributes not to wind up with a table that has the wrong number of cells in a row or column. This generally yields unpredictable results.

Initially a web designer's best friend, tables have fallen out of favor recently because robots and editing software have difficulty understanding them due to their complexity. When tables are coded by hand, the author generally knows what kind of content will go into the cells. However, when tables are generated by server-side scripts drawing content from a database, it is less certain what content, if any, will go into a given row or cell. Therefore, extra care is needed to deal with null data values and edge conditions.

LINKS AND ANCHORS

Links are the lifeblood of the Web, and Hypertext is the name of the Markup Language. That said, "link" is a strange word. It is both a noun and a verb, and its use is loose. And how can a link be hyper? Two elements in HTML, the anchor and area elements, when used with an href (hypertext reference) attribute, create hyperlinks. A third element, the link element (<link/>), can also create hyperlinks when used with certain attributes. It is a document head element providing a means for web authors to link the current document to other resources on the Web. The link element is discussed further in the section "Page Head Information" in Chapter 5.[3]

The anchor element, <a></a>, in HTML5 is allowed to contain any other content and markup, including nested block elements. It should not, however, contain any markup that responds to mouse clicks or finger taps. It is rare in practice to code a link that spans multiple block elements such as paragraphs and lists. Such constructions may be more difficult for search robots to understand than if the separate paragraphs and list items were each linked to the same URL. It is also more difficult to maintain a consistency of link styling if links span multiple elements.

Because the introduction of the first graphical web browsers in 1993, the default formatting behavior for browsers is to underline the text content of an anchor element and make it blue (linked images get a blue border). One of the first browser enhancements was to give both web authors and browser users the ability to change the style and color of links. A distinctive look for links is an important branding tool for website designers, and a consistent look for linked text items is an important aid to navigation.

The area element, <area/>, is a content-free, self-closing element that does not affect the rendering of a web page. It is used to specify that a subarea of an image is hyperlinked to a Web resource. The area element must always be the child of a map element, which can be referenced by an image element elsewhere on the page. Like the anchor element, the area element becomes a hyperlink when used with an href attribute whose value is a valid URL.

---

3. Any HTML element, actually, can create a hyperlink if that element has an event handler attribute to detect an appropriate user action and can execute an instruction to set the document's location to a new URL.

Unlike with the anchor element, a browser does not indicate the linked sub-areas of an image. The map and area elements are explained in the section "Inline Images."

UNIFORM RESOURCE LOCATORS

The URL format permits almost any resource on the Internet to be addressed, whether that resource is an HTML file on a web server or another Internet resource, such as a file on an FTP server. The URL has several parts, not all of which are required for the URL to be valid. In order of appearance, they specify the following:

1 The **protocol** method to be used to access the resource

2 A **username** if the resource requires authentication

3 The **hostname** of the server providing the resource

4 A **port** number to be used on the server

5 The directory **path** to the resource

6 The **filename** of the resource

7 The **anchor** name or ID of an element in the HTML document

8 **Parameters** to be passed to the resource

Various delimiters separate the parts, as follows:

protocol://username@hostname:port/path/filename#anchor?parameters

The method for accessing resources on ordinary web servers is http, which stands for Hypertext Transport Protocol. Secure web servers are accessed with the https method. Other protocol methods access Internet services other than the Web.

The file protocol method is used to access resources on the local computer. This is the implied protocol when using the Open command on the browser's File menu. The username, hostname, and port parts of the URL are not used with the file protocol. The file protocol method should never be used in a web page on a remote web server.

The mailto protocol method signals that the browser should open a new message in the user's email client. The recipient's email address comes immediately after the colon (:) following the protocol. For example:

```
<a href="mailto:info@logocorp.com"
   title="Request for information">Email Us</a>!
```

In addition, there are a number of special browser protocol methods. Replacing http or https with view-source causes most browsers to display the HTML source code of a Web resource. The javascript protocol, followed by a valid JavaScript expression after the colon, causes the browser to execute that expression. For example, type the following into a browser's location window and press Enter:

javascript:document.write('<h1>Hello</h1>');

The port number is the server's version of a telephone extension number. The default is port 80 for the http protocol. Most websites are accessible on that port, so it rarely needs to be entered. Secure servers use a different default port.

To link to another HTML document in the same directory as the current one, only the filename is needed. A user agent fills in the missing information from the current document's URL before sending the request to the web server. This is called **relative URL addressing**, and it is the preferred way to write hyperlinks in documents that reside within the same website. The following example provides a link to the file spotdata.html:

Data has a cat named **<a href="spotdata.html">Spot</a>**.

Relative addressing makes a website portable. As long as the files reside in the same logical directory, none of the relative links need to be updated when the collection is moved to another server or domain. To link to a specific place in the destination page, follow the filename with a pound sign (#) and the id of the HTML element that corresponds to that place in the destination page:

<a href="spotdata.html#habits">Spot</a>

If the file is in a subdirectory of the directory containing the current file, the anchor element's link to the preceding file would be written like this:

<a href="pets/spotdata.html">Spot</a>

The double-dot (../) shorthand can be used to write a link to a resource in the parent directory of the current file:

<a href="../officers/">List of Officers</a>

This code references a directory on the web server rather than a single file. This is a request to the web server for the default index file in that directory, usually index.html. If the web server cannot find a default index file, it has the option of returning an index listing of all files in that directory. A URL beginning with a single slash is a request to get a resource from the website's document root. This is called **root URL addressing**. A single slash with no path or file information is a shorthand request for the website's home page:

```
<a href="/">Enterprise Home</a>
```

Full URL addressing must be used if the file or resource is on a different server than the current file. The protocol method and the server's hostname must be specified:

```
<a href="http://enterprise.ufp.mil/pets/spotdata.html">Spot</a>
```

Optional parameters can be sent to a web server resource by adding a question mark (?) to the end of the URL with a list of name-value pairs separated by ampersands (&). Usually, the resource is a server-side script that knows what to do with the parameters. For example, the following anchor element could represent a link to a server-side script named show_log:

```
<a href="/officers/show_log?rank=captain&stardate=1512.2"> ... </a>
```

The show_log script has access to the information in the parameters and knows that the request is for the captain's log, stardate 1512.2. It uses that information to dynamically build a reply page to send back to the requesting browser. The parameters are also available to client-side scripts embedded in an HTML file—even an HTML file generated by a server script—so every URL request has multiple dynamic possibilities.

ANCHOR STATES

The link created by an anchor or area element can be in one of four states: normal, hover, active, or visited. The normal state is a link that has not been visited by that browser in recent history. The active state occurs when the anchor or area element has focus and has been "activated." For standard PC browsers this occurs when a mouse down event has been detected and the browser is waiting for the user to release the button. A link is in the visited state if it has been visited before in recent history. The length of time a link remains in the visited state is a function of the browser's preference settings. Clearing a browser's history resets the state of any visited links to normal.

The colors that a browser uses to indicate the normal, active, and visited states to the user can be set with link, alink, and vlink attributes of the body element, as shown next. These attributes were introduced before there was support for CSS. CSS is the preferred way of styling hyperlinks.

```
<body link="darkblue" alink="red" vlink="grey">
```

In CSS, the state of an *anchor* element can be selected for rule assignment using the pseudo-selectors: link, hover, active, and visited. The following CSS rules set the same values as the attributes in the preceding body tag and change the background color when the user's mouse hovers over an anchor element. Other CSS statements in the document's styles can set different values for specific elements and classes of elements.

```
<style type="text/css">
  a           { color: blue; }
  a:active  { color: red; }
  a:visited { color: green; }
  a:hover    { background-color: yellow; }
</style>
```

These states are also available to client-side scripts as document object properties. Changes in the state of an anchor can be detected using event handler attributes such as onmouseover, onmouseout, onfocus, onblur, onclick, onmousedown, and onmouseup.

ANCHOR ATTRIBUTES

In addition to the href and name attributes, anchor and area elements can have the target and title attributes. The target attribute provides a means for Web authors to have links open in a new window. The target attribute provides the name of the browser window in which to open the requested document. If no existing window has that name, a new window is created with that name. The special target name "_blank" always opens a new window with no name.

A window's name is an internal name that can be used by scripts in one document to play with the elements of another document loaded into a different window. It is not the same as the window title, which is set by the title attribute in the document's head section. The title attribute can set the window title in cases where the requested document is not an HTML resource and does not have a title element of its own, such as with a JPEG image or text file. For example:

```
<a href="http://area51.mib.gov/library/M2plans.jpg"
   target="_blank"
   title="Top Secret Plans">Mark II Saucer</a>
```

Most browsers display the value of an anchor element's title in a small yellow tooltip box when the user's mouse hovers over the element for a couple of seconds. Robots love title attributes and consider the information they contain valuable. title attributes are important for search engine optimization.

INLINE IMAGES

An image is worth a thousand words on the Web as well. Images make a web page more attractive. The images on a page give readers information that cannot be gleaned from the text. For example, a simple line graph is more informative than a table of numbers. Images function importantly as page design elements.

Three image formats are widely used on the Web. Graphics Interchange Format (GIF) works well for simple line drawings and illustrations with plain blocks of color. GIF format is limited to 256 colors in a single image but does permit one color in the image's palette to be treated as fully transparent by the displaying browser or other software. Joint Photographic Experts Group (JPEG) format permits the use of millions of colors and is suitable for photographs and illustrations with gradient colors. JPEG images feature a variable compression setting that can be used to balance image quality with file size. The last format, Portable Network Graphics (PNG) format, can be used for either simple illustrations or colorful photographs. It has an efficient fixed compression algorithm, so file sizes are reasonable. It also has alpha transparency that can be controlled by CSS settings and manipulated by client-side scripts. This makes it possible to fade the image in and out in response to a user's activity.

To include an inline image on a page, use the self-closing image tag, <img/>. No paragraph breaks or additional white space around the image are implied. If text flow around the image is not specified, the image is inserted into the text like a single odd-sized character. Unlike an image in a page layout program, which can be anchored to a specific spot on the page, an inline image on a Web page is part of the text in which it is embedded. An inline image can be placed anywhere a text character can be placed.

The image tag has two important, required attributes. The source attribute, src, provides the URL of the file containing the image data. The URL in a source attribute follows the same rules as a URL in the href attribute of an anchor or area element. The alternative text attribute, alt, is used to specify an alternative description of the image that can be read by robots and displayed by browsers if the image is unavailable or cannot be displayed for some reason. The alternative text should not be considered a description of the image. It is replacement text content for situations where an image cannot be displayed.

Example 2.22 displays a page with two small, inline images. The second image is the anchor of a link and is given a blue border, as shown in Figure 2.22. Note the use of the align attribute in the second image tag to align the "top" of the image with the top of the line of text it is embedded in.

Example 2.22: Inline images

```
<!DOCTYPE html>
<html>
<head>
        <title>Example 2.22</title>
</style>
</head>

<body>
<h1>Inline Images</h1>
<p>Have you seen this person?
    <img src="mystery_man.png" alt="Mystery Man"/></p>
<p><a href="report.html"
        title="Report sighting"><img src="bigYes.png" alt="Yes"
                                        align="top"/></a>
        Please let us know.</p>
</body>
</html>
```

Figure 2.22: A web page with two inline images

An inline image behaves on a web page as if it were a large character of text. This is the key to understanding how to use images on a Web page. It not only means that anywhere a text character can go, an inline image can go; it also means that inline images are bound to adjacent characters (or other inline images) the same way as letters are bound into words. This sequence of image elements:

```
<img src="..." alt=""/>
<img src="..." alt=""/>
<img src="..." alt=""/>
```

is not the same as this sequence:

```
<img src="..." alt=""/><img src="..." alt=""/><img src="..." alt=""/>
```

In the former case, the carriage returns ending each line in the HTML source are treated as white space between the images. If the images together are wider then the containing element, it word-wraps on those spaces. In the latter case, there are no spaces between the images. They are like the characters in a three-letter word. If the containing element is narrower than the total width of the three images, horizontal scrolling may be enabled. Or depending on the properties of the containing element, the images can either be clipped or allowed to overflow into adjacent content.

A large image, especially one that is wider than it is high, should be placed by itself by enclosing it in an HTML block element that can take the `align` attribute, such as a division, heading, or paragraph. For example, the following HTML centers an image over a caption:

```
<div align="center"><img src="images/300-8.gif" alt="book
cover"/><br/>
Cover of the First Edition</div>
```

There is even an element for enclosing an image: the figure element, which can supply a caption with the `figcaption` child element.

```
<figure>
  <img src="images/300-8.gif" alt="book cover"/><br/>
  <figcaption>Cover of the First Edition</figcaption>
</figure>
```

The figure element is not limited to images. It can be used with any content that can in some way be separated from the main part of the document, including tables and code samples. The figcaption element is optional. There should not be more than one in any figure. The figure element aids search engine optimization by distinguishing images that are part of the content from images that are purely decorative. The figure and figcaption elements also make it possible to compile a "list of figures" for a document.

When images are taller than they are wide, text and other content can be directed to flow around the image, either on the right or left side by giving the value "left" or "right", respectively, to the image element's align attribute. But, when the align attribute has one of the values: "top", "middle", or "bottom", it specifies how the image should be aligned with the adjacent text. The default is to align the bottom of an image with the baseline of the text. A value of "top" aligns the top of the image with the top of the tallest character in the current line, as illustrated in Figure 2.22. The value of "middle" aligns the middle of the image with the baseline of the text.

Two additional attributes, hspace and vspace, can be used to control the amount of horizontal and vertical space around a floating image. However, using the CSS padding property provides more control. The image element's border attribute applies only when the image is inside an anchor tag. Its value is the size of the border in pixels. A value of 0 turns off the border. This is useful when it is otherwise obvious that the image represents a hypertext link.

The image element can also be specified with height and width attributes. These attributes can have values in pixels. Their function in the image tag is performance-related. If specified, the height and width attributes allow the browser to reserve a space of that size in the appropriate place on the page. This allows the browser to continue formatting the page while the image is being downloaded, speeding up the process for the reader. If the height and width attribute values are not the same as the corresponding dimensions of the image, the browser scales the image to that size. However, this has its limitations. Scaling up reduces an image's quality, and scaling down wastes resources because it takes the same amount of time to download the image, regardless of its displayed size.

Fun effects can be achieved by setting an image's height or width to a percentage value. The HTML code in Example 2.23 creates a colorful bar (trust me, it has all the colors of the rainbow), as shown in Figure 2.23. In reality it is a square 16-by-16-pixel image that has been scaled up with height and width attributes in its image element.

Example 2.23: HTML code for image scaling

```
<!DOCTYPE html>
<html>
<head>
<title>Example 2.23</title>
</head>

<body>

<h1>Wide Style</h1>
<img src="rainbow_sq.gif" height="32" width="100%" alt=""/>

</body>
</html>
```

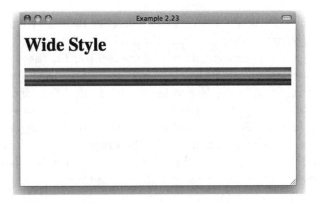

Figure 2.23: A scaled-up image

Imagemaps are an extension to the concept of document linking. An imagemap is an ordinary image upon which a set of subareas have been defined, each of which is a hyperlink to a different URL. An image becomes imagemapped when the usemap attribute is added to the image element with a value that matches the name or id attribute value of a map element placed elsewhere in the document. The map element contains a set of area elements as it immediate children, as in the following snippet of HTML code that could define a button bar:

```
<img src="images/bbar.gif" alt="" usemap="#bbar"/>

<map name="bbar">
   <area shape="rect" href="top.html"  coords="0,0,49,29"/>
   <area shape="rect" href="prev.html" coords="50,0,99,29"/>
   <area shape="rect" href="next.html" coords="100,0,149,29"/>
</map>
```

In this HTML, three rectangular shapes are defined upon the image at the locations specified in the coords attributes, which take values specifying the top-left and bottom-right corners of the hyperlinked area. The first area, linked to top.html, begins at the top-left corner of the image and extends to a point 49 pixels from the image's left edge and 29 pixels below the top edge of the image. The remaining two area elements define similar areas to the right of the first.

Imagemapped areas can overlap. In this case, the URL associated with the first area element that matches the coordinates of the reader's mouse click is the one taken. To provide a default URL for clicks on the image that are outside any defined areas, a final area element with coordinates encompassing the entire image area can be added. The href attribute is optional, but an onclick event handler can be used to alert the user. For example:

```
<area shape="rect" coords="0,0,200,29" onclick="alert('You missed!')"/>
```

AUDIO AND VIDEO

The video element is used to play videos or movies. The audio element is used for audio data such as music, recorded speech, ringtones, and other sounds. Both elements are containers. The content inside is fallback content intended for older web browsers that do not support the element. This allows plugins to be tried, or text to be shown to the users, informing them of alternative means to access the medium.

Both elements take the following attributes:

src   The URL of the file to be played.

autoplay The media file should begin playing when the page is loaded.

preload The media file should be loaded into the browser before being played.

loop   When finished, the media file should be replayed.

controls   Displays a set of controls to let the user control the playing of the medium.

The autoplay, preload, loop, and controls attributes are Boolean. As a general rule, if autoplay is specified, the controls attribute should also be provided so that the user can turn off the player.

Additionally, the video element supports width and height attributes to set the size of the playing area in pixels. If no height or width is supplied for a video element, the browser should create a player that displays the video in a 300-by-150-pixel area.

The video element's optional poster attribute provides the URL of an image file that the browser can display while video data is loading or before a movie is played. This can be a frame of the video or a title screen. Example 2.24 shows how to construct a video element with a fallback to use an Adobe Flash plugin if the browser does not support HTML5 video. The Flash code is incomplete. Only the framework is shown to give you an idea of how it might be coded.

Example 2.24: Using the HTML5 video element with a Flash fallback

```
<!DOCTYPE html>
<html>
<head>
<title>Example 2.24</title>
</head>

<body>
<video src="author.mp4" width="600" height="300"
       poster="author.jpg" controls>

<!-- Use a Flash player if no HTML5 video -->
  <object...>
    <param.../>
    <param.../>
    <embed...></embed>
  </object>

</video>
```

```
</body>
</html>
```

How Example 2.24 will be displayed, or *if* it will be displayed, depends on your browser. Figure 2.24 shows how the video is displayed using Google's Chrome browser.

Figure 2.24: Google Chrome's built-in video player with controls enabled

Alternatively, the source of the video or audio data can be provided in a source element that can have a type attribute to identify specific media formats and encodings. If used, the source element must be a direct child of the video element and come before any fallback content. For example:

```
<video autoplay controls>
  <source src="flick.mp4"
          type="video/mp4; codecs='avc1.42E01E, mp4a.40.2'"/>
  <!-- fall-back content -->
</video>
```

A discussion of the various types and encodings of audio and video data is beyond the scope of this book. The W3C's draft HTML5 specification has a list of the supported media type values and corresponding source elements.[4] It is reproduced here:

4. http://dev.w3.org/html5/spec/Overview.html#the-source-element

H.264 Simple baseline profile video (main and extended video-compatible) level 3 and Low-Complexity AAC audio in MP4 container

```
<source src='video.mp4' type='video/mp4; codecs="avc1.42E01E,
mp4a.40.2"'/>
```

H.264 Extended profile video (baseline-compatible) level 3 and Low-Complexity AAC audio in MP4 container

```
<source src='video.mp4' type='video/mp4; codecs="avc1.58A01E,
mp4a.40.2"'/>
```

H.264 Main profile video level 3 and Low-Complexity AAC audio in MP4 container

```
<source src='video.mp4' type='video/mp4; codecs="avc1.4D401E,
mp4a.40.2"'/>
```

H.264 High profile video (incompatible with main, baseline, or extended profiles) level 3 and Low-Complexity AAC audio in MP4 container

```
<source src='video.mp4' type='video/mp4; codecs="avc1.64001E,
mp4a.40.2"'/>
```

MPEG-4 Visual Simple Profile Level 0 video and Low-Complexity AAC audio in MP4 container

```
<source src='video.mp4' type='video/mp4; codecs="mp4v.20.8,
mp4a.40.2"'/>
```

MPEG-4 Advanced Simple Profile Level 0 video and Low-Complexity AAC audio in MP4 container

```
<source src='video.mp4' type='video/mp4; codecs="mp4v.20.240,
mp4a.40.2"'/>
```

MPEG-4 Visual Simple Profile Level 0 video and AMR audio in 3GPP container

```
<source src='video.3gp' type='video/3gpp; codecs="mp4v.20.8,
samr"'/>
```

Theora video and Vorbis audio in Ogg container

```
<source src='video.ogv' type='video/ogg; codecs="theora, vorbis"'/>
```

Theora video and Speex audio in Ogg container

```
<source src='video.ogv' type='video/ogg; codecs="theora, speex"'/>
```

Vorbis audio alone in Ogg container

```
<source src='audio.ogg' type='audio/ogg; codecs=vorbis'/>
```

Speex audio alone in Ogg container

```
<source src='audio.spx' type='audio/ogg; codecs=speex'/>
```

FLAC audio alone in Ogg container

```
<source src='audio.oga' type='audio/ogg; codecs=flac'/>
```

Dirac video and Vorbis audio in Ogg container

```
<source src='video.ogv' type='video/ogg; codecs="dirac, vorbis"'/>
```

Theora video and Vorbis audio in Matroska container

```
<source src='video.mkv' type='video/x-matroska; codecs="theora, vorbis"'/>
```

Input Forms

Isn't it great that the Web not only gives us information but can take it from us as well? Since its early days, HTML has been able to accept user input using forms with well-defined input field types and controls. This forward-looking addition to HTML had the effect of establishing websites as more than hyperlinked collections of documents—a website can be an application!

In HTML5, a form is a `block` element that serves as a container for collections of `input` elements and controls. A form can contain any other markup and content, with the exception of another `form` element. Although multiple forms can exist on the same web page, the most common approach is to have a single form on a page that submits the user's input to a server-side CGI program. The CGI program then returns a page that acknowledges the submission or reports an error to the user. The CGI program is also responsible for doing something with the user's input, such as performing calculations, updating databases, or emailing the information to someone. It is beyond the scope of this book to teach CGI or database programming. However, there are free CGI programs to format and email the user's input.

The form element has two important attributes: action and method. The action attribute's value is the URL of the server resource that is sent the form's contents appended to the HTTP request the browser generates upon form submission. The method attribute tells the browser how to send that input. If it has the value "post", the browser adds to the HTTP request header a name=value pair for each input field. If the method attribute has the value "get", the browser appends the name=value pairs to the end of the URL in the action attribute. Most CGI scripts are written to accept post requests. Some CGI scripts also accept get requests, but some reject get requests as a security precaution. A typical form element looks something like this:

```
<form method="post" action="/cgi-bin/save_info.cgi">...</form>
```

The action attribute's value is a URL, and that can be a "mailto" URL such as this:

```
<form method="post" action="mailto:info@example.com">...</form>
```

In this case, when the form is submitted, the browser opens a new email message using the user's email program with the name=value pairs in the body of the message.

The children of the form element create text input fields, selection menus, checkboxes, radio buttons, and submit and reset buttons. For historical reasons, most of this functionality is implemented through the input element and the particular form depends on the value of its type attribute.

If an input element has a type attribute with the value "text", it creates a single line input field. This code, for example:

```
<input type="text" name="fullname" size="60"/>
```

creates an input field 60 characters wide. A browser accepts more than this number of characters typed into the field unless the input tag also includes a maxlength attribute. Adding a maxlength attribute is a good idea just in case the server-side CGI script neglects to check the input rigorously enough.

An input element with "text" as the value of the type element accepts any text string that does not contain a line break. Other type attribute values create text input fields with restrictions on what the user can enter:

url
: The input must be a valid URL, complete with protocol and hostname parts.

email
: The input must represent an email address or a comma-separated list of email addresses.

password
: The input is treated as a text field, but the user's input is obscured as it is entered.

number
: The input must represent an integer or a real number.

However, the default type for the input element is text, so if the type element is missing or its value is unrecognized, the browser just creates an ordinary text input field. Therefore, although having these nice built-in types is convenient, you cannot rely on pre-HTML5 browsers to do the input checking for you.

Example 2.25 shows the use of text input fields in a simple form. The required attribute is added to some of the input elements to prevent the user from leaving those fields blank. The value attribute is used to initialize the field requesting a URL and to indicate to the user that a full web address is being requested. Most elements within a form permit the use of a value attribute to set an initial value for the field.

Within the form element, there must be some provision for users to submit their entries. This is usually provided by an input element with the type attribute's value set to submit, which creates a button. Likewise, an input element with the type attribute's value set to reset gives the user a button that clears all entries from the form's fields and starts over.

Example 2.25: A simple form with input elements

```
<!DOCTYPE html>
<html>
<head><title>Example 2.25</title></head>
<body style="padding: 0px 36px;">
```

continues

Example 2.25: A simple form with input elements *(continued)*

```
<h2 align="center">Join Us!</h2>

<form method="post" action="mailto:info@example.com?subject=new+user">
  <fieldset style="background-color: #eee">
    <legend><strong>Entry Form:</strong></legend>

    <p>Your Name:
    <input type="text" name="fullname" size="40" required/></p>

    <p>Your Email:
    <input type="email" name="email" size="40" required/></p>

    <p>Your Age:
    <input type="number" name="age" size="3" required maxlength="3"/>
    <small>You must be over 18 years of age</small></p>

    <p>Web Page:
    <input type="url" name="web" value="http://" size="40"/></p>
  </fieldset>

  <p><input type="submit"/> <input type="reset"/></p>

</form>

</body>
</html>
```

Figure 2.25 shows how the page created by Example 2.25 appears in a typical browser. The fieldset element used in Example 2.25 is an optional block element that groups form input and control elements. By default, a thin border is drawn around a fieldset. Example 2.25 applies a light gray background for additional highlighting by using a style attribute. A legend element provides a title for the fieldset.

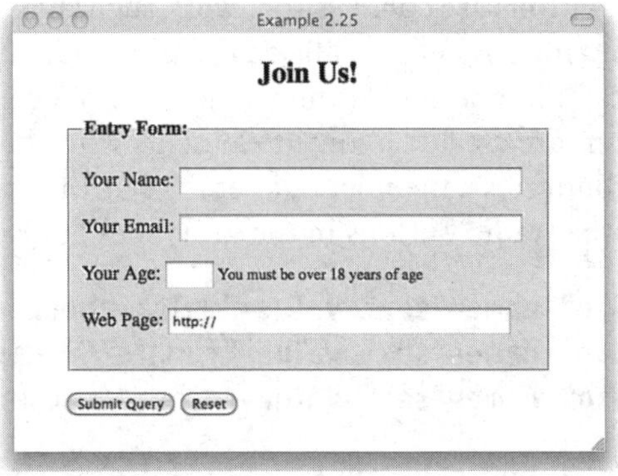

Figure 2.25: A simple form with input elements

In browsers that permit tabbing from one field to the next, the ordering of the fields is the same as the ordering of the elements in the code. This behavior can be changed by adding a `tabindex` attribute to the form element:

```
<input type="text" name="addr" size="40" tabindex="20"/>
```

Wherever an ordering such as the `tabindex` attribute is used, I recommend specifying numbers in increments of 10 to make it easier to insert new items or rearrange the ordering later.

In the preceding form example, if a user entered the values `Betty Boop`, `bboop@example.net`, and 16 for the Name, Email, and Age fields, respectively, the user's browser, if properly configured, would create a new email message addressed to `<info@example.com>` with the subject `new user`. The following string would appear in the body of the message:

```
fullname=Betty+Boop&email=bboop%40example.net&age=16&web=
http%3A%2F%2F
```

The string is encoded using a method called URL encoding. Plus signs (+) are substituted for blanks, and other special characters are replaced by a percent sign (%) followed by the character's hexidecimal ASCII code. The `name=value` pairs are separated from each other by the ampersand (&) character.

This is not as user-friendly as we would like. Most websites, therefore, use a general-purpose form-to-email CGI script such as Matt's Formmail script to receive the contents of the input form and format it nicely for emailing.

But before we go too much further, let's see what else can be done with the input element using other values for the `type` attribute. Take radio buttons, for instance. Radio buttons are controls that work such that one and only one button is "on" at any time. When you click a different radio button, the button that was on goes "off," and the button you just clicked becomes the "on" button. Radio buttons are created by input elements with the type attribute set to "radio". A radio button is a member of a set if it has the same value for its name attribute as other radio buttons in the same set.[5] For example:

```
<input type="radio" name="sex" value="male" checked/>Male
<input type="radio" name="sex" value="female"/>Female
<input type="radio" name="sex" value="other"/>Other
```

The value attribute supplies the value that the form returns if the corresponding button is the last one clicked when the form is submitted. Note that no default value is returned if the user ignores a group of radio buttons. Any default value must be specified by adding the checked attribute, as in the preceding code snippet. If more than one element in a group of radio buttons has the checked attribute, the last one encountered becomes the default.

Enclosing an input element and its description in a label element extends the button's sensitivity. For example:

```
<label><input type="radio" name="sex" value="female"/>Female</label>
```

Clicking the word "Female" is the same as clicking the adjacent button. This is a friendly interface item that users appreciate. Adding a for attribute to the label element allows the author to place the label somewhere else on the page, such as in another table cell. The for attribute's value matches the id attribute's value of the associated control, as in this code snippet:

```
<tr>
  <th align="right">
    <input type="radio" name="sex" id="choice-other" value="other"/>
  </th>
  <td align="left">
    <label for="choice-other">Other</label>
  </td>
</tr>
```

An input element with a type attribute value of checkbox creates a single checkbox. Unlike radio buttons, each checkbox stands alone and has a unique

---

5. This is an exception to the rule that names should be unique.

name. The value that a checkbox has when the form is submitted is given by the input element's value attribute. It defaults to "on" if checked and the value attribute is missing. Only elements that the user checks are sent to the server as a name=value pair upon form submission. Before the form is submitted, all checkboxes have a value whether they are checked or not. If a client-side script needs to examine the value of a checkbox, it must also test that element's checked property.

An input element with a type attribute value of hidden creates an element that is inaccessible to the user. Its purpose is to provide a data value in the form of a name=value pair to the CGI script receiving the input or a client side script handling page events. Hidden fields can provide configuration information or identify the page submitting the form. Example 2.26, shown in a moment, uses hidden fields.

One additional input element is worth mentioning. If the type attribute has the value "file", the browser presents both an input text field and a Browse button for the purpose of selecting a file to upload from the user's local PC. For this to work correctly, the form element must have its method set to post and the attribute enctype set to "multipart/form-data". Because this changes how the form's input is sent to the server, check with your webmaster before writing code that uploads files.

For multiline text input in a form, a textarea is used. Unlike the input element, the textarea element is a block element and a container. A textarea element is usually written with rows and cols attributes to set the initial size of the input area. The content, which is treated like text without markup in a preformatted element, is its initial value.

Example 2.26 includes all the form elements discussed so far. For the action attribute, the URL of a form-to-email script is used. The script accepts input from hidden values to set the subject and recipient of the email message it will send from the server. Furthermore, it recognizes certain input names. In particular, by using "fullname" and "email" for the names of the input fields for that information, the script uses the values of those fields to construct the message's From address, such as "Betty Boop" <bboop@example.net>.

Example 2.26: An input form that calls a form-to-email CGI script

```
<!DOCTYPE html>
<html>

<head><title>Example 2.26</title></head>
```

continues

Example 2.26: An input form that calls a form-to-email CGI script *(continued)*

```
<body style="padding: 0px 36px;">

<h2 align="center">Join Us!</h2>

<form method="post" action="/cgi-bin/formmail.cgi">
<!-- Set hidden fields for email subject and recipient -->
    <input type="hidden" name="subject" value="new user"/>
    <input type="hidden" name="recipient" value="info@example.com"/>

    <fieldset style="background-color: #eee">
    <legend><strong>Entry Form:</strong></legend>

<!-- text input fields -->
    <p>Your Name:
    <input type="text" name="fullname" size="40" required/>
    </p>

    <p>Your Email:
    <input type="email" name="email" size="40" required/>
    </p>

    <p>Your Age:
    <input type="number" name="age" size="3" required maxlength="3"/>
    <small>You must be over 18 years of age</small>
    </p>

    <p>Web Page:
    <input type="url" name="web" value="http://" size="40"/>
    </p>

<!-- radio buttons -->
    <p>Gender:
    <label><input type="radio" name="sex"
                    value="male" checked/>Male</label>
    <label><input type="radio" name="sex"
                    value="female"/>Female</label>
    <label><input type="radio" name="sex"
```

```
                  value="other"/>Other</label>
   </p>

<!-- checkboxes -->
   <p>I'm interested in: <br/>
   <label><input type="checkbox" name="aches"/>Aches</label><br/>
   <label><input type="checkbox" name="cakes"/>Cakes</label><br/>
   <label><input type="checkbox" name="fakes"/>Fakes</label><br/>
   <label><input type="checkbox" name="lakes"/>Lakes</label><br/>
   <label><input type="checkbox" name="rakes"/>Rakes</label><br/>
   </p>

<!-- textarea for comments -->
   <textarea name="comnt" rows="6" cols="50" onfocus="this.value='';">


   Use this space for comments
   </textarea>
  </fieldset>

<!-- submit and reset buttons  -->
  <p align="right">
  <input type="submit" value="Join"/>
  <input type="reset"  value="clear"/>
  </p>
</form>

</body>
</html>
```

A little bit of JavaScript is added to the textarea element to clear the initial message when the user gives it focus with a mouse click or finger tap:

onfocus="this.value='';"

Figure 2.26 shows how the form created with Example 2.26 appears in a typical browser. Unfortunately, unlike the other examples in this chapter, you cannot test how this form works offline. You need a web server and form-to-email CGI script. Search the Web for "formmail.cgi" to find a copy you can upload to your server if there isn't one there already. Be sure to read the instructions in the README file to learn how to prevent your script from being used by spammers.

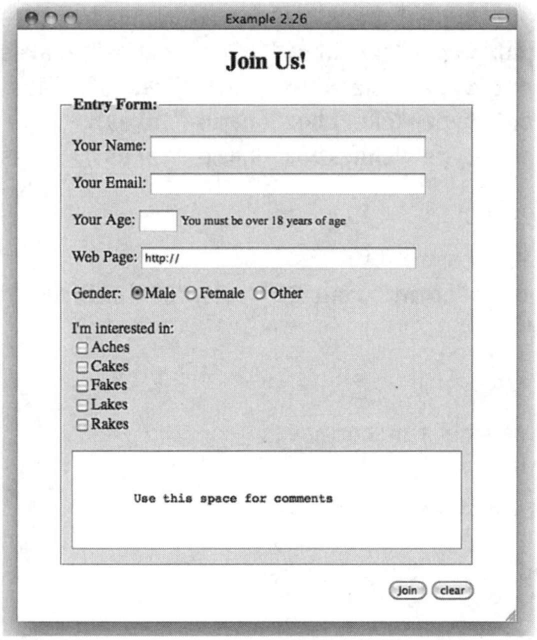

Figure 2.26: Input form with input text fields, radio buttons, and checkboxes

The select element provides a method of creating single- and multiple-choice inputs. As with radio buttons and checkboxes, the user is presented with a collection of predefined choices. However, the select element is represented on the web page as a single, compact form control. The select element is a container with one or more option elements as its only permitted child elements. For example, the "gender" question in Example 2.26 could be presented as a select element with the following code:

```
<p>Gender:
    <select name="sex">
        <option value="male">Male</option>
        <option value="female">Female</option>
        <option value="other">Other</option>
    </select></p>
```

To permit the user to select multiple choices from a menu, add the `multiple` attribute to the `select` element. For example, as an alternative to the check-boxes in Example 2.26, this code can be used:

```
<p>I'm interested in:
   <select name="interests" multiple>
      <option value="aches">Aches</option>
      <option value="cakes">Cakes</option>
      <option value="fakes">Fakes</option>
      <option value="lakes">Lakes</option>
      <option value="rakes">Rakes</option>
   </select></p>
```

Figure 2.26a shows how a typical browser displays the two sample `select` elements. Note how much of a difference adding the `multiple` attribute makes. Without the attribute, the `select` element creates a drop-down menu that is activated when the user clicks the control. The activated menu exists above other page elements and overlaps them. Because of these differences, web developers often use HTML tables to lay out the various elements of a form. This is an acceptable exception to the rule that HTML tables should only be used to mark up tabular information. When using tables, however, remember that a `form` element may be inside a table cell (`th`, `td`) element, or that an entire table element can be inside a form, but a form may not break a table. A `form` element, for instance, cannot be a direct child of a table body (`tbody`) or table row (`tr`) element.

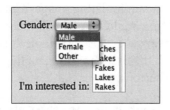

Figure 2.26a: Single- and multiple-choice select elements

With the `multiple` attribute, the `select` element creates an open menu that is aligned with the text it is embedded in. The `select` element is positioned so that the baseline of its last item is aligned with the baseline of the surround-ing text. By using various alternative clicks (which are device- and operating-system-specific), the user can select none, one, or many of the options.

There is another important difference. The select element without the multiple attribute always returns a value that, by default, is the first option item. The select element with the multiple attribute does not return a value if the user does not leave any of the options selected when the form is submitted. To override this behavior, the selected attribute can be added to any option element. For example:

```
<option value="quakes" selected>Quakes</option>
```

THE HTML5 CANVAS

The canvas element is one of HTML5's most exciting new additions. As the name implies, the canvas element creates a rectangular drawing surface on a web page with a height and width given by the value of the height and width attributes. The canvas element is a block element. Its content is fallback material for browsers and other user agents that do not support the canvas element. The fallback content should not contain other block elements but may contain images and other inline markup.

```
<canvas id="c1" width="360" height="360">
 Sadly, your browser doesn't support the <em>canvas</em> element.
</canvas>
```

What happens on the canvas is controlled by scripts. The canvas application programming interface (API) provides several dozen methods or functions for drawing lines, arcs, and rectangles; filling areas with patterns and colors; writing stylized text; manipulating images and video; and other fun activities. Covering all of this would take a book in itself, but we can look at a quick example to see how canvases work. Example 2.27 has a 400-by-400-pixel canvas element upon which the user can draw smaller squares of different colors by clicking various buttons.

Example 2.27: HTML code for using the canvas element

```
<!DOCTYPE html>
<html>
<head>
<title>Example 2.27</title>
</head>
```

```
<body style="text-align: center; margin: 1in;">

<canvas id="square" width="400" height="400"
        style="border: thin solid">
Sadly, your browser does not support the <em>canvas</em> element.
</canvas>

<div>
<button onclick="draw('red')">red</button>
<button onclick="draw('orange')">orange</button>
<button onclick="draw('yellow')">yellow</button>
<button onclick="draw('green')">green</button>
<button onclick="draw('aqua')">aqua</button>
<button onclick="draw('blue')">blue</button>
<button onclick="draw('violet')">violet</button>
</div>

<script type="text/javascript">
/* Get the canvas element and establish a drawing context */
  var canvas = document.getElementById("square");
  var square = canvas.getContext("2d");
  var offset = 0; var sqsize = 400;

/* function to draw a filled square */
  function draw(color) {
      square.fillStyle = color;
      square.fillRect(offset, offset, sqsize, sqsize);
      if (sqsize > 40) { offset += 20; sqsize -= 40; }
  }
</script>
</body>
</html>
```

The canvas element defined in Example 2.27 is blank to begin with. It has
a light border around it just so we can see where it is in this example. There
is no requirement to visually display a canvas element before any drawing
takes place. Each of the buttons below the canvas calls the draw function when
clicked, with the associated color name as an argument to the function. The

draw function draws a 400-by-400-pixel rectangle filled with the color provided by the argument. Each time a colored square is drawn in response to a user's button click, the origin point for the next square is moved down and to the right 20 pixels, and the size of the square is reduced by 40 pixels.

Figure 2.27 shows how the code from Example 2.27 looks in a HTML5 browser after all seven buttons have been clicked in order from left to right.

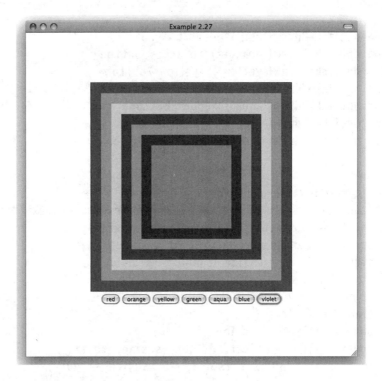

Figure 2.27: A web page with an interactive canvas

SUMMARY

Here are the important points to remember from this chapter:

▸ HTML code consists of markup elements, comments, and character entities.

▸ Markup elements provide the semantic information for user agents to understand page content. CSS provides instructions for styling and presenting the content.

▸ The Document Object Model (DOM) provides a mapping between HTML page elements and their content to data objects that can be manipulated by client-side scripts written in JavaScript and other languages.

▸ Markup elements can have attributes. Attributes change how an element looks or behaves without changing the semantic meaning of the element's content.

▸ There are two types of HTML markup elements—block elements, which change content flow, and inline elements, which do not. A block element can be floated so that other content wraps around it.

▸ The anchor and area elements create hyperlinks when given an href attribute with a URL value. Hyperlinks can have relative, root, or full addressing.

▸ Inline images are like big characters of text. Unless floated, they are aligned with their adjacent content and participate in the content flow.

▸ HTML5 adds native support for audio and video content. The audio and video elements provide fallbacks to other methods of media support for older browsers.

▸ The new HTML5 canvas element gives web developers an interactive drawing area in which image data can be manipulated with JavaScript.

Elements
of Style

3

Cascading Style Sheets (CSS) is a major piece of the art of web programming. It is the technology that gives a web page its distinctive look and feel. In this chapter you will learn how to use CSS to modify the layout and typography of a web page to create web pages with style.

CASCADING STYLE SHEETS

A cascading style sheet is a set of statements that applies rules to the various elements of a web page, specifying the layout, typography, and other properties that those elements should assume when displayed by web browsers or by WYSIWYG editing software. We speak of these properties as being in the presentation layer of the web page as distinct from the semantic description provided by the HTML markup of the page's content. CSS allows us to create web pages that are more visually striking. At the same time they are simpler, easier to maintain, more accessible, and friendlier to search engine robots and other user agents. These entities are concerned more with the meaning and relevance of content on the Web than with how a particular page looks. CSS also lets you create a web page with different presentation rules depending on the type of device, or medium, accessing the page, such as a text-to-speech reader for the visually impaired.

The CSS statements associated with a web page can appear in one or more places:

▶ In files referenced by link elements in HTML documents

▶ In style elements in the head of an HTML document

▶ In style attributes in individual markup elements

Putting CSS statements in separate CSS files allows those statements to be used throughout the website. A CSS file is a text file containing only CSS statements. (No HTML is allowed.) A link element in an HTML document's head section connects the CSS file to the HTML document when the relationship attribute, rel, is set to stylesheet. For example:

```
<link rel="stylesheet" href="styles.css" media="screen"/>
```

The media attribute provides context to the browser so that it can have different CSS instructions depending on the kind of device reading the web page. The value "screen" means a general-purpose web browser running on a PC display. The HTML4 values for the media attribute are tty, tv, projection, handheld, print, screen, Braille, aural, and the default value all. The media attribute is optional and could have been omitted from the link element just shown.

HTML5 extends the versatility of the media attribute by permitting "query expressions" that can test for specific device characteristics to determine whether the CSS rules should apply. This is a very powerful feature with syntax that is a bit too complicated to go into in detail. Here is a simple example of a media query in a link to a style sheet:

```
<link rel="stylesheet" media="screen and not(color)" href="bw.css"/>
```

CSS style sheets for complex websites can be quite long. Often, several hundred rules may be required for an entire site. Many web developers separate the CSS styles into two files—one for the layout and positioning rules, and one for typography and colors. Looking at the HTML source of a page on such a site, you might see something like this:

```
<link rel="stylesheet" href="styles.css"/>
<link rel="stylesheet" href="layout.css"/>
```

As an alternative, CSS in a style element or CSS file can import other CSS files using the import directive. An import directive begins with the "at" sign followed by the word "import" and a URL expression. For example:

```
<style type="text/css">
@import url(reset.css); /* Reset CSS */
```

```
/* Import corporate style sheet  */
@import url(http://example.com/css/hq.css);

/* Local styles begin here  */

  body { padding: 36px; }
</style>
```

An import directive must appear before any other CSS statements with the exception of comments and other import directives. Because imported files can also contain import directives, it is possible to construct infinite loops if you are not careful.

CSS statements in a document's style element apply only to that document. As a general rule, style elements in a document head should be placed after any style sheets referenced in link elements. All rules for a given HTML element are combined. If the browser has more than one CSS rule to apply to a given element property, the last one found will apply.

A CSS statement consists of a selector expression that determines which HTML elements the statement applies to, followed by one or more rules enclosed in curly braces. Each rule is composed of a property name and a value expression separated by a colon (:). Each rule is separated from the preceding rule by a semicolon (;). For example, the following CSS statement causes all level-three headings in a document to be rendered in a bold, red font:

```
h2 { font-weight: bold; color: red; }
```

The actual layout of a CSS statement is flexible. Blanks, carriage returns, tabs, and other white space are ignored, allowing the author to format a style sheet for readability. Comments can be added for even more readability. The CSS statement just shown could be written like this without any difference in meaning:[1]

```
h2 {                    /* multiple lines */
  font-weight:bold;     /* don't matter   */
  color:red;
}
```

---

1. The final semicolon before the closing curly brace can be omitted. I put it there because, like many programmers, I'm always adding to my previous work, and because the extra punctuation is inconsequential. A missing semicolon between two CSS statements will cause both statements to be ignored.

When a CSS statement is provided as the value of an HTML element's style attribute, only the property names and value expressions are used; the selector expression and curly braces are omitted. The CSS statement just shown applied to a particular level-two heading in a document would be written like this:

```
<h2 style="font-weight:bold; color:red;">...</h2>
```

CSS rules in the value of an HTML element's style attribute take precedence over any rules previously in effect for that element's properties. In the following HTML, the level-two heading will be bold, italic, and blue when viewed in a typical browser:

```
<!DOCTYPE html>
<html>
<head>
<title>Example 3.0</title>
<style type="text/css">
  h2  { font-style: italic; color: red; }
</style>
</head>

<body>
<h2 style="color:blue; font-weight: bold">Earthquakes!</h2>
</body>
</html>
```

The normal order of the cascade can be overridden by adding an exclamation point (!) and the important keyword after a CSS rule. For example, changing the rule for the h2 element in the preceding code to this

```
h2  { font-style: italic; color: red !important; }
```

instructs the browser to ignore any further settings of h2 elements' color property, unless those settings also include the important keyword. As a result, the level-two heading will be bold italic and red.

The important keyword becomes very useful with content management systems and blogging software. It is often common with such software for plugins and other code to dynamically insert CSS style elements and attributes directly into the document's head and body elements. If you only have access to the style sheet, and your changes are blocked by the generated CSS rules after the style sheet is loaded, using !important can put you back in control.

CSS SELECTORS

CSS statements, whether in a style sheet file or style element in the head section of a document, begin with a selector expression that determines which elements the statement's rules apply to. The simplest case is a named HTML element like the h2 selector in the style element in the preceding section. The following examples have just the selector portion highlighted in bold:

```
body { font-family: arial,sans-serif; }
h1   { font-size: 21pt; }
a    { color: blue; text-decoration: none; }
p    { line-height: 1.4em; }
```

Actually, the simplest case is just an asterisk, which means all elements. The following CSS statement

```
*    { font-family: arial,sans-serif; }
```

instructs the browser to use the Arial font (or a generic sans serif font if Arial is unavailable) to render every element. This is different from setting the body element's font-family to arial,sans-serif. The body's font family is not inherited by some elements, such as the code and pre elements, which would keep their default monospace font. The asterisk is better used as a descendent term to select all elements that are nested within a specified element.

An individual HTML element can be selected if it has an id attribute. In this CSS statement, the value of the id attribute is appended to a named HTML element with a hash sign (#)[2] in between:

```
h2#main-title { margin-top: 20px; }
```

Because the value of any element's id attribute must be a unique name within a document, the HTML element name can be omitted. The preceding code is more commonly written as follows:

```
#main-title { margin-top: 20px; }
```

A selector expression can refer to elements in a given class. In other words, the element is selected if it has a class attribute with a matching value. In the CSS, the class name is appended to the element name with a period:

```
p.in-a-box { border: thin solid black; }
```

---

2. Technically, this is called the *octothorpe* (eight points) character.

This code applies a thin black border to all paragraph elements in the page with that `class` attribute value, as in

```
<p class="in-a-box">...</p>
```

Different kinds of HTML elements can be selected by their `class` attribute values as well. A CSS statement beginning with a dot followed by a class name is the same as `*.classname` and applies the style rule to every element that has that `class` attribute value.

Any number of selector expressions can be grouped into a single expression by separating the individual expressions with commas. For example, to style a page so that all headings are in a different font family than the body text, use CSS statements like these:

```
body { font-family: georgia,times,serif; }
h1,h2,h3,h4,h5,h6 { font-family: verdana,helvetica,sans-serif; }
```

The values for the `font-family` property are usually given as a list of preferences. In this code, all headings are rendered in the Verdana font if it exists on the reader's computer. If the Verdana font is not found, the browser uses Helvetica. If that's not found, the browser can use the default sans serif font to render the headings. See the section "Typography" for more on font properties.

An element can be selected based on its status as the descendent of another element just by separating the two element names with blanks. For example, this code sets the color of all links inside a block quote to dark green:

```
blockquote a { color: darkgreen; }
```

Here are some more examples of descendent selectors:

```
table td a { text-decoration: none; }     /* not underlined */
#main-title strong { font-size: 120%; }
footer address a.email { font: bold 10pt courier,monospace; }
div.aside ul { background-color: rgb(100,100,100); }
div.aside li { color: white; list-style-type: square; }
```

A descendent element is selected no matter how deeply it is nested inside the parent element. To select an element that is the first-generation child of a parent element, the following syntax is used:

```
body > div { margin-top: 0px; margin-bottom: 36px; }
```

This applies the margin settings to only the top-level divisions in the body of the page, not to any divisions nested within other elements. Only direct child elements are selected, no grandchildren or other distant relatives. Example 3.1 shows two identical unordered lists with IDs list1 and list2. Each has lists nested within its list items.

Example 3.1: Selecting elements in nested lists

```
<!DOCTYPE html>
<html>
<head>
<title>Example 3.1</title>
<style type="text/css">
li          { padding: .25em; border: thin solid black; }
li li       { background-color: #ccc; width: 6em; }
#list2 > li { float: left; list-style-type: none; margin-right: 5px; }
h3          { font:  12pt verdana; }
</style>
</head>

<body style="padding: 36px;">
<h3>Planetary List 1:</h3>     <!-- first list -->

<ul id="list1">
 <li>Mercury</li>
 <li>Venus</li>
 <li>Earth
     <ul>
       <li>Moon</li>
     </ul>
 </li>
 <li>Mars
     <ul>
       <li>Deimos</li>
       <li>Phobos</li>
     </ul>
   </li>
</ul>
```

continues

Example 3.1: Selecting elements in nested lists *(continued)*

```
<h3>Planetary List 2:</h3>     <!-- second list -->

<ul id="list2">
 <li>Mercury</li>
 <li>Venus</li>
 <li>Earth
    <ul>
      <li>Moon</li>
    </ul>
 </li>
 <li>Mars
    <ul>
      <li>Deimos</li>
      <li>Phobos</li>
    </ul>
  </li>
</ul>
</body>
</html>
```

The first CSS statement in the head section's `style` element

```
li    { padding: .25em; border: thin solid black; }
```

places a 1-pixel border around every list item, at every depth, and gives each item a bit of padding to make it look nicer. The second CSS statement

```
li li    { background-color: #ccc; width: 6em; }
```

selects only list items that are descendents of other list items. Those nested list items have a gray background and a limited width. Finally, the third CSS statement selects just the top-level list items of the second list, causing the items to be floated into a horizontal bar. The list bullets are removed, and 5 pixels of margin is added to separate the top-level items:

```
#list2 > li { float: left; list-style-type: none; margin-right: 5px; }
```

This HTML is displayed by a browser in a manner similar to Figure 3.1. Note that the nested lists of moons are the same in both lists; only the top-level list items are changed in the second list by the preceding CSS statement.

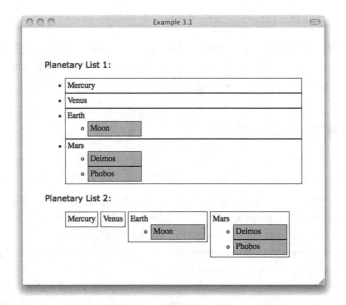

Figure 3.1: Nested horizontal and vertical lists

The use of a plus sign (+) between two element names indicates a selection based on the status of an element as an adjacent sibling to another element. For example, if this CSS statement

```
h3 + ul   { margin-top: 0; }
```

were added to the style element in Example 3.1, it would reduce the margin of space between level-three headings and the list items that immediately follow them. But it would not affect the nested lists, because they are not adjacent to the headings.

Document elements can be selected based on whether the element has a particular attribute, or whether the element has an attribute with a particular value. A CSS statement such as this

```
a[name]  { color: cyan; }
```

selects any anchor element that has a name attribute. Such anchors are usually the in-page destinations of hyperlinks. The preceding CSS highlights all such elements by coloring them cyan. To select an HTML element by the value of an attribute, follow the name with an equals sign (=) and the value in quotes:

```
input[type="text"] { background-color: #ffff99; }
```

input elements exist within interactive forms (see Chapter 2, "The HTML Language") and come in a variety of types, including checkboxes, radio buttons, and text fields. The preceding CSS statement provides a light yellow background color to input text fields like this:

```
<input type="text" size="32"/>
```

PSEUDO-CLASSES AND PSEUDO-ELEMENTS

Pseudo-classes extend the capability of CSS statements to select HTML elements based on certain states or circumstances. Pseudo-elements allow for the selection of specific parts of a document element, such as its first line of text. The pseudo-class or pseudo-element name is appended to the rest of the selection expression, separated by a colon (:).

The most common use of pseudo-classes is to detect and style the various states of links created by anchor elements. For example, the following four CSS statements set the colors of hyperlinked text, depending on whether the link is in its normal state, whether the mouse is hovering over the link, whether the link is active (hover and hold down the mouse button), and whether the link is in the visited state:

```
a:link    { color: blue;   }
a:hover   { color: green;  }
a:active  { color: red;    }
a:visited { color: purple; }
```

Because these four link states are mutually exclusive and represent all the possible states of a hypertext link, it is usually not necessary to specify the link state. In other words, the first statement just shown could be written as a { color: blue; } with the same result. The link pseudo-class is included to enable authors to overwrite previously set CSS rules for the same element.

Modern browsers permit all elements to have the hover state, not just links created by the anchor element.[3] In theory, other elements can have link, active, and visited states. But this is not defined in CSS, and browser manufacturers might or might not implement such features.

---

3. Currently, Internet Explorer version 6 is the only browser with significant market share that recognizes the hover state only with anchor elements.

The focus pseudo-class is used in a similar way to select elements when they have focus. Typically, this applies to input and other form elements when the user's cursor is positioned in the element and text can be entered from the keyboard into the element. The following CSS statement gives a light-yellow background only to the text input element that currently has the keyboard's focus. This is a nice user interface feature, especially when you present the user with a long form that has many input elements:

```css
input[type="text"]:focus { background-color: #ffff99; }
```

Other elements can have keyboard focus. Anchor elements, for example, can have focus if the browser permits the user to press the Tab key to move sequentially through page links.

The first-child pseudo-class selects an element if it is the first child of its parent element. Example 3.2 illustrates this feature using a simple horizontal list of links. Figure 3.2 shows how this HTML appears in a browser.

Example 3.2: The first-child pseudo-class

```html
<!DOCTYPE html>
<html>
<head>
<title>Example 3.2</title>
<style type="text/css">
  body { font-family: sans-serif; }
  a    { text-decoration: none; }   /* don't underline links */

  li { float: left;                 /* horizontal list */
       padding: .25em;
       margin-right: 5px;
       border: 2px black outset;    /* shaded buttons */
       list-style-type: none; }

  li:first-child   { background-color: black; }
  li:first-child a { color: white; }
</style>
</head>

<body>
<ul>
```

continues

Example 3.2: The first-child **pseudo-class** *(continued)*

```
    <li><a href="home.html">Home</a></li>
    <li><a href="about.html">About</a></li>
    <li><a href="contact.html">Contact Us</a></li>
</ul>
</body>
</html>
```

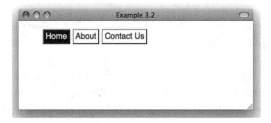

Figure 3.2: A horizontal menu styled with the first-child **pseudo-class**

CSS3 greatly expanded the list of pseudo-classes with additional structural classes that, like :first-child, permit the selection of any element based on its relationships to other elements in the DOM. These include the following:

:root	The root of the document
:nth-child(n)	An element that is the *n*th child of its parent
:nth-last-child(n)	An element that is the *n*th child of its parent, counting from the last one
:nth-of-type(n)	An element that is the *n*th sibling of its type
:nth-last-of-type(n)	An element that is the *n*th sibling of its type, counting from the last one
:first-child	An element that is the first child of its parent
:last-child	An element that is the last child of its parent
:first-of-type	An element that is the first sibling of its type
:last-of-type	An element that is the last sibling of its type

:only-child	An element that is the only child of its parent
:only-of-type	An element that is the only sibling of its type
:empty	An element that has no children or text

Pseudo-elements are similar to pseudo-classes but select a portion of the element's content instead of the entire element. The first-line and first-letter pseudo-elements are the most commonly used. Example 3.3 shows how to create a "drop cap" letter using the first-letter pseudo-element applied to a first-child pseudo-class. Only the first character of the first paragraph in each division is enlarged to 300 percent of its normal size. Figure 3.3 shows how a browser displays this code.

Example 3.3: Using the first-letter pseudo-element to create a "drop cap" letter

```
<!DOCTYPE html>
<html>
<head>
<title>Example 3.3</title>
<style type="text/css">
  body { padding: 0 36px; font-family: cursive; }
  h3   { text-align: center; }
  div p:first-child:first-letter { font-size: 300%; color: #999; }
</style>
</head>

<body>
<h3>The Raven</h3>
<div>
  <p>Once upon a midnight dreary, while I pondered, weak and weary,
Over many quaint and curious volume of forgotten lore&mdash;</p>
  <p>While I nodded, nearly napping, suddenly there came a tapping, As
of some one gently rapping, rapping at my chamber door.</p>
</div>
</body>
</html>
```

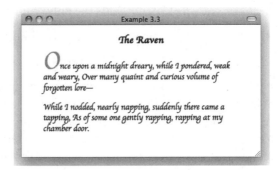

Figure 3.3: Styling an initial "drop cap"

The before and after pseudo-elements select the points just before and after, respectively, the element, allowing the author to insert content at those points. Here are two examples:

```
p.joke:after   { content: url(/icons/smiley.gif); }
a[href]:before { content: "[LINK] "; }
```

The first CSS statement inserts a smiley-face icon (if the image file exists at the URL provided) after any paragraph that has a class attribute with the value joke. The second statement inserts the text [LINK] before any anchor element that has an href attribute. It should be emphasized that using the before and after pseudo-elements is not an acceptable means of inserting meaningful content into a page. The content will not be visible to robots or other user agents that ignore CSS.

Now that you understand how to select HTML elements in CSS, it is time to look at the various element properties that can be set in CSS statements. Typography—the specification of font families, styles, weight, size, and color—is the foremost class of these properties.

TYPOGRAPHY

The font family or typeface sets the document's tone. CSS lets you set both specific fonts and generic font families. Although there are now mechanisms for embedding fonts in a document, by and large, most web pages depend on the fonts resident in the reader's device used to display the page. The web author may write a CSS rule calling for a specific font, such as Copperplate or Futura, but if the reader does not have those specific fonts in his device, the browser substitutes a different font.

Note: Font files that reside on a web server and are made available for downloading to be used in a web page are called *webfonts*. All modern browsers support the use of webfonts to some extent, but there is no common accepted standard for the file formats.

In the late 1990s, Microsoft released a set of core fonts for the Web and made it available as a free download for both Windows and Macintosh computers. Microsoft later ended the free download policy but continued to ship the core fonts with its operating systems and Office products. Over time, this collection of "safe web fonts" has been expanded and today includes Helvetica, Arial, Arial Black, Times, Times New Roman, Courier, Courier New, Palatino, Garamond, Bookman Old Style, Avant Garde, Verdana, Georgia, Comic Sans MS, Trebuchet MS, Impact, Tahoma, and others.

Helvetica is a general-purpose sans serif font with a wide range of applications. It is one of the most commonly used fonts. Along with Times and Courier, it was a native font on PostScript printers. Arial is an updated version of Helvetica that has been optimized for both screen and print. Times is a serif font designed for newspaper text. Times New Roman is an updated and optimized version of Times that is better for screen reading. Courier and its updated cousin, Courier New, are monospace fonts that provide the feel of typewritten text. Verdana is a sans serif font with wide lowercase letters, making it suitable for headlines but generally not for body text. Tahoma is about halfway between Verdana and Arial. Comic Sans MS has an informal, hand-drawn feel. Impact and Arial Black are dramatic fonts well suited for titles and headings.

The following font properties can be specified in a CSS statement: `font-family`, `font-style`, `font-size`, `font-weight`, and `font-variant`. Here are some examples in which I've highlighted the properties and values:

```
p        { font-family: Arial, Helvetica, sans-serif; }
h3       { font-style: italic; }
ul       { font-size: 1.2em; }
p.alert  { font-weight: bold; }
h4       { font-variant: small-caps; }
```

The `font-family` property takes a comma-delimited string of names. The first name is the preferred font to be used, and the remaining names are successive fallbacks in case a font is not resident on the reader's device. Authors are encouraged to place a generic font family name as the last fallback choice. Most browsers recognize the generic font family names listed in Table 3.1.

Table 3.1: Font families recognized by most browsers

Family Name	Properties	Examples
sans-serif	Proportional, without serifs	Helvetica, Arial, Geneva, Verdana, Tahoma
serif	Proportional, with serifs	Times, Times New Roman, Georgia, Bookman Old Style
monospace	Fixed-width; code or typewriter style	Courier, Courier New, Monaco, Andale Mono
cursive	Curved strokes; handwriting style	Comic Sans MS, Lucida Handwriting
fantasy	Anything unusual	Papyrus, Klingon

To test your browser's styling of these generic font families, copy the code shown in Example 3.4 into the body of an HTML file or anywhere else you can enter HTML code to create a page you can display. Figure 3.4 shows how this code rendered in my browser.

Example 3.4: HTML code for displaying generic font families

```
<p style="font-size: 14pt">
  <span style="font-family:sans-serif">sans-serif &mdash;
abcdefghijklmnopqrstuvwxyz</span><br/>
  <span style="font-family:serif">serif &mdash;
abcdefghijklmnopqrstuvwxyz</span><br/>
  <span style="font-family:monospace">monospace &mdash;
abcdefghijklmnopqrstuvwxyz</span><br/>
  <span style="font-family:cursive">cursive &mdash;
abcdefghijklmnopqrstuvwxyz</span><br/>
  <span style="font-family:fantasy">fantasy &mdash;
abcdefghijklmnopqrstuvwxyz</span>
</p>
```

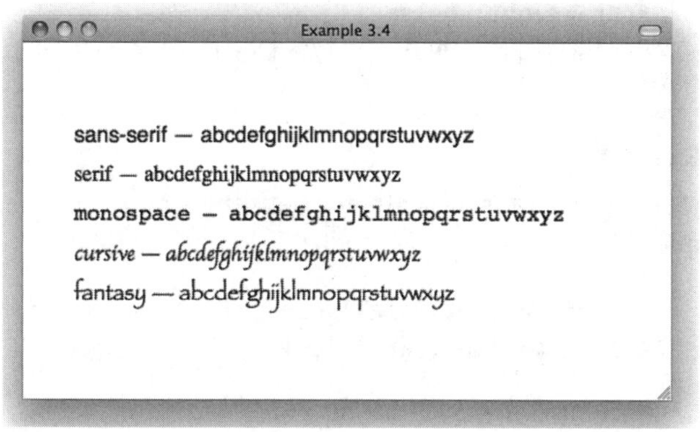

Figure 3.4: Generic font families displayed

FONT STYLE

The font-style property can have any one of four values: normal, italic, oblique, or inherit. The normal style is a font with vertical strokes. Inherit means to adopt the font-style property of the parent element. Italic style is slanted in the forward direction of the text. Oblique is also slanted, but simply. That is, an oblique style is achieved by slanting the normal style, whereas an italic style may be a separate font resource with different serifs on the characters or altered punctuation symbols. In the vast majority of cases this won't make a difference and should not be relied on as an element of design. Here are a couple examples:

```
address      { font-style: italic; }
h4 cite      { font-style: normal; }
```

FONT WEIGHT

The font-weight property can have the values normal, bold, and inherit. It can also have the relative values bolder and lighter. Or it can take one of the following "hundred" weights: 100, 200, 300, 400, 500, 600, 700, 800, or 900. 100 is the lightest, and 900 is the boldest. There is no guarantee that a browser will render text with a font weight of 700 any differently than text with a weight of 600, because this can depend on other font properties, such as font-family, font-size, and font-style. Here are a couple examples:

```
p.intro em   { font-weight: bold; }
li:first     { font-weight: 900;  }   /* the bolder the better */
```

FONT VARIANT

The font-variant property is basically for defining small-caps text. Here are a couple examples:

```
h3.post-title { font-variant: small-caps; }
#outline dt   { font-variant: normal; }
```

FONT SIZE

The font-size property provides a wide range of values to specify how big the characters should appear. It can be given in pixels or as a named, relative, or absolute size value. The named sizes are like clothing sizes:

```
xx-small
x-small
small
medium
large
x-large
xx-large
```

Relative values include the keywords smaller and larger; length values using the em, ex, and px units; and percentages. The absolute size values are lengths of inches (in), centimeters (cm), millimeters (mm), points (pt), or picas (pc).

The medium value should be about 16 pixels, although that may vary among browsers, especially browsers on mobile devices. Example 3.5 displays a number of different font sizes using the :before pseudo-element to self-describe each span element. This trick will not work with older versions of Internet Explorer. Figure 3.5 shows how this code displays in my Firefox browser.

Example 3.5: HTML source code for displaying font size values

```
<!DOCTYPE html>
<html>
<head>
<title>Example 3.5</title>
<style type="text/css">
```

```
  body { padding: 24px; }
  span:before { content: attr(style); }
</style>
</head>

<body>
<span style="font-size: 16px;"></span>
<p>
  <span style="font-size: xx-small;"></span><br/>
  <span style="font-size: x-small;"></span><br/>
  <span style="font-size: small;"></span><br/>
  <span style="font-size: medium;"></span><br/>
  <span style="font-size: large;"></span><br/>
  <span style="font-size: x-large;"></span><br/>
  <span style="font-size: xx-large;"></span>
</p>
<p>
  <span style="font-size: smaller;"></span><br/>
  <span style="font-size: larger;"></span><br/>
  <span style="font-size: 1em;"></span><br/>
  <span style="font-size: 100%;"></span>
</p>
</body>
</html>
```

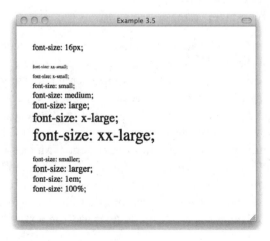

Figure 3.5: font-size **values displayed**

Points and picas are traditional typographic measures. There are 12 points to a pica and 6 picas to an inch. Therefore, a font size of 18 points is equivalent to 1.5 picas, or .25 inches. Ems and exes are also typographic measures. Like a percentage value, they specify sizes relative to the element's computed size rather than an absolute number of units. When type was set using individual letters cast in lead alloy, font sets included spacer characters of different sizes. An em-quad was a square space just large enough to contain an uppercase M. Exes are squares the size of a lowercase x. Obviously, a larger font will have larger ems and exes in absolute terms. However, in CSS, one em is equivalent to 100 percent of the current font size. To illustrate, consider the following three CSS statements:

```
#main            { font-size: medium; }
#main p.first    { font-size: 1em; }
#main p.second   { font-size: 100%; }
```

In a division element with id="main", the two nested paragraphs with classes first and second will have the same font size, measured in pixels, if they are in the same font family. If the two paragraphs are of different font families, they may appear to have different font sizes. An em measure is only a guideline for font designers, who are free to make their letters larger or smaller as they please. Here are some examples:

```
blockquote  { font-size: 18pt; }
p.event     { font-size: 16px; }
#intro      { font-size: 7mm; }
address     { font-size: 1.75em; }
```

Font sizes given in pixels are relative to the browser's viewport and therefore are dependent on the resolution of the reader's display device and the viewer's distance from the display. Pixels are not simple screen dots anymore. However, as a rough guide, a 17-inch monitor (measured diagonally) set to a resolution of 1024 by 768 pixels is very close to 72 pixels per inch. Because this is now considered the low end of display screen technology, most PC users are looking at a screen with approximately 96 pixels per inch. Mobile and tablet users may have resolutions and relative pixel sizes more or less than that.

Specifying a font size in pixels can provide the exact control a web author needs to align text elements with images or other text elements. No matter what font family a reader's browser may substitute, the text will still occupy the same number of screen dots. For example, the code in Example 3.6 creates a page header that keeps the alignment of the various elements when the page is resized in a reader's browser. Figure 3.6 shows how this looks in most browsers.

Example 3.6: Using font sizes in pixels for alignment

```html
<!DOCTYPE html>
<html>
<head>
<title>Example 3.6</title>
<style type="text/css">
  #d1 { font-size: 64px; width: 4em; float: left; }
  #d2 { font-size: 32px; font-variant: small-caps; }
</style>
</head>

<body>
<div id="d1" style="font-family: Gill Sans;">LOGO</div>
<div id="d2">The Company Tagline<br/>
            The Company Motto</div>
<hr/>
<div>Company Content</div>
</body>
</html>
```

Figure 3.6: A logo area aligned using pixel font sizes

It cannot be stressed enough that font sizes are inexact. Web authors are strongly encouraged to use relative sizes specified in em and percentage units in their CSS statements and leave it to the readers to set the overall metrics.

FONT

To save web authors time, CSS has a shorthand notation for specifying font properties. It is conveniently called the font property. It has two formats:

```
font: <font-style> <font-variant> <font-weight> <font-size>
<font-family>
```

or

```
font: <keyword>
```

In the first format, the font-style, font-variant, and font-weight property values are optional. The font-size and font-family values are required. The second format sets the font to match one of the fonts used by the operating system for user interface elements. The acceptable keywords are caption, small-caption, icon, menu, and message-box. The keyword inherit may also be used to indicate that the font properties should be taken from the parent element. Here are some examples:

```
p      { font: bold 120% Verdana, Tahoma, sans-serif; }
h2     { font: italic 18pt Times, "Times New Roman", serif; }
code   { font: message-box; }
cite   { font: italic large Georgia,Times,serif; }
```

When using the shorthand font property, font family names that contain blanks should be enclosed in double quotes to avoid confusion. However, when you specify the CSS in a style attribute, double quotes are already in use for the entire attribute value, so the font family name should be enclosed in single quotes. For example:

```
<h2 style="font: italic 18pt Times,'Times New Roman',serif;">...</h2>
```

The keyword values are seldom used. One of the problems with keyword values is that the text is rendered in a fixed size determined by the operating system and unaffected by any font-size property set for the element. However, the line-height property is dependent on the font-size property, and it *is* affected! This is illustrated in Example 3.7 using the self-describing element trick of Example 3.5.

Example 3.7: Using keyword font property values

```
<!DOCTYPE html>
<html>
<head>
<title>Example 3.7</title>
<style type="text/css">
  body { padding: 24px; }
  p:before, span:before { content: attr(style); }
</style>
</head>

<body>
<p style="font: bold x-small sans-serif;"><br/>
  <span style="font: caption;"></span><br/>
  <span style="font: small-caption;"></span><br/>
  <span style="font: icon;"></span><br/>
  <span style="font: menu;"></span><br/>
  <span style="font: message-box;"></span>
</p>

<p style="font: bold x-large sans-serif;"><br/>
  <span style="font: caption;"></span><br/>
  <span style="font: small-caption;"></span><br/>
  <span style="font: icon;"></span><br/>
  <span style="font: menu;"></span><br/>
  <span style="font: message-box;"></span>
</p>
</body>
</html>
```

Figure 3.7 shows how the keyword font properties of Example 3.7 appear in a browser. Note how the second paragraph has expanded line height but the displayed font sizes are the same as the first paragraph.

Figure 3.7: Keyword font properties and their relation to font size and line height

COLORS

Perhaps just as important as typography, color adds information and sets expectations for the tone and mood of a page. The color property takes a color value or the inherit keyword and sets an element's foreground color. This includes the color of any text, the color of any list bullets, and the color of any border the element may have, provided it is not otherwise set by a border or border-color property.

Color values may be specified in any of five formats: color names, RGB values, RGB percentages, and short and long hexadecimal values. Color names are the easiest and include most of the colors in the basic crayon box:

```
red        orange     yellow     green

blue       teal       aqua       fuchsia

lime       maroon     navy       olive

purple     black      gray       silver

white
```

These 17 colors are from the CSS2.1 specification. The CSS3 specification expanded the number of names to 140 colors, matching the set of color names in the X11 window standard, including brown, pink, tan, cyan, magenta, gold, and the ever-popular chartreuse. For example:

```
p.crazy { color: chartreuse; }
```

In general, authors are advised to use colors from the set of 17 names to ensure that their colors are displayed correctly on the widest variety of devices.

Color values can be precisely defined by giving a triplet of values for the component colors red, green, and blue (RGB). Each component color is represented by a number from 0 to 255, or by a percentage from 0 percent to 100 percent, signifying how much of that color to contribute—from none to the display's maximum brightness. If all the component colors have the same value, the resulting color will be along the gray scale. Here are a couple examples:

```
.nav li a  { color: rgb(0,0,51); }      /* very dark blue */
address    { color: rgb(255,255,255); } /* white */
```

Colors can also be specified using hexadecimal (base 16) notation. The long-format hexadecimal notation is a hash mark (#) followed by six hexadecimal digits. A hexadecimal digit is one of the digits from 0 to 9 or a letter from a to f, standing in for the numbers 10 through 15. The digits are grouped into pairs. The first two digits represent the red component, the second two represent the green component, and the last two represent blue. Table 3.2 shows the 17 CSS2.1 colors and their corresponding decimal, percentage, and hexadecimal values.

Table 3.2: CSS2.1 colors

Color Name	RGB Decimal	RGB Percentage	Hexadecimal
black	rgb(0,0,0)	rgb(0%,0%,0%)	#000000
white	rgb(255,255,255)	rgb(100%,100%,100%)	#ffffff
red	rgb(255,0,0)	rgb(100%,0%,0%)	#ff0000
yellow	rgb(255,255,0)	rgb(100%,100%,0%)	#ffff00
green	rgb(0,128,0)	rgb(0%,50%,0%)	#008000
aqua	rgb(0,255,255)	rgb(0%,100%,100%)	#00ffff

continues

Table 3.2: CSS2.1 colors (continued)

Color Name	RGB Decimal	RGB Percentage	Hexadecimal
blue	rgb(0,0,255)	rgb(0%,0%,100%)	#0000ff
fuchsia	rgb(255,0,255)	rgb(100%,0%,100%)	#ff00ff
gray	rgb(128,128,128)	rgb(50%,50%,50%)	#808080
silver	rgb(192,192,192)	rgb(75%,75%,75%)	#c0c0c0
orange	rgb(255,170,0)	rgb(100%,67%,0%)	#ffaa00
olive	rgb(128,128,0)	rgb(50%,50%,0%)	#808000
lime	rgb(0,255,0)	rgb(0%,100%,0%)	#00ff00
teal	rgb(0,128,128)	rgb(0%,50%,50%)	#008080
purple	rgb(128,0,128)	rgb(50%,0%,50%)	#800080
navy	rgb(0,0,128)	rgb(0%,0%,50%)	#000080
maroon	rgb(128,0,0)	rgb(50%,0%,0%)	#800000

Many years ago computer monitors could display only 256 colors (including black and white). Of these 256 colors, only 216 of them would reliably display the same on both Windows and Macintosh computers. This set was referred to as the "web-safe" color set. These web-safe colors are distributed evenly throughout the entire set of colors such that they occur whenever all the components are even multiples of 20 percent, which is the same as multiples of 51 decimal. Converted to hexadecimal, web-safe colors occur when all the components have one of these values: 00, 33, 66, 99, cc, or ff. An example is #3366ff.

Today, most devices, including mobile devices, can display thousands or millions of colors. Sticking to web-safe colors is not as important as it once was. Nevertheless, many web designers still use web-safe colors because they are easier to remember and it helps keep the colors consistent from page to page.

CSS also accepts a shorthand hexadecimal notation consisting of the hash sign followed by three hexadecimal digits. The idea is that each of the three digits will be duplicated so that #f00 is equal to #ff0000 (red), for example, or #666 is equal to #666666 (dark gray).

BACKGROUND PROPERTIES

There is little point in controlling the foreground color of text if there isn't also a way to specify background colors. The background-color property does just that, using the same color value notation as the foreground color property. For example:

```
body          { background-color: #eee; }   /* very light gray */
ul.hilite     { background-color: yellow; }
div.tip       { background-color: rbg(204,204,255); }   /* light blue */
```

The background color fills the entire area occupied by the element, including the padding and extending to the outer edge of the border. The HTML code in Example 3.8 features a division with a fat dotted border. The result is shown in Figure 3.8.

Example 3.8: HTML and CSS for background colors

```
<!DOCTYPE html>
<html>
<head>
<title>Example 3.8</title>
<style type="text/css">
body { background-color: #aaa; }    /* light gray page        */
div  { color: white;                /* white text and border */
        width: 100px;
        height: 160px;
        margin: 36px;
        font-size: 4em;
        border: 10px dotted;        /* not a solid border    */
        background-color: #333;     /* dark gray background   */
    }
</style>
</head>

<body>
<div align="center">1&cent;</div>
</body>
</html>
```

Figure 3.8: Background colors and element borders

The background-color property can also have the keywords transparent and inherit as values. inherit means to use the same background color as the element's parent element, and transparent means to cancel any background color the element has and let the parent element's background show through.

In addition to colors, an element's background can be filled with an image using the background-image property and a URL value. CSS provides three additional background properties to manage the position of the background image. Here is an example showing all the background properties:

```
div.cute {
    background-color: pink;
    background-image: url(images/cute.png);
    background-repeat: no-repeat;
    background-attachment: fixed;
    background-position: top center;
}
```

Note that URLs in CSS are written without quotes and, in a stylesheet file, are relative to the stylesheet's location rather than the location of the HTML file. In addition to a URL, the background-image property can have the keyword value none to remove any background image from previous settings.

Preference is given to the background image over the background color. If a background image completely fills the element, none of the background color will show unless the image itself has transparent areas. The background-repeat property controls how the image fills the element if it is smaller than the element's width and/or height. The possible values are repeat, no-repeat, repeat-x, repeat-y, and inherit. The default is repeat.

A designer can achieve interesting effects with repeating patterns. For example, a page featuring a gradient background that is light at the top of the page, gradually getting darker toward the bottom, can be created with an image that is only 1 pixel wide by specifying a background-repeat value of repeat-x.

The background-position property controls where the background image is initially positioned with respect to the element. Authors can provide a value to this property in three different ways:

1 Using the keywords left, center, or right, and top or bottom, to position the background image with respect to the left, right, top, and bottom edges of the element. Positioning the background image with respect to the center of the container keeps the center of the background image fixed to the center of the container even as the containing element is dynamically resized.

2 Using a pair of percentages specifying relative offsets from the top-left corner of the element. If only one number is provided, it is taken as the horizontal offset, and the vertical offset is set to 50%.

3 Using a pair of lengths specifying an absolute horizontal and vertical off-set from the top-left corner. Negative numbers are permitted and cause the background image to be shifted outside the element's boundaries and clipped.

Following are some examples of the background-position property. Note that no comma separates the pair of values:

```
background-position: bottom center;
background-position: 0px 20px;
background-position: 50% 50%;
```

The final background property, background-attachment, controls how the background image moves in response to the scrolling of the foreground content. The three possible values are scroll, fixed, and inherit. The default value, scroll, means that the background image scrolls with the foreground content. The fixed value means that the background image is fixed in place with respect to the document's window. This alignment is maintained for all scrolled elements, not just the document body.

In a manner similar to the `font` property, the various background properties can be combined into one rule using the `background` property. The ordering is color, image, repeat attachment, and position. For example:

`body { `**`background: white url(shading.png) repeat-y static 0px 10px; }`**

This format is encouraged because it is more widely supported among older browsers and is shorter to type. Any property values not specified are given their default values.

TEXT PROPERTIES

The important CSS properties that affect the appearance of text include `text-align`, `text-decoration`, `text-indent`, `text-transform`, `line-height`, `letter-spacing`, `word-spacing`, `white-space`, and `vertical-align`. Unlike the font, background, and some other properties, there is no shorthand form to combine the various individual properties that set the characteristics of element text.

TEXT-ALIGN

The `text-align` property controls the horizontal alignment of content within an element. The permissible values are `left`, `right`, `center`, `start`, `end`, `justify`, and `inherit`. The `justify` value instructs browsers to add letter and word spacing to the text so that each line of text—except, perhaps, the last—occupies the full width of the element minus any padding and border. The last line of justified text can be controlled with the `text-align-last` property, which accepts the same values as the `text-align` property. Authors are cautioned to use justified text only in the simplest cases. An element with mixed font families, sizes, and styles may display poorly in some browsers when the text is justified.

TEXT-DECORATION

This property allows web authors to add certain effects to element text. The permissible values are `underline`, `overline`, `line-through`, `blink` (which browsers are not required to support), and `inherit`. Values can be combined in a single statement. However, subsequent settings of the `text-decoration` property will override any previous rules in effect for the same element. Proposed CSS3 extensions for refining the line that a browser draws above, below, or through the text include the `text-line-color` and `text-line-style` properties.

Text decoration is most commonly used to turn off the underlining of anchor elements where it is obvious that the content is linked, as with navigation buttons, for example:

`#nav li a { `**`text-decoration: none; }`**

Example 3.9 illustrates the use of several text decorations. Figure 3.9 shows how these properties appear in my browser.

Example 3.9: Various text decorations

```
<!DOCTYPE html>
<html>
<head>
<title>Example 3.9</title>
<style type="text/css">
  p.p1 { text-decoration: underline ; }
  p.p2 { text-decoration: line-through; }
  p.p3 { text-decoration: overline; }
  p.p4 { text-decoration: overline underline; }
  p.p5 { text-decoration: overline underline line-through; }
</style>
</head>

<body style="padding: 20px;">
<p class="p1">Deck the halls</p>
<p class="p2">With boughs of holly</p>
<p class="p3">Fa la la la la, la la la la</p>
<p class="p4">'Tis the season to be jolly</p>
<p class="p5">Fa la la la la, la la la la</p>
</body>
</html>
```

Figure 3.9: Using the text-decoration property

TEXT-INDENT

The text-indent property does just what you expect: It indents the first line of text in a paragraph or other block element. It can take either an absolute length or a percentage. Negative values are permitted and cause the text to be outdented. Here are some examples:

```
h2      { text-indent: -2em; }
main p { text-indent: 1%;    }
#t1 td { text-index: .25in; }
```

TEXT-TRANSFORM

This property provides a means to control the case of an element's text. The permissible values are uppercase, lowercase, capitalize, none, and inherit. The property can be applied to any body element. It is a useful tool for dealing with listings and menus generated by blogging software or other content-management systems. For example, you can display the same marked-up list of links as uppercase in a menu bar at the top of the page, but with smaller lowercase letters in the page footer.

LINE-HEIGHT

The principal use of the line-height property is to control how far apart the lines are in a paragraph or other block element, but there are subtle aspects to its effects. The height of a line is the minimum distance from its baseline to the baseline of the line just above it. That is usually set at 1.2 times the font size of the line's tallest character, but it is only a minimum value; no maximum value is implied. Thus, each line in a block of text can have a different line height. Because the normal behavior is to calculate the line height from the font size, it is common to specify the line-height property using a relative unit. For example:

```
#content p { line-height: 1.6em; }
ul.page-list li { line-height: 180%; }
```

The difference between what the browser calculates for the height of a line and the line's maximum computed font size is called "leading" and is pronounced like the metal that plumbers once used. Half of the leading is added above the characters on each line, and half goes below. If the leading is negative, as can happen when working with absolute values in pixels, points, inches, centimeters, or millimeters, lines of text can overlap each other. Here are some examples:

```
#nav li   { line-height: 200%; }
#p.intro { line-height: 1.6em; }
#content p { line-height: 1.6em; }
```

Web authors are cautioned to avoid setting line heights except for simple text elements such as paragraphs, which are expected to consist of multiple lines. Relative units such as ems, exes, pixels, and percentages generally work better with heights than absolute units. The keyword normal is a permissible value, and it is useful to reset line heights for generated elements. As a general rule, you should not set the line height for any element unless you also set the font size for that element or you know what the computed font sizes and units will be.

Example 3.10 has four paragraphs of text, each set to a different line height.

Example 3.10: Setting line heights

```
<!DOCTYPE html>
<html>
<head>
<title>Example 3.10</title>
<style type="text/css">
  p:before { content: attr(style) " ";  }
</style>
</head>

<body>
<p style="line-height: normal;">Lorem ipsum dolor sit amet, ...</p>
<hr/>
<p style="line-height: 100%;">Lorem ipsum dolor sit amet, ...</p>
<hr/>
<p style="line-height: 1.5em;">Lorem ipsum dolor sit amet, ...</p>
<hr/>
<p style="line-height: 10px;">Lorem ipsum dolor sit amet, ...</p>
</body>
</html>
```

Figure 3.10 shows how this looks in a typical browser. Notice how the second paragraph, with a `line-height` value of 100%, has less spacing between the lines than the first paragraph, which has a `normal` line height. This is because normal line height is 1.2 em, or 120 percent of the font size.

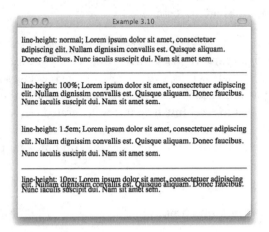

Figure 3.10: Paragraphs with varying line heights

LETTER AND WORD SPACING

The `letter-spacing` property sets the amount of space between letters. The value of the property can be a length with a units designator or the keyword `normal` or `inherit`. The normal value is equivalent to 0 em. Negative values are permitted, which has the effect of making the letters look cramped. The `word-spacing` property similarly sets the spacing between words and takes the same values as the `letter-spacing` property. However, the distinction of what is and what is not a word can be browser- and language-dependent. As with the `letter-spacing` property, 0 is equivalent to normal.

Example 3.11 has code for three paragraphs with different letter spacing. I've used the Verdana font for the text because it already has a generous amount of width in the characters. It uses the same Latin nonsense as Example 3.10, but, as you can see in Figure 3.11, the effect is quite different.

Example 3.11: Letter spacing and word spacing

```
<!DOCTYPE html>
<html>
<head>
```

```
<title>Example 3.11</title>
<style type="text/css">
 p { font-family: verdana,sans-serif; }
 p:before { content: attr(style) " ";  font-weight: bold; }
 h4.wide  { word-spacing: 2em; }
</style>
</head>
<body>

<h4 class="wide">Paragraphs with different <em>letter-spacing</em></h4>

<p style="letter-spacing: normal;">Lorem ipsum dolor sit amet, ...</p>
<hr/>
<p style="letter-spacing: -1px;">Lorem ipsum dolor sit amet, ...</p>
<hr/>
<p style="letter-spacing: 0.5em;">Lorem ipsum dolor sit amet, ...</p>
</body>
</html>
```

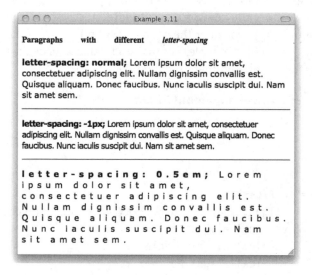

Figure 3.11: Paragraphs with different letter-spacing values

WHITE SPACE

The normal removal of excess white space in an element can be modified with the white-space property. The permissible values for this property are normal, nowrap, pre, pre-wrap, pre-line, and inherit. The nowrap value prevents the browser from wrapping the line until a line-break character (<br/>) is encountered or the end of the element is reached. Content extending beyond the width of the element is usually clipped.

The pre value of the white-space property causes the element to be treated in the same manner as the pre HTML element. All line breaks and white space in the element are respected and preserved. The pre-line value instructs the browser to preserve line breaks but do normal excess white space removal within each line. The pre-wrap value does somewhat the opposite, allowing the browser to break lines that are too long for the width of the element, while preserving the excess white space within each line. Neither the pre-wrap nor pre-line property is used very much.

VERTICAL-ALIGN

The vertical-align property is most useful in aligning elements in table cells, but it can be specified for any element. When applied to table elements, the permissible values are the keywords top, middle, and bottom. To understand how these values work, consider the code shown in Example 3.12, which has a three-row-by-three-column table. Because each table data cell is taller than the image it holds, vertical alignment is called for.

Example 3.12: Vertical alignment in table cells

```
<!DOCTYPE html>
<html>
<head>
<title>Example 3.12</title>
<style type="text/css">
  td,th     { height: 150px; width: 72px; text-align: center; }
  #row1     { vertical-align: top; }
  #row2     { vertical-align: middle; }
  #row3     { vertical-align: bottom; }
</style>
</head>
```

```
<body>
    <table border="1" cellspacing="0">
        <tr id="row1">
            <th>top align</th>
            <td><img src="img001.jpg" alt=""></td>
            <td><img src="img002.jpg" alt=""></td>
            <td><img src="img003.jpg" alt=""></td>
        </tr>
        <tr id="row2">
            <th>middle align</th>
            <td><img src="img001.jpg" alt=""></td>
            <td><img src="img002.jpg" alt=""></td>
            <td><img src="img003.jpg" alt=""></td>
        </tr>
        <tr id="row3">
            <th>bottom align</th>
            <td><img src="img001.jpg" alt=""></td>
            <td><img src="img002.jpg" alt=""></td>
            <td><img src="img003.jpg" alt=""></td>
        </tr>
    </table>
</body>
</html>
```

Figure 3.12 shows the result in a typical browser.

In a block element with normal word wrapping, text of different sizes is aligned on its baselines, and the tallest character (or inline image) in each line sets the height of that line's inline box. The inline box can be thought of as a virtual element with properties that can change dynamically as the user changes window sizes, font preferences, and so on. The vertical-align property can be used to align text within the text's inline box. This inline box's height may be more or less than the line-height property's value for the block element if it is set with a fixed value.

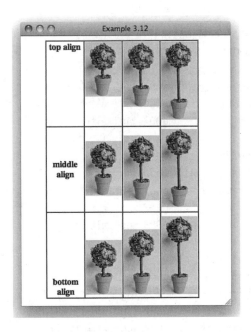

Figure 3.12: Images and text vertically aligned in a table

In addition to the three values top, middle, and bottom that are applicable to table elements, the vertical-align property can have an offset value specified in fixed or relative units. For example:

```
span.upper { vertical-align: 10px; }
p.under    { vertical-align: -1em; }
div.topper { vertical-align: 50%; }
```

The vertical-align property can also take one of the following keyword values: super, sub, text-top, or text-bottom. super and sub move the text to positions appropriate for superscripts and subscripts. They should be equivalent to the effects of using the <sup> and <sub> HTML elements. text-top and text-bottom instruct the browser to align the top or bottom, respectively, of the text's inline box with the top or bottom of the parent element's content area.

BOX PROPERTIES

Every HTML block element has a set of box properties that define the characteristics of the rectangular area that element occupies on the web page.

HTML inline elements also can have box properties as a consequence of their participation in lines of the content flow, as we saw with respect to setting the line-height and vertical-align properties. The box properties discussed in this section are height, width, margin, padding, and border.

HEIGHT AND WIDTH

The height and width properties of a block element are the dimensions of the rectangle the element's content occupies. Width and height specifications are ignored for inline elements. However, you can change the apparent height of an inline element by adding or subtracting leading with the line-height property.

The area that the element takes up on the page is usually larger than the specified height and width property values because it includes the padding, border, and margin amounts. This is important to remember when working with background images, which extend into the padding and under the element's border, as shown in Figure 3.8 earlier in the chapter.

Both the width and height properties can be given values using a length and units designator. Negative values, however, are not allowed. The two properties can also have the keyword values auto and inherit. auto is the default value. For height, auto means to compute a height sufficient to contain the content as currently flowed. Element height is, in a sense, conserved. The computed value is the minimum required. In most instances it is counterproductive to set an element's height to a specific value unless the heights of all child elements are known. Among the exceptions are table elements and labels matched to backgrounds.

In contrast, an element's width is not constrained. The computed value is the largest value that will fit the element with its margins, padding, and borders within the width of the parent element. It is for this reason that you must specify widths when working with floating elements:

```
#col1,#col2 { width: 48%; float: left; }
ul.nav li    { height: 1.4em; }
```

As a general rule, web authors should set an element's width when it is necessary to make the element narrower than it would normally be. Web authors also should set an element's height when it's necessary to make the element taller than normal. If more precise control is needed, the author can use the min-height, min-width, max-height, and max-width properties, which are recognized by most modern browsers. As you might expect, these properties set constraints on the browser's computed widths and heights.

MARGINS AND PADDING

Most HTML elements are rendered with some amount of space between them. For elements without a border, this space is composed of margin and padding on each of the element's four sides. For elements with a border, the margin is the amount of space on the outside of the borders, and the padding is the amount of space on the inside of the border. Both the margin and padding properties can take any size value, including a percentage value and the keyword auto. A margin value can be negative and will cause an element's position to be shifted, possibly to overlap another element. A negative padding value is effectively taken as 0. It will not cause the content to be shifted into the border or margin areas.

Example 3.13 is an HTML page with three paragraphs, each one having different margin and padding values. The first paragraph has a 0 margin and 2 em of padding. The third paragraph reverses that with a 2 em margin and 0 padding. The paragraph in the middle has 1 em each of margin and padding. The text is from a children's story by the English mathematician Charles Lutwidge Dodgson.[4] All body elements are given a light gray background to illustrate the effects. Figure 3.13 shows how the HTML appears in a typical browser.

Example 3.13: Use of margin and padding for block elements

```
<!DOCTYPE html>
<html>
<head>
<title>Example 3.13</title>
<style type="text/css">
  body * { font-family: Comic Sans MS,cursive; background-color: #ccc; }
  #p1 { margin: 0em; padding: 2em; }
  #p2 { margin: 1em; padding: 1em; }
  #p3 { margin: 2em; padding: 0em; }
</style>
</head>

<body>
<p id="p1">In a minute or two the Caterpillar took the hookah out of
its mouth and yawned once or twice, and shook itself. </p>
```

---

4. Writing under the pseudonym Lewis Carroll in *Alice's Adventures in Wonderland*.

```
<p id="p2">Then it got down off the mushroom, and crawled away in the
grass, merely remarking as it went,</p>

<p id="p3">"One side will make you grow taller, and the other side will
make you grow shorter."</p>
</body>
</html>
```

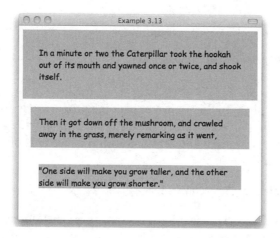

Figure 3.13: An element with different amounts of margin and padding

Notice that there are a few pixels of space between the first paragraph, which has 0 margins, and the edges of the browser's window. Where does this space come from? A bit of experimentation shows that this space is the body element's margin! This is a bit illogical. You might expect the body element to have some amount of padding so that content doesn't mash up against the window's edges, but it should not need any margin to separate itself from other content elements, because there are none. The body element does, in fact, have a parent element, the html element, that can be given margins, padding, borders, and background that will be recognized by most browsers. However, how browsers should behave at the extreme margins is not well defined. Web developers should avoid assigning any styles to the html element.

The body element's default margin amount may be due to historical reasons, but it does have a consequence. Unlike other HTML elements, any background color or image assigned to the body element is extended to the edges of the browser's window. In other words, the document body acts as if it has a 0 margin and a few pixels of padding when it comes to backgrounds, but its margin controls the position of its child elements. A web author must explicitly set the body's margin to 0 to eliminate the default space between the edges of the browser's window and any content elements.

The margin and padding properties are actually shorthand notations for sets of properties:

margin-top	padding-top
margin-right	padding-right
margin-bottom	padding-bottom
margin-left	padding-left

Any single value given to the margin or padding properties is applied to the margins or padding on each side of the element. This shorthand notation allows the author to specify different amounts on each side of an element in the following manner:

```
p.intro { margin: 0 .5em 20px .5em; }
```

The ordering is clockwise: top, right, bottom, left. Therefore, the preceding rule is the same as this one:

```
p.intro {
  margin-top: 0;         /* zero amounts do not need units */
  margin-right: .5em;
  margin-bottom: 20px;
  margin-left: .5em;
}
```

When given a value consisting of fewer than four amounts, the existing amounts are recycled. Thus, this

```
p.intro { padding: 0 2%; }
```

is the same as this:

```
p.intro { padding: 0 2% 0 2%; }
```

BORDERS

Element borders are created by using one or more of the border properties to set values for the width, color, and style of the border. The border-width property can take any nonnegative numeric value or one of the keywords thin, medium, thick, or inherit, with medium as the default value. The permissible values for the border-style property are none, hidden, solid, dotted, dashed, double, ridge, groove, inset, outset, and inherit. The default for all HTML elements is a border with a style of none. Therefore, an element must have its border-style property set to some other value for a border to appear. Older browsers may not support all values. Example 3.14 illustrates the use of a table to display the different border style values. Figure 3.14 shows how this code appears in a typical browser.

Example 3.14: Using a table to display border styles

```
<!DOCTYPE html>
<html>
<head>
<title>Example 3.14</title>
<style type="text/css">
 body { font: bold 9pt Tahoma,Verdana,sans-serif;   }
 td { border-width: 5px; padding: 1em; background-color: #ddd; }
 td:before { content: attr(style); } /* insert style content */
</style>
</head>

<body>
<table border="0" width="100%" cellspacing="8">
  <tr>
    <td style="border-style: none"></td>
    <td style="border-style: hidden"></td>
    <td style="border-style: solid"></td>
    <td style="border-style: dotted"></td>
    <td style="border-style: dashed"></td>
  </tr>
  <tr>
    <td style="border-style: double"></td>
    <td style="border-style: ridge"></td>
    <td style="border-style: groove"></td>
```

continues

Example 3.14: Using a table to display border styles *(continued)*

```
      <td style="border-style: inset"></td>
      <td style="border-style: outset"></td>
   </tr>
</table>
</body>
</html>
```

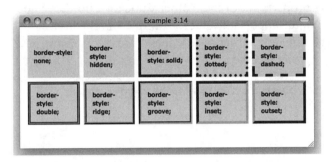

Figure 3.14: Ten different border style types

The border-style value of hidden appears to have the same effect as the value none. That is, both values cause the browser to draw a border with a 0 width. This is unfortunate, because it would be useful to keep the border's space and color without showing it. Consider the following HTML, which sets up a horizontal menu of two links:

```
<style type="text/css">
   li        { list-style-type: none; float: left; padding: 1em; }
   li a      { text-decoration: none; }
   li a:hover { border-style: solid; }
</style>


. . .


<ul>
   <li><a href="here.html">link 1</a></li>
   <li><a href="there.html">link 2</a></li>
</ul>
```

When the reader's mouse hovers over the first link in the list, a medium border is drawn around it. However, this border takes up an additional number of pixels on the right and left of the link and pushes the second link to the right. Coding this

```
li a { border-style: hidden; }
```

doesn't help. The following CSS is needed to toggle the link borders on and off without shifting the following elements to the right:

```
li a        { border-style: solid; border-color: transparent; }
li a:hover  { border-style: solid; border-color: black; }
```

The border property is a shorthand method for setting color, style, and width in one statement. The ordering does not matter. For example:

```
div.greeting    { border: 2px solid rbg(220,240,250); }
#sidebar .widget { border: white dotted; }
#main .button   { border: #456 3px outset; }
```

Each of the four sides of an HTML block element has its own set of border properties by using one of the following:

border-top-width	border-top-color	border-top-style
border-right-width	border-right-color	border-right-style
border-bottom-width	border-bottom-color	border-bottom-style
border-left-width	border-left-color	border-left-style

A shorthand notation can also be used. The border-width, border-style, and border-color properties can each take up to four values to specify the values for the top, right, bottom, and left borders, respectively. Also, the four properties border-top, border-right, border-bottom, and border-left can use the same shorthand notation as the border property. Here are some examples:

```
p { border-right: thin solid gray; }
p { border-style: none none solid none; } /* just a bottom border */
p { border-color: red blue; }
```

Highlighting elements that you want to draw attention to by giving them borders is a nice touch. But borders with rounded corners are cool! CSS3 includes the border-radius property for this purpose. Currently, the border-radius property is not supported by all browsers. However, several browser manufacturers have added proprietary CSS properties to set border corners. These are -moz-border-radius for Mozilla browsers such as Firefox, and -webkit-border-radius for Webkit browsers (Safari and Chrome). Internet Explorer does not support border-radius as of IE version 8. Authors are encouraged to use all proprietary properties when coding CSS for rounded corners for the best results across all browsers. For example:

```
p.welcome {
  border: medium solid blue;
  border-radius: .5em;
  -moz-border-radius: .5em;
  -webkit-border-radius: .5em;
}
```

Example 3.15 demonstrates the creation of borders with rounded corners for browsers built on the Mozilla engine, such as Firefox. Figure 3.15 shows how the HTML is displayed on the Firefox browser.

Example 3.15: HTML for borders with rounded corners

```
<!DOCTYPE html>
<html>
<head>
<title>Example 3.15</title>
<style type="text/css">
  body { font: 9pt Tahoma,Verdana,sans-serif; padding: 1em; }
  p { padding: 1em; background-color: #ddd; }
</style>
</head>

<body>
<p style="border: 2px solid; -moz-border-radius: 10px;">
border: 2px solid;<br/>-moz-border-radius: 10px;</p>
<p style="border: 6px outset; -moz-border-radius: 6px;">
border: 6px outset;<br/>-moz-border-radius: 6px;</p>
<p style="border: 6px dashed; -moz-border-radius: 10px;">
border: 6px dashed;<br/>-moz-border-radius: 10px;</p>
</body>
</html>
```

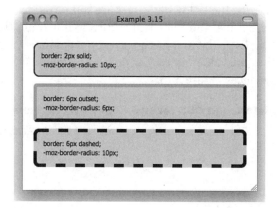

Figure 3.15: Rounded corners

LIST STYLES

CSS provides three properties that help authors create lists with style: list-style-type, list-style-position, and list-style-image. A fourth shorthand property, list-style, allows the author to specify all list properties in a single statement. List properties can be applied to list and list item elements. A list item element that doesn't have its own list style properties set inherits those property values from its parent list element. Here are some examples of list-style:

```
ul.nav      { list-style-type: none; }
li.selected { list-style: url(images/check.gif) inside; }
```

The set of permissible values for the list-style-type property has undergone some changes over time. The CSS2 specification has about 20 values, whereas CSS2.1 has only a dozen. The draft specification for CSS3 expands the permissible values a couple orders of magnitude with support for many national language symbol sets.

The list-style-image property allows a web designer to use a custom image for a list bullet. The list-style-position property has three permissible values: inside, outside (the default), and inherit. The outside value places the marker some distance outside the list item's border. How far outside is browser-dependent. The inside value places the item marker inside the list item's content box as if it were an inline element. You can easily see the difference by putting a border around the list items, as shown in Figure 3.16.

For unordered lists, the following values are supported by most browsers: none, disc, circle, square, and inherit. Figure 3.16 illustrates the first four of these values in two lists. The first has a list-style-position value of outside, and the second has the value inside. Example 3.16 contains the HTML and CSS code that produces Figure 3.16.

Example 3.16: HTML and CSS for two lists with different list-style properties

```
<!DOCTYPE html>
<html>
<head>
<title>Example 3.16</title>
<style type="text/css">
  body { padding: 1em; }
  ul li { border: 1px #999 solid; padding: .25em; }
  lh { font-weight: bold; }
  li:before { content: attr(style); }
  #l1 { list-style-position: outside; }
  #l2 { list-style-position: inside; }
</style>
</head>

<body>
<ul id="l1">
      <lh>Outside position</lh>
      <li style="list-style-type: none;"></li>
      <li style="list-style-type: disc;"></li>
      <li style="list-style-type: circle;"></li>
      <li style="list-style-type: square;"></li>
</ul>

<ul id="l2">
      <lh>Inside position</lh>
      <li style="list-style-type: none;"></li>
      <li style="list-style-type: disc;"></li>
      <li style="list-style-type: circle;"></li>
      <li style="list-style-type: square;"></li>
```

```
</ul>
</body>
</html>
```

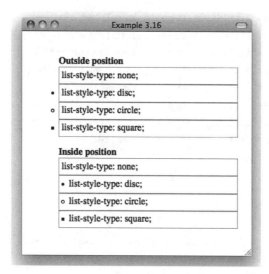

Figure 3.16: List style positions and list style types

For ordered lists the appropriate list-style-type values are decimal, decimal-leading-zero, lower-roman, upper-roman, lower-alpha, upper-alpha, lower-greek, and armenian.

In the ordered list element shown in Example 3.17, each list item is given one of these ordered values. Figure 3.17 shows the result in a typical browser.

Example 3.17: HTML and CSS for displaying ordered list style types

```
<!DOCTYPE html>
<html>
<head>
<title>Example 3.17</title>
<style type="text/css">
 body { padding: 1em; font-family: sans-serif; }
 li:before { content: attr(style); line-height: 1.5em; }
</style>
</head>
```

continues

Example 3.17: HTML and CSS for displaying ordered list style types *(continued)*

```
<body>
    <ol>
        <li style="list-style-type: decimal;"></li>
        <li style="list-style-type: decimal-leading-zero;"></li>
        <li style="list-style-type: lower-roman;"></li>
        <li style="list-style-type: upper-roman;"></li>
        <li style="list-style-type: lower-alpha;"></li>
        <li style="list-style-type: upper-alpha;"></li>
        <li style="list-style-type: lower-greek;"></li>
        <li style="list-style-type: armenian;"></li>
    </ol>
</body>
</html>
```

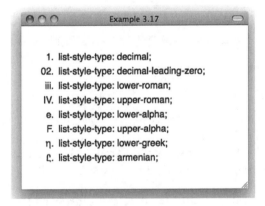

Figure 3.17: An ordered list showing eight different style types

There is order even in unordered lists. The list-style-type property sets the type of list as well as the marker used. An ordered list element behaves just like an unordered list element if the list-style-type value is disc, circle, or square. Likewise, an unordered list element behaves just like an ordered list element if its list-style-type value is one of the keywords for an ordered type. Every list has an internal counter that keeps track of the array of list items no matter if

the list tag is ul, ol, menu, or dl. If the value of the list-style-type property is
one of the sets of numbers or alphabets, the number or letter corresponding
to the counter value is used as the marker for that list item. This is illustrated
in Figure 3.18, which was generated with the HTML and CSS code shown
in Example 3.18. The last list item in the second list illustrates the syntax for
using the list-style-image property.

Example 3.18: HTML and CSS for mixed list-style-type values

```
<!DOCTYPE html>
<html>
<head>
<title>Example 3.18</title>
<style type="text/css">
 body  { padding: 1em; font-family: sans-serif; }
 ol,ul { float: left; margin: auto 1.5em; }
</style>
</head>

<body>
    <ol>
      <li>This</li>
      <li style="list-style-type: circle;">is</li>
      <li style="list-style-type: lower-roman;">an</li>
      <li style="list-style-type: square;">ordered</li>
      <li>list</li>
    </ol>
    <ul>
      <li>This</li>
      <li style="list-style-type: circle;">is</li>
      <li style="list-style-type: decimal;">an</li>
      <li style="list-style-type: lower-latin;">UNordered</li>
      <li style="list-style-image: url(peace.gif);">list</li>
    </ul>
</body>
</html>
```

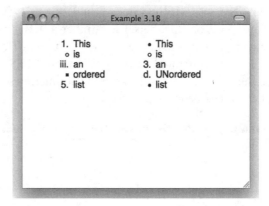

Figure 3.18: Ordered and unordered lists with different list-style-type values

CSS Positioning

HTML elements that are part of the normal content flow in a document are said to have *static* positioning. But web authors are not required to go with the flow. Any HTML element can be positioned precisely on the browser's page by setting the CSS positioning properties: position, top, right, bottom, and left.

The position property can have one of four values:

- ▸ static   This is the default. Normal, floated, and inline elements fill the browser's window in the same order as presented in the HTML source.

- ▸ relative   The element's position is offset by some amount from its static position. The space the element formerly occupied is preserved so that all other document elements keep their original positions.

- ▸ absolute   The element is removed from the document flow and positioned with respect to an ancestor element. The space the element occupied is closed up, and other HTML elements are repositioned as if the element was never there.

- ▸ fixed   The element is removed from the document flow and positioned with respect to the browser's window. Like absolute, the space it occupied is removed, and other elements act as if it never existed.

The top, right, bottom, and left properties determine how far the positioned element is offset from the edges of its containing element. They can be given length values consisting of a positive or negative number and units designator, a percentage value, or the keyword auto or inherit. The auto value is the default and keeps the element in the same place with respect to its containing element.

The notion of an element's containing element needs some explanation. When a block element has absolute positioning, its containing element is its closest ancestor that does not have static positioning. If no such ancestor element exists, the containing element is the document's html element. This means that each element that is not statically positioned has its own steam of content flow, and an absolutely positioned element can only jump out of its own place in the current stream. For example, suppose an absolutely positioned element has a great-grandparent element that is already outside the document flow. The element is positioned with respect to the edges of its great-grandparent.

When an element has fixed positioning, it jumps out of all streams in the document flow and is offset relative to the document window without regard for the status of any ancestors. A fixed positioned element does not scroll along with the document's content. You often see such elements as extra toolbars at the top of the window or as feedback buttons at the sides or bottom.

The containing element for a relatively positioned element is the rectangle containing the element, along with its padding, borders, and margins. All positioned block elements retain their padding, borders, and margins.

The offset amounts set by the top, right, bottom, and left properties are measured, on each respective side, from the inner edge of the border (if there's no border, from the inner edge of the margin) to the outer edge of the element's corresponding margin. Example 3.19 illustrates how this works.

Example 3.19: HTML to demonstrate CSS positioning

```
<!DOCTYPE html>
<html>
<head>
<title>Example 3.19a</title>
<style type="text/css">
  body    { padding: 1em; font-family: sans-serif; border: dotted; }
  #d1     { width: 200px; height: 200px; border: dashed; }
  #d2     { width: 50%; height: 50%; border: solid; }
</style>
</head>
```

continues

Example 3.19: HTML to demonstrate CSS positioning *(continued)*

```
<body>
<div id="d1">
  <div id="d2"></div>
</div>
</body>
</html>
```

There is no content in these elements. In each example, the document body consists of the same two nested divisions with borders to show their size and positioning. The body element has a dotted border, the outer division has a dashed border, and the inner division has a solid border. Figure 3.19a shows how the code of Example 3.19a is displayed in a typical browser.

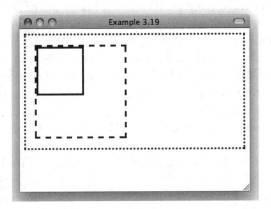

Figure 3.19a: Nested divisions with static positioning

The outer division, d1, has a height and width of 200 pixels. The inner division, d2, has its `height` and `width` properties set to 50%, which makes it a 100-by-100-pixel square occupying the top-left quadrant of its parent, which sits within the body element's 1 em of padding.

You can edit the CSS statement for the inner division to set absolute positioning:

```
#d2  { width: 50%; height: 50%; border: solid;
       position: absolute; }
```

Saving and reloading the example displays something similar to Figure 3.19b. Because the top, right, bottom, and left properties all have the default value of auto, the inner division's top-left corner is in the same place as it was in Figure 3.19a. But since it is no longer in the document flow, its height and width are now 50 percent of its containing element: the viewport coinciding with the document's html element. Thus, the inner division is half the height and width of the browser's window and will grow and shrink as the window is resized. Try it!

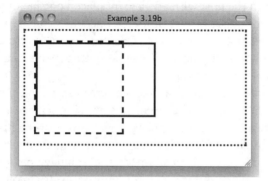

Figure 3.19b: A division with absolute positioning and auto offset

Finally, add some offset to the position of the inner division as shown in the following CSS statement, save, and reload the example again. Figure 3.19c shows the result that I saw using Firefox.

```
#d2   { width: 50%; height: 50%; border: solid;
        position: absolute;
        top: 0; right: 0; }
```

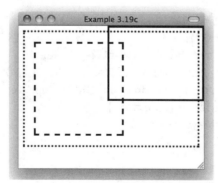

Figure 3.19c: An absolutely positioned element offset with respect to the viewport

As shown in Figure 3.19c, the right edge of the inner division, with its solid border, is now 0 pixels from the viewport's right edge and 0 pixels from its top. It is actually outside the body element's border!

When does it make sense to use positioning? It is such a powerful tool that authors are cautioned to use it sparingly and only for exceptional needs. For example, suppose you are composing a blog post, and you want to complement the information in the post with an element placed outside the post's content area, such as in the page's header or footer. Such an element might serve as a call-to-action link or a reminder icon. CSS positioning is also useful for the proper placement of tooltip boxes, asides, and drop menus that are made to appear in response to a user's actions.

The HTML code shown in Example 3.20 creates a simple horizontal navigation menu with second-level drop menus by using relative and absolute positioning. When the reader's mouse pointer hovers over a first-level list item, its nested list's display property is changed from none to block. Because the first-level list item is relatively positioned, its absolutely positioned child list occupies the same space as its parent. It is only necessary to offset the nested list 1 em down from the top and 0 pixels from the left edge to position it properly.

This technique works in most modern browsers. The links are just dummy entries. It is left as an exercise for you to flesh out this skeleton code into an attractive and useful navigational element.

Example 3.20: HTML skeleton code for creating a two-level horizontal drop menu

```
<!DOCTYPE html>
<html>
<head>
<title>Example 3.20</title>
<style type="text/css">
  ul { padding: 0; margin: 0; list-style: none; }
  li { float: left; position: relative; width: 8em; }
  li ul { display: none; position: absolute; top: 1em; left: 0; }
  li > ul { top: auto; left: auto; }
  li:hover ul { display: block; }
</style>
</head>

<body>
```

```
<ul>
  <li><a href="#">Apples</a>
    <ul>
      <li><a href="#">Red Delicious</a></li>
      <li><a href="#">Gala</a></li>
      <li><a href="#">Macintosh</a></li>
    </ul>
  </li>

  <li><a href="#">Oranges</a>
    <ul>
      <li><a href="#">Navel</a></li>
      <li><a href="#">Valencia</a></li>
      <li><a href="#">Blood</a></li>
    </ul>
  </li>
</ul>
</body>
</html>
```

Figure 3.20 shows how this appears in a typical browser. The window on the right shows the drop menu for oranges activated by the mouse pointer's hovering on the link.

Figure 3.20: Creating a simple drop menu

OTHER CSS PROPERTIES

We have not covered all of CSS. A number of important properties control the fundamental display characteristics of an HTML element. This section covers the properties display, visibility, overflow, float, and clear.

DISPLAY AND VISIBILITY

The display property controls how a browser will display an element. This is not as simple as it first appears. This property has many permissible values. Among the most important are none, inline, block, inline-block, and run-in.

It is important to remember when using the display property that it does not actually change the nature of an element; it changes only how the browser displays it. A paragraph that is declared inline still retains its box properties, including its padding, and borders. More important, declaring a paragraph inline does not allow you to nest that paragraph inside another paragraph. A paragraph cannot be inside another paragraph, no matter what their display properties are set to.

The display property is useful when you're dealing with generated content that must appear in contexts it was not originally intended for. For example, suppose you want to simply list the titles of blog posts by a certain author, but the blogging software only generates such information marked up as an unordered list of links. Example 3.21 shows how to set the display property of the list items to inline so that the information is displayed more like a paragraph.

Example 3.21: Using the display property to make a list display inline

```
<!DOCTYPE html>
<html>
<head>
<title>Example 2.21</title>
<style type="text/css">
 ul.post-listing li { display: inline; font-style: italic; }
 ul.post-listing li:after { content: ','; }  /* add a comma */
</style>
</head>

<body>
<ul class="post-listing">         <!-- generated content -->
  <lh>Posts by the author:</lh>
  <li><a href="/?p=1">What happened yesterday</a></li>
  <li><a href="/?p=2">What's happening now</a></li>
  <li><a href="/?p=3">What will happen tomorrow</a></li>
</ul>
</body>
</html>
```

Figure 3.21 shows how this HTML appears in a typical browser.

Posts by the author: *What happened yesterday*, *What's happening now*, *What will happen tomorrow*,

Figure 3.21: Showing how a list can be changed into a paragraph with the `display` **property**

Note that even though the list items have lost their bullets and are displayed inline, the list itself still has its block properties, including the extra left margin that lists typically have. This is probably not exactly what you wanted. You can fix it by adjusting the list's margin with another CSS statement like so:

`ul.post-listing { margin-left: -2em; }`

Sometimes the opposite action is necessary: changing a collection of inline elements, such as anchor or span elements, into block elements so that they display as paragraphs would. But perhaps the most important use of the `display` property is to make items appear and disappear in response to a user's action. The HTML code and CSS in Example 3.22 cause the first paragraph to disappear when the mouse button is held down over the "missing" link. It reappears when the button is released. No new page is loaded when this happens because the link's `href` attribute points to the currently loaded page.

Example 3.22: Disappearing an element by using the `display` **property**

```
<!DOCTYPE html>
<html>
<head>
<title>Example 3.22</title>
<style type="text/css">
 a:active + p { display: none; }   /* the paragraph after the link */
</style>
```

continues

Example 3.22: Disappearing an element by using the display
property *(continued)*

```
</head>

<body>
<a href="#">Something is missing.</a>
<p>The following sentence is false.</p>
<p>The previous sentence is true.</p>
</body>
</html>
```

Figure 3.22 shows how this code is displayed in two browser windows. In the window on the right, the mouse is on the link, and the mouse button is held down, causing the first paragraph to disappear.

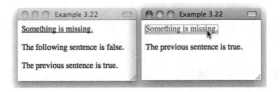

Figure 3.22: Changing the display **property of a sibling element using the**
:active **pseudo-class**

Changing an element's display property from block to none has the effect of making it look as if the element never existed on the page. The content following the element is moved up to occupy the space the element once occupied. Of course, the element still exists and can be accessed by scripting methods.

If the visibility property were used in Example 3.22 instead

```
a:active + p { visibility: hidden; }
```

the paragraph after the link still disappears, but the space it occupied remains. The final paragraph does not move up to take its place.

Setting a block element's display property to the value inline-block instructs the browser to treat the element the same way an inline image is treated. The element loses its margins to become part of the content flow of its parent element but keeps its other box properties, including height, width, padding, and borders. If the inline-block element is embedded in text, a browser aligns the baseline of its bottom line of text with the baseline of the parent's text. Example 3.23 illustrates this relationship.

Example 3.23: HTML and CSS coding for inline-block elements

```
<!DOCTYPE html>
<html>
<head>
<title>Example 3.23</title>
<style type="text/css">
 #faq p.pad { display: inline-block;
              border: thin dotted; padding: 1px;
              font: bold small sans-serif; }

 #faq p.mad { position: relative;
              bottom: -1em; }
</style>
</head>

<body>
<div id="faq">
  The reason that the numbers on a keyboard are arranged
  <p class="pad">7 8 9<br/>4 5 6<br/>1 2 3</p>
  while the keys on a telephone are
  <p class="pad mad">1 2 3<br/>4 5 6<br/>7 8 9</p> is ...
</div>
</body>
</html>
```

Figure 3.23 shows how this code appears in a typical browser. Notice how the second inline block paragraph's position is offset to align the middle line (4 5 6) with the baseline of the parent element's text. The offset works out to an even –1 em because the embedded paragraphs have a small font size. If the embedded elements had the same font size as the parent element, the offset would be –1.2 em, because that is the normal ratio of line height to font size, and it is close to the ratio of medium to small in font size values.

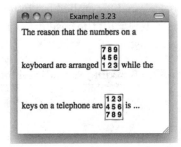

Figure 3.23: Paragraphs embedded as inline-block elements

HTML elements with a display value of run-in are another form of hybrid element. This setting provides a means to mash one element into the beginning of the following block element. This is a useful technique when you run out of ideas on what to do differently with your headings. Example 3.24 shows how a heading can be made to flow into the following element as if it were an inline part of that element.

Example 3.24: The level-four heading is incorporated into the following paragraph[5]

```
<!DOCTYPE html>
<html>
<head>
<title>Example 3.24</title>
<style type="text/css">
 body { border: thin solid; padding: 0 1em; }
 h4.smerge { display: run-in;
 padding-right: 0.5em;
 font: large sans-serif; }
</style>
</head>

<body>
<h4 class="smerge">Market Smarts:</h4>
<p>The question is not whether the passerby wants to buy
your lemonade but whether he is thirsty.</p>
</body>
</html>
```

---

5. This is using the Safari browser. At the time this was written, the display property value of run-in was not recognized by Firefox's HTML parser.

Figure 3.24 shows how the merged elements look in a browser. Note how the level-four heading keeps its font size and family.

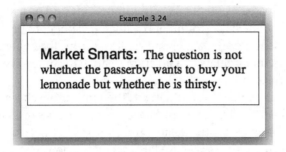

Figure 3.24: Creating a run-in heading to a paragraph

OVERFLOW

When working with content management systems and generated content, it often happens that the amount of content for an element may be more than the element can accommodate. This is where the overflow property comes in handy. The default value is visible for all elements, meaning that content visibly overflows the edges of the element. The other permissible values are hidden, scroll, auto, and inherit. The value of hidden causes any excess content to be clipped at the element's edges. No options are available that permit the reader to see the clipped-off content.

The scroll value instructs the browser to allow the user to see content that has overflowed the containing element. Browsers usually do this by providing scrollbars and/or enabling swipe motions on touch-sensitive devices such as iPads, e-readers, and tablet computers. The scroll value says to enable scrolling whether overflow exists. The auto value, on the other hand, instructs the browser to enable scrolling only if necessary.

FLOAT AND CLEAR

Any HTML block element can be made to float so that it moves to either the left or right extent of its containing element, and the remaining content flows around it. This is what happens with an image element that has its align attribute set to either left or right. The containing element for a floated element is its most recent ancestor element. The floated element retains its margins and padding. For an element floated left, web authors typically set the left margin and padding to 0 to make its left edge align with the left edge of the content above and below it. They also provide enough right margin or padding to visually separate the element from the content flowing around it. The opposite is applied to right-floated elements. Whether to use margin or padding depends on where you want the background of the floated element to be.

A floated element is both part of and removed from the content flow of its parent element in that it floats to a position relative to some ancestor element, yet it affects all the elements following it.

In addition to the values left and right, the float property can have the values none and inherit. A float value of none does not cause an element to sink. The value exists because it is the default and a means to turn off the floating behavior of an element that may have been set by previous CSS statements. The inherit value means to adopt the parent's float property value. This is rarely used. Authors are encouraged to be explicit in the settings of floated elements.

The clear property, applied to an element, defines the sides of the element on which no other element may float. The permissible values are left, right, both, and none. The effect of setting clear: both; on an element that follows a floating element is to add enough space above the cleared element so that its top edge moves below the bottom of the floated object. If the element in question is already clear of all floating elements, no additional space is added. The right and left values can be used to fine-tune an element's clearing behavior. The value none means that no clearing is to be done. It exists only to override any previous CSS clear values in effect for the element.

SUMMARY

Here are the important points to remember from this chapter:

▸ Cascading Style Sheets (CSS) provide the means to efficiently specify presentation layouts and styles for an entire site. CSS also provides precise control over the presentation of any given element on any given web page.

▸ Every CSS statement is composed of a selection expression followed by one or more rules enclosed in curly braces. Each rule is composed of a property name, one or more values appropriate to that property, and an optional importance marker.

▸ CSS includes pseudo-elements and pseudo-classes that can select elements by their status (such as hover) or by their circumstance (such as first-letter) to achieve stylish typographic effects.

▶ Font properties are dependent on the fonts that reside on the readers' devices and the resolution of their monitors. Web authors need to understand that what they see on their computer is not what someone else may see.

▶ Foreground and background colors can be specified using color names, decimal, hexadecimal, and percentage red-green-blue values. Images can be used as backgrounds for any element.

▶ Block elements are displayed with settable padding, borders, and margins. Borders and list bullets come in a variety of styles.

▶ Document elements can be removed from the normal content flow and explicitly positioned anywhere in the browser's viewport.

▶ Elements can be displayed in a manner contrary to their nature using the display property. Block elements can be made to flow like an inline element inside other content, and inline elements can be made to act like blocks.

Using HTML

Chapter

4

This chapter covers the use of HTML in various applications, including blogging, using Google Docs, selling on eBay, working on wikis, and email marketing. When the Web was introduced, HTML's inventor, Tim Berners-Lee, said that few people would ever learn HTML. He expected that most HTML would be written by software applications. Twenty years later we find that he got it half right. A mind-boggling amount of content is marked up in HTML and added to the Web every second by web-based software applications and services. Yet people using the Web do understand HTML, at least at the basic level of knowing that the headings, paragraphs, lists, and links they see are the result of simple markup tags embedded in the content.

Many websites allow for the limited input of HTML code to create formatted content that will appear on other web pages. YouTube, for example, provides snippets of HTML code on its video pages that can be copied and pasted into a web page to embed a video. If you work on the Web, the more knowledge of HTML, CSS, and JavaScript you have, the more you can do on the Web.

In this chapter, you will learn how to use HTML and CSS in content you input to a website. Because many services filter out or disable any HTML that might be dangerous, the level of HTML used in this chapter is on the simple side. It doesn't assume that you have either the access or the tools to build a complete website. This task is covered in Chapter 5, "Building Websites."

TOOLS OF THE TRADE

The most important tool for working with HTML is the View Source option, available from a menu or toolbar on most browsers. Choosing this option displays the HTML document's source code that the browser received in response to its request for that web page. Modern browsers do a good job of color-highlighting the various elements so that it is easy to differentiate between the raw content and the HTML elements and their attributes. Every web page's HTML source code is available for you to inspect and learn from.

Figures 4.1 through 4.4 show the location of the View Source option in the Internet Explorer, Firefox, Safari, and Chrome web browsers.

Figure 4.1: Location of the View Source option in Microsoft's Internet Explorer

Figure 4.2: Location of the View Source option in Mozilla Firefox

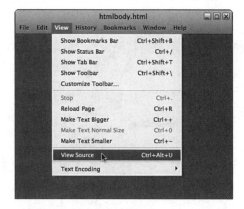

Figure 4.3: Location of the View Source option in Apple's Safari browser

Figure 4.4: Location of the View Source option in Google Chrome

In Figure 4.4, notice that at the bottom of the menu is an option called Inspect element. This opens an advanced tool that allows the user to inspect a document element's properties, including its CSS settings, HTML attributes, event handlers, and relationship to the DOM. Even better, the element inspector allows you to select a document element and edit many of its properties in situ. For example, you can turn individual CSS styles on and off and change values and see their immediate effect in the browser's window.

The element inspector is available in all four of the browsers shown in the preceding figures. You can access it in Firefox, Safari, and Chrome by Alt-clicking an element and choosing Inspect Element from the context menu. In Internet Explorer you must select Developer tools from the Tools menu. Figure 4.5 shows how the Element Inspector looks in Google Chrome when you inspect a paragraph element.

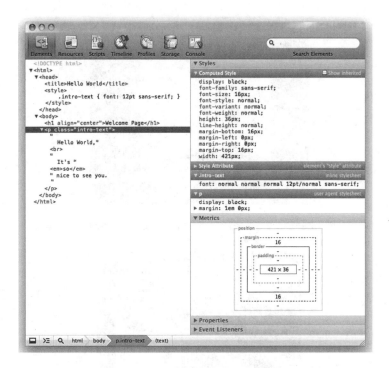

Figure 4.5: The Element Inspector in Google Chrome

As shown in Figure 4.5, the Element Inspector has many powerful features, including the graphic display of an element's box properties. It provides a nicely formatted listing of the HTML source code and the CSS associated with each document element. It is also interactive, changing the displayed properties and values as you mouse over the various page elements.

The other tools, accessible from the Element Inspector's menu bar, offer additional information on the resources used by the page, as well as how the browser loaded them. The Console tool is invaluable for debugging faulty JavaScript functions. I encourage you to become familiar with these tools even if you do not intend to get very deep into Web programming.

Other tools are available to help you work with HTML entirely through your browser. Firebug for the Firefox browser is one of my favorites, as is the Web Developer tools collection. Search the Internet for add-ons and extensions to your favorite browser with keywords such as "web developer," and you will find several that are free and easily installed.

Blogging

Blogging has grown tremendously in recent years to become an important channel for people to develop and share content on the Web. Modern blogging software, such as WordPress and Movable Type, go beyond the posting of articles and comments with powerful content-management capabilities. Major media websites are powered by blogging software.

Blogging can be experienced in two ways. If you run your own blog, you have complete control of a website, including its structure, appearance, and operation. As the owner, you have administrator privileges, including the ability to add other users to your blog in various roles. Posting privileges vary according to the user's role. Administrators, editors, and authors can publish articles on a blog. Contributors can submit articles that are then approved by an editor or administrator for publication. Blogs can also have subscribers. These are registered users who, depending on the software, may be allowed to comment on articles and see private posts.

A number of blogging services provide almost all the functionality of running your own blog, but without the monthly hosting fees and administrative responsibility of maintaining your own website. These services include Word-Press.com, Blogger, TypePad, Windows Live Spaces, and others. They make it easy to publish content on the Web while limiting some of the functionality you would have if you owned the website. WordPress.com, for example, does not allow JavaScript and limits the content management functions. And although you can put CSS rules into individual HTML style attributes in a post, you must pay a small yearly fee to be able to edit the global CSS style sheet and give the site your own look.

Whether you run your own blog, use one of the blog hosting services, or have posting privileges on someone else's blog, Web-based blogging software usually provides a post editor that accepts input in two modes: a visual, what-you-see-is-what-you-get (WYSIWYG) mode and an HTML source edit mode. Figure 4.6 shows the post/page editor in WordPress in the visual editing mode. This editor is called TinyMCE. It is a free, open-source, JavaScript-based editor for HTML from Moxiecode.com. Its extendibility and easy integration into other web software make it a popular editor for blogs and other content management systems.

The two tabs in the upper right of Figure 4.6 labeled Visual and HTML are for switching between the two editing modes. Below those tabs is a double-row toolbar with buttons for creating strong and emphasized text (the **B** and *I* buttons), unordered and ordered lists, and block quotes (the " button). A drop menu labeled "Format" has options to mark up paragraphs, address blocks, preformatted areas, and six levels of headings. There are buttons for setting text color, inserting images, making links, and entering character entities. In short, TinyMCE can do a lot of HTML, but there is also a lot of HTML that it doesn't do. It doesn't let you create tables, insert horizontal rules, or add element backgrounds, borders, and floating elements other than images. If you need any of those features in a blog post, HTML editing mode is essential.

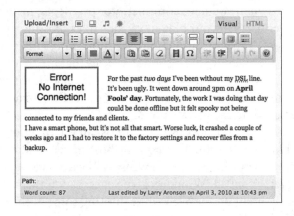

Figure 4.6: The TinyMCE editor in WordPress

To create the floating red box shown in Figure 4.6, first I switched the editor to HTML mode. Then I pasted the following HTML code into the editor before the content I previously entered in Visual mode:

```
<div style="float: left; width: 25%; margin-right: 1em; padding: 0.5em;
border: solid red; font: large sans-serif; text-align: center;">Error!
No Internet Connection!</div>
```

In this situation, you must be careful about extra white space in the content. WordPress assumes that any line breaks are intentional and will inserts break and paragraph elements to preserve the lines as you see them in visual mode. Figure 4.7 shows the same post content using the TinyMCE editor in HTML mode. The line break after the word "Error!" is intentional in this case.

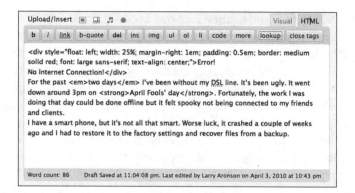

Figure 4.7: The TinyMCE editor in HTML editing mode

If you can edit the CSS style sheet for the blog, the division's style attribute with its CSS rules can be replaced with an id and/or class attribute:

```
<div class="red-box" id="no-internet-error">Error!
No Internet Connection!</div>
```

It helps to be specific in creating names for classes and IDs. In the style sheet for the site, the following CSS statements would reproduce the formatting:

```
div.red-box { padding: 0.5em; border: solid red; }

#no-internet-error {
   font: large sans-serif; text-align: center;
   float: left; width: 25%; margin-right: 1em;
}
```

When the HTML is in place, you can switch the editor back to visual mode to continue editing the post, including the text inside the red box. If more extensive editing in HTML is needed, there is an option in each WordPress user's profile settings to turn off visual editor mode and only accept input into the post editor as is, complete with any HTML markup. I highly recommend doing this when pasting code snippets or widget code that was copied from other web services.

Although the TinyMCE editor has no provisions for entering table elements, it does in fact recognize HTML tables, and outlines the table cells and lets you edit the cells' contents. If you are running your own blog, you can extend TinyMCE's functionality with plug-ins that add tools for creating tables, horizontal rules, and so on.

If you find TinyMCE too limited for your needs, there are other alternatives. Any stand-alone editor that produces HTML markup can be used to compose a post, and the HTML can then be copied and pasted into the blog's post editor in HTML mode. Final editing can be done in the blog editor's visual mode. Searching the Web for "HTML editors" or "WYSIWYG Web editors" will provide you with many suggestions on and reviews for such applications.

Even though it offers the option to save a document as a web page, Microsoft Word is not a good tool for creating HTML code. A Microsoft Word document that has been saved in web page format has an awesome amount of extra markup that binds the saved HTML file to Microsoft Office's XML name space. This extra markup ensures that you can move and copy the document contents from Word to PowerPoint to Excel to Outlook and back, keeping most of the typography and layout intact. For those who insist on using Microsoft Word for everything, the TinyMCE editor used in WordPress and other blogging software has a toolbar button specifically for entering content edited in Microsoft Word. Figure 4.8 shows the paste-from-Word toolbar icon circled. When it is clicked, the input window form appears over the grayed-out page.[1]

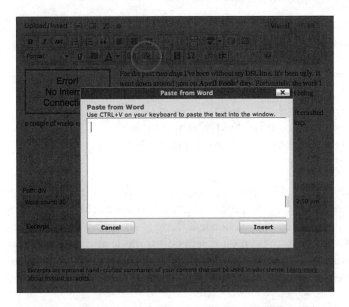

Figure 4.8: The Paste-from-Word feature in WordPress' TinyMCE editor

---

1. This effect is called *exposing*, and it is used to give a previously hidden element exclusive focus. A pop-up window, on the other hand, is a new browser window, opened by a script, containing a complete HTML document.

A far better tool for creating Web content is Microsoft's Windows Live Writer—a free Windows desktop application that can be downloaded from Microsoft's Windows Live support website. Live Writer presents much of the same user interface as TinyMCE but has a better layout and supports editing many of the features that TinyMCE misses.

Figure 4.9 shows the editing of a new blog post using Windows Live Writer. The post contains an embedded map from Bing, Microsoft's search portal. It was inserted into the post by clicking the link in the right sidebar's Insert menu. (The arrow is pointing to it.)

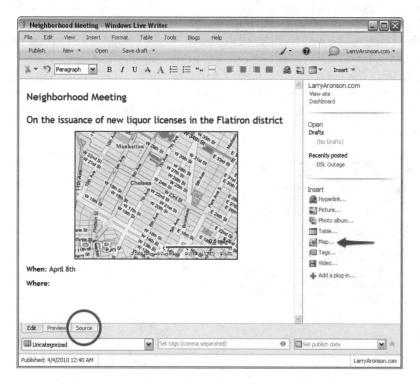

Figure 4.9: Windows Live Writer post editor

To let you see and edit the HTML source code created by Windows Live Writer, a Source tab is provided in the lower-left portion of the editing screen (circled in Figure 4.9). What makes Windows Live Writer a great blog editor is its capability to connect to any blog that supports the Atom Publishing Protocol. This means that Windows Live Writer can import a blog's CSS settings to provide a Preview mode to see what the formatted page will look like when published. It can also import, edit, and save an existing post or draft. Windows Live Writer can even publish directly to a blog, complete with categories, tags, and publication date.

There are several places on a blog where content with limited HTML markup can be entered but no built-in editor is available. This includes post excerpts, comments on posts, and category and other item descriptions. A good example is the practice of coding an excerpt for a post. On some blogs, excerpts can appear in post listings, search result pages, RSS feeds, and email digests.

A common practice among bloggers is to code a post excerpt with a thumbnail version of the post's principal image. You can do this by hand, of course, but it's easier to use a post editor's HTML or Source option. To illustrate this, I used Windows Live Writer to create a blog post about the America's Cup trophy from the content of Example 2.6 in Chapter 2, "The HTML Language." After saving the entry to my blog as a draft post, I switched to Source mode and made a number of edits appropriate for a blog excerpt. Figure 4.10 shows the excerpt as edited in Windows Live Writer.

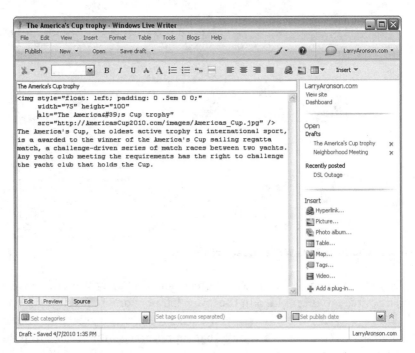

Figure 4.10: Creating a blog post excerpt using Windows Live Writer

In addition to shortening the text, I made changes to the image element. These changes from Example 2.6 appear in bold text in the following code snippet:

```
<img style="float: left; padding: 0em 0.5em 0em 0em;"
    width="75" height="100"
    alt="The America&#39;s Cup trophy"
    src="http://AmericasCup2010.com/images/Americas_Cup.jpg"/>
```

Because the excerpt may appear in contexts outside of the blog, I replaced the image element's class attribute, which referred to a CSS statement in the blog's style sheet, with explicit CSS rules in a style attribute. The padding between the floating image and the text was reduced because the image will be scaled to a smaller size by the explicit values of the width and height attributes. Finally, a full URL is used to reference the image, again because the excerpt may appear on external websites. All that remains to be done is to copy the code from Windows Live Writer and paste it into the excerpt input box on the blog editing page.

Similar blog editors exist for Apple computer users. MarsEdit, for example, shown in Figure 4.11, provides the same features as Windows Live Writer. It is not free but can be purchased for a reasonable price. In contrast to Windows Live Writer, MarsEdit's editing window is always in HTML mode. A separate preview window (shown under the editing window in the figure) shows how the edited markup will appear in a browser. The preview window operates in real time, reflecting changes as they are made in the editing window. A drop-down menu on the right provides easy access to common HTML elements and includes the capability to add your own favorites. As with Windows Live Writer, you can publish directly to a blog from MarsEdit, complete with categories, tags, and other options.

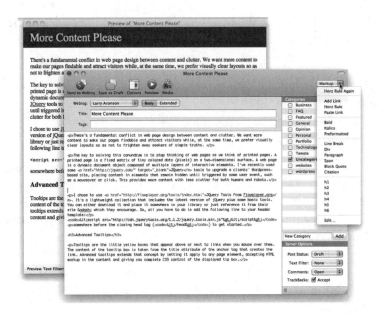

Figure 4.11: Editing a blog article using MarsEdit for Apple Macintosh computers

GOOGLE DOCS

Google Docs is a collection of office productivity application services accessible "from the cloud." That is, both the application software and all created documents exist on Google's Internet servers and not on each individual user's personal computer. This allows documents to be accessed and worked on from any browser on any computer connected to the Web. Having the documents in the cloud also allows them to be shared and edited collaboratively.

Google Docs provides applications for the creation and editing of four types of documents: word processing documents, spreadsheets, presentations, and input forms. Content in any document type can be copied and placed into other types of documents. Forms are automatically tied to spreadsheets for storage of content entered into form fields. In this respect, an input form is just a different view of a spreadsheet.

Figure 4.12 shows the management page of Google Docs. After logging into a Google account, you go to http://docs.google.com. The management page, also called the Explorer, allows the user to organize documents into folders, create new documents, and share them. On the left side of Figure 4.12, the Create New menu has been clicked to show the options for creating a new document.

Whereas popular desktop applications such as Microsoft Office are focused on creating precisely formatted printed documents, Google Docs' approach is Web-centric. In fact, Google Docs documents are saved as HTML files and can be published directly to the Web. If the user wants to print a document, it is converted to a PDF file and downloaded to the user's personal computer for printing locally.

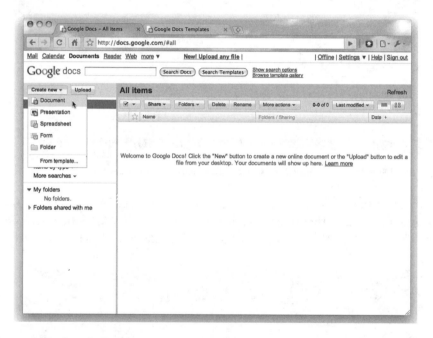

Figure 4.12: Google Docs management page

Google Docs' word processing application reflects the semantic markup approach of HTML. Its WYSIWYG user interface is quite similar to that of the TinyMCE and Windows Live Writer editors. A Styles menu provides a choice of formatting a paragraph, a block quote, or one of the six HTML heading styles. The Font menu offers the most commonly available Web fonts: Arial, Arial Black, Arial Narrow, Times New Roman, Garamond, Georgia, Tahoma, Trebuchet MS, Verdana, Comic Sans MS, and Courier New. An Insert menu lets you insert links, images, tables, and other HTML document objects.

Suppose we want to create a Google Docs document with two columns of block-justified text. It might be an article for a local newsletter we are collaborating on. We start with a new Google Docs document and select the Edit HTML option from the Edit menu, as shown in Figure 4.13.

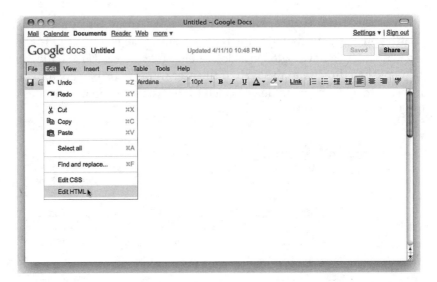

Figure 4.13: Editing a document in Google Docs' word processor

Note that there is a menu item, just above Edit HTML, for editing the CSS. We will make use of that shortly. Figure 4.14 shows the HTML editing window into which the HTML code from Example 2.7 in Chapter 2 has been pasted.

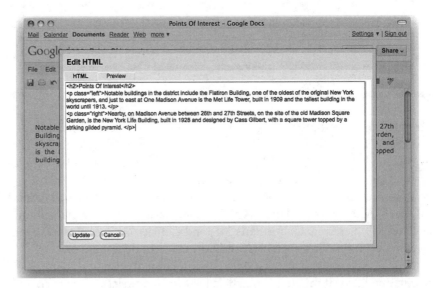

Figure 4.14: The HTML editing mode in Google Docs' word processor

After clicking the Update button to save our input, we can choose the Edit CSS option from the Edit menu. Then we can enter the rules for formatting the level-two heading and defining the two classes for floating the paragraphs. Figure 4.15 shows the CSS editing window with the CSS statements from the style element in the head section of Example 2.7 in Chapter 2 pasted in.

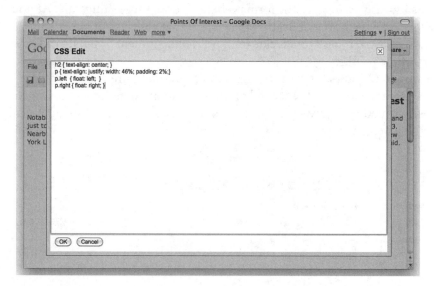

Figure 4.15: Entering CSS Statements for a Google Docs document

Clicking the OK button saves the CSS so that it is applied to the HTML elements in the document. The final result is shown in Figure 4.16.

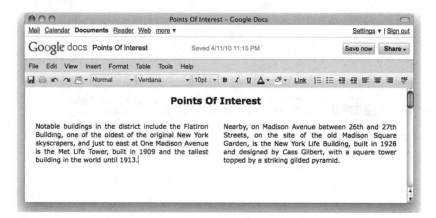

Figure 4.16: A two-column newsletter-style article edited in Google Docs

Although both Google Docs' spreadsheet application and the presentation editor make it possible to publish those types of documents directly to the Web, neither lets you directly edit the HTML source code. However, the spreadsheet application's forms generator and the presentation editor have a very nice feature: They both provide HTML code that embeds those documents into any web page. The forms generator does this intelligently. Although the form can be made public, the spreadsheet that collects the public's input remains private unless you decide to share that document or publish a summary of the results.

Figure 4.17 shows the creation of a simple questionnaire using Google Docs' forms generator. The second of three questions, a multiple-choice item, is being edited in Figure 4.17. You can rearrange the questions by clicking and dragging items to new locations.

Figure 4.17: An input form edited using Google Docs' forms generator

The Embed option on the More actions menu on the blue menu bar exposes a window containing HTML code that can be copied and pasted into a web page. This code is an iframe element, which lets you embed one HTML document inside another. For example:

```
<iframe src="http://spreadsheets.google.com/
embeddedform?formkey=dENZMHFKE6MQ" width="760" height="716"
frameborder="0" marginheight="0" marginwidth="0">Loading...</iframe>
```

The URL of the embedded document is given in the src attribute. The actual content of the iframe container, "Loading...," is displayed while the browser is fetching the embedded document.

This HTML embed code can be pasted into any web page, including a blog post. Figure 4.18 shows the questionnaire presented as a plain web page. Additional options in the forms generator can be set to control what happens after the Submit button is clicked. You can either display a summary of the results or return the user to the form for more input.

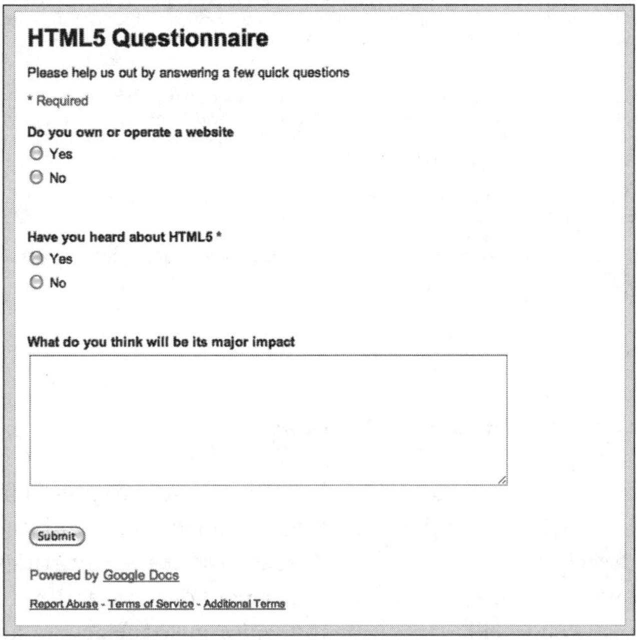

Figure 4.18: The input form of Figure 4.17 as shown on the Web

eBay Selling

eBay, the popular online auction site, has enabled people around the world to sell their used and excess products efficiently. However, the success of eBay means that any given product often has many competing merchants. The secret to getting the best price for your goods on eBay is creating an attractive selling page with content that highlights the product's features in a way that gives potential customers confidence in the seller.

The eBay product creation page is a form with various fields for information about the product you want to sell. In the middle of the page is an editor for entering the product's description. The editor features Standard and HTML modes for composing the description. Figure 4.19 shows this editor, into which I've entered content for auctioning an old vinyl EP.

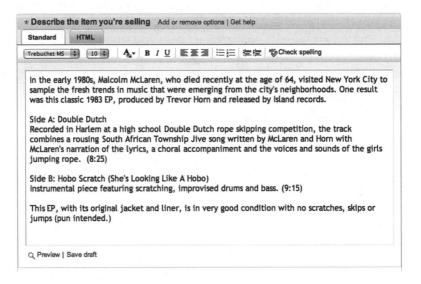

Figure 4.19: eBay's product description editor

Product images that will appear on the selling page are entered in another form and will be automatically scaled and positioned on the finished selling page. In the description, however, I would like to style the song titles as headings, marked with citation elements for the benefit of the search robots. To do this, I need to switch to HTML editing mode. Because the generated HTML source code is a bit dense, I'll copy it to my favorite HTML editor to clean it up and make my changes. Here is the HTML that I will paste back into the editor:

```
<h2 align="center">Rare Malcolm McLaren EP</h2>
<div style="font: 14pt 'Trebuchet MS', sans-serif">
<p>In the early 1980s, Malcolm McLaren, who died recently at the age of
64, visited New York City to sample the fresh trends in music that were
emerging from the city's neighborhoods. One result was this classic
1983 EP, produced by Trevor Horn and released by Island records.</p>
<h3 style="margin-bottom: -1em">Side A: <cite>Double Dutch</cite></h3>
<p>Recorded in Harlem at a high school double dutch rope skipping
competition, the track combines a rousing South African Township Jive
song written by McLaren and Horn with McLaren's narration of the
lyrics, a choral accompaniment and the voices and sounds of the girls
jumping rope. (8:25)</p>
<h3 style="margin-bottom: -1em">Side B: <cite>Hobo Scratch (She's
Looking Like A Hobo)</cite></h3>
<p>Instrumental, featuring scratching, improvised drums and bass.
(9:15)</p>
<p>This EP, with its original jacket and liner, is in very good
condition with no scratches, skips or jumps (pun intended.)</p>
</div>
```

Figure 4.20 shows the product description section of the finished eBay selling page for my record.

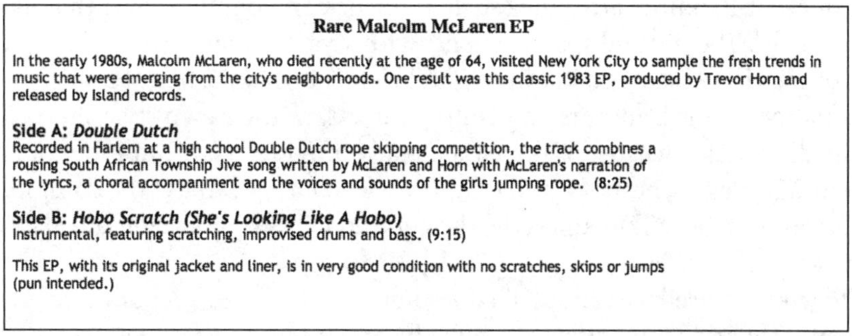

Rare Malcolm McLaren EP

In the early 1980s, Malcolm McLaren, who died recently at the age of 64, visited New York City to sample the fresh trends in music that were emerging from the city's neighborhoods. One result was this classic 1983 EP, produced by Trevor Horn and released by Island records.

Side A: *Double Dutch*
Recorded in Harlem at a high school Double Dutch rope skipping competition, the track combines a rousing South African Township Jive song written by McLaren and Horn with McLaren's narration of the lyrics, a choral accompaniment and the voices and sounds of the girls jumping rope. (8:25)

Side B: *Hobo Scratch (She's Looking Like A Hobo)*
Instrumental, featuring scratching, improvised drums and bass. (9:15)

This EP, with its original jacket and liner, is in very good condition with no scratches, skips or jumps (pun intended.)

Figure 4.20: Product description section on an eBay selling page

WIKIPEDIA

Wikipedia, the free online encyclopedia, describes itself as "a multilingual, web-based, free-content encyclopedia project based on an openly-editable model." Wikipedia is collaboratively written by mostly anonymous Internet users. Anyone with Internet access can write and submit changes to Wikipedia articles. It is one of the largest reference websites, with more than 91,000 active contributors working on more than 15,000,000 articles in more than 270 languages. And it is another web service that lets you input content with HTML markup.

Wikipedia does not have a dual-mode content editor. Instead, its online editor uses a special markup language, wikitext, for composing and editing articles using square brackets and other delimiters to separate the markup from the content. Wikipedia's wikitext editor accepts an input mix of wikitext tags and permitted HTML markup, including comments and these elements:

h1	h2	h3	h4	h5	h6	div
p	blockquote	pre	table	tr	td	th
ul	ol	li	dl	dt	dd	span
strong	cite	em	abbr	caption	code	var
del	ins	small	sub	sup	tt	b
i	hr	br				

Common attributes such as id, class, style, height, and width are allowed, but not event-handling attributes such as onclick and onmouseover that have script values. The div and span elements with style attributes are available for controlling the presentation of individual elements in an article. For more presentation control, authors and editors can attach their own style sheets to a Wikipedia article. Because Wikipedia already provides a large number of predefined CSS classes, authors, and editors are encouraged to use the common CSS styles. In true Wikipedia style, the common CSS style sheet is a collaborative wiki-work article.

The wikitext used by Wikipedia does not accept HTML anchor or image elements. Those document objects must be created using wikitext tags. In wikitext, an anchor element is created by putting the URL and label, separated by a blank, inside square brackets. If the link is to another Wikipedia article, then only the article's title should be in double square brackets. The following code snippet, for example, is marked up content with a wikitext link to another Wikipedia article:

The wat can be reached by road from **[[Chiang Mai]]**. From the car park, at the temple base visitors can climb 309 steps for free to reach the pagodas or there is a tram.

Figure 4.21 shows the Wikipedia editor with the preceding content and markup. Clicking the Show preview button at the bottom of the panel displays the result above the editing window's toolbar.

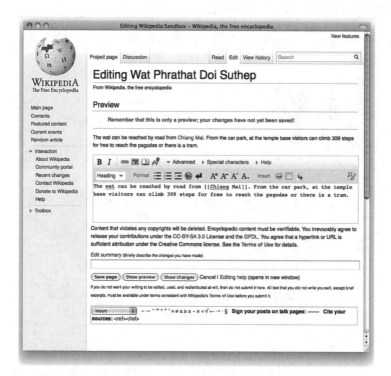

Figure 4.21: The Wikipedia article editor

Placing images in a Wikipedia article is a little more complicated. Wikipedia allows only images in articles that have been uploaded to Wikipedia and checked for appropriate use and correct copyright information. Every Wikipedia image lives on a media page that provides this reference information. This approach is understandable. If Wikipedia permitted external images to appear in articles, it wouldn't know, from one moment to the next, if that image were replaced with a different image that was inappropriate for the article.

Figure 4.22 shows the media page for an image of Wat Prahthat, the temple in Thailand referred to in the article being edited in Figure 4.21. The image has the filename Entrance_to_wat_prahthat_doi_suthep.jpg. The wikitext tag to insert the full-size image into an article, centered, with a border and the caption "Wat Prahthat," would be as follows:

```
[[image:Entrance_to_wat_prahthat_doi_suthep.jpg|
frame|border|center|Wat Prahthat]]
```

Figure 4.22: A Wikipedia file page for an image

It is estimated that less than 1 percent of all visitors to Wikipedia edit or contribute articles. Nonetheless, as Wikipedia grows, it may eventually have an article about a subject near and dear to you, and you will want to edit that article to fix the mistakes other people have made. To learn more about wikitext and editing Wikipedia articles, search Wikipedia's help section.

HTML Email

Up to this point, we have described uses of HTML only within the framework of the Web. HTML, however, has other uses. In fact, it is probably safe to say that we receive more HTML formatted messages in our email inboxes every day[2] than the number of web pages we visit. With the advent of iPhones, BlackBerrys, and other email-capable mobile devices, HTML is with us everywhere we go.

HTML in email presents particular challenges. From a technical perspective, an HTML email message is actually an attachment to a message using the Multipurpose Internet Mail Extensions (MIME) standard. It is up to the receiving email client whether to display the original text-only message or the HTML marked-up attachment. It also decides whether to display any other attachments (such as images) inline or as attached files. An email client may be a stand-alone email application such as Microsoft's Outlook or Apple's Mail programs; a Web-based application such as Google's Gmail, Yahoo! Mail, or Microsoft's Hotmail; or a wide variety of clients on just about any device connected to the Internet. Support for HTML, even in the more popular email clients, is not as strong as with the major Web browsers: Firefox, Internet Explorer, Safari, Chrome, and Opera. In addition, specific issues with input forms, JavaScript functions, and CSS can be frustrating to both email senders and recipients.

Most of the popular email clients, both Web-based and stand-alone applications, do not permit the direct entry and editing of HTML markup in messages. This is true even though they feature WYSIWYG editing environments and tools that generate HTML markup. It is possible to get around these limitations by composing a message using an HTML editor, displaying the result in a Web browser, copying the result from the browser, and pasting it into an email message. However, this method is cumbersome and offers no guarantee that the message your recipients see will look like the preview you saw before sending it.

Most email messages do not need the kind of formatting that goes into a web page. Simply being able to make text bold or italic, to change the typeface or size, or to give it some color is enough. After all, email messages are personal. They are not analyzed and indexed by search engines, so the semantic description function of HTML is unimportant. Yet we receive dozens of highly formatted messages every day. This raises the questions of where all these HTML email messages—newsletters, product promotions, and other

---

2. Most of which is discarded as spam.

solicitations—come from and what tools are used to create them. The answer is: from email marketing services.[3]

Constant Contact is one of the more popular email marketing services. A Constant Contact customer creates and maintains a database of email recipients with the service and composes formatted emails using Constant Contact's web-based editor and online templates. Constant Contact charges a monthly fee for its service based on the number of recipient email addresses.

Constant Contact's approach is to build an email as a series of sections or blocks. Rather than bringing the entire email message into the editor, only one block is edited at a time. The editor has many of the same features as other WYSIWYG editors, including a button for directly editing a block's HTML content. Figure 4.23 shows the beginning of the editing process for a newsletter, with the introductory paragraph being edited. The section being edited

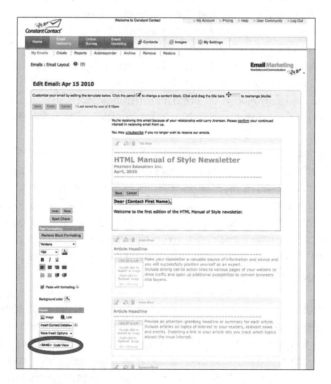

Figure 4.23: Editing an HTML email using Constant Contact

---

3. Spammers do not use commercial email marketing services. They use custom spamming software that directly connects to outgoing email servers. Such spamming software is installed by Internet worms and other malware on the ordinary computers of unsuspecting users.

appears in the center of Figure 4.23. Instead of a typical toolbar, Constant Contact provides a tool palette in the left sidebar. At the bottom of that palette, the button that activates HTML editing mode is circled.

HTML editing mode exposes the HTML source of your email. Like most generated HTML, the code is a bit dense. It includes Constant Contact's special tags for inserting the recipient's name and other mail-merge features. To work with the HTML, it is useful to copy the source code into a dedicated HTML editor and then paste it back into Constant Contact when done. It is also useful to download Constant Contact's *Code View Users Guide* and become familiar with its special tags and features. Figure 4.24 shows HTML editing mode in action.

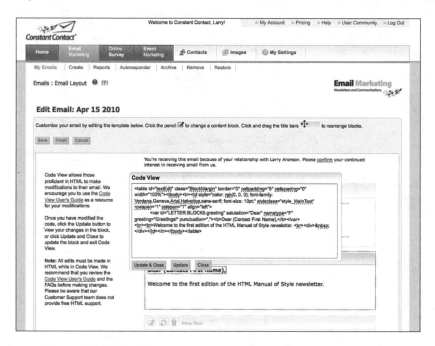

Figure 4.24: Using HTML Code View mode of Constant Contact's editor

In addition to allowing you to directly edit the HTML source code of an email message, Constant Contact lets you directly edit the CSS style sheet that controls the presentation of the email message. The style sheet contains many predefined CSS classes specific to the template chosen for the message. These classes can be modified and added to as required. Figure 4.25 shows the CSS style sheet editor with the classes defined for Constant Contact's basic template.

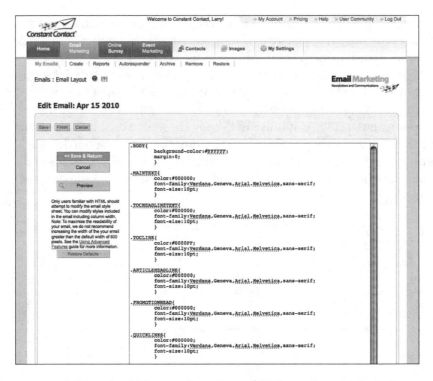

Figure 4.25: Editing the CSS style sheet for an HTML email message in Constant Contact

Summary

Here are the important points to remember from this chapter:

► Many services on the Web that allow users, subscribers, and customers to create content or edit personal profile information have a means for entering both content and HTML markup. These services vary in the type of online editor they provide and the range of HTML markup allowed.

► Blogging software lets you create complete websites without any knowledge of HTML. However, knowledge of HTML and a good HTML editor will enable you to create better websites.

► Many websites have created their own markup languages that mix a subset of HTML with proprietary tags for features unique to their service. Wikipedia is an example of such a service.

► Varying HTML support among the many different email clients makes it difficult and impractical to compose messages directly with HTML markup. Email marketing services such as Constant Contact simplify the process for commercial email senders.

Building Websites

DEVELOPMENT APPROACHES

WEBSITES

ORGANIZATION AND NAVIGATION

PAGE HEAD INFORMATION

SEARCH ENGINE OPTIMIZATION

AVOIDING COMMON MISTAKES

Chapter

5

In the preceding chapter we looked at a number of ways to use HTML to create content for use with various web services. In this chapter, we will concentrate on creating complete, stand-alone websites. There are, of course, different approaches to this end, and it always helps to spend time up front to analyze the requirements of the new website and the context in which it will operate.

After you have chosen an appropriate development approach, you can build a framework for your website that will accommodate the web pages and other resources that will be offered to site visitors. You can rough out each type of web page, marking up the semantics in HTML, applying layout and styles with CSS, and adding behaviors with JavaScript and other client-side scripting languages. This chapter explores the subjects of page construction and website navigation, with examples showing a variety of techniques to achieve different design objectives.

Finally, this chapter includes a section on Search Engine Optimization (SEO) and offers some tips for avoiding common mistakes.

DEVELOPMENT APPROACHES

The first questions to ask when you're thinking about creating a website are What is the purpose of the website? What will it accomplish? Does a website have to be built to accomplish that purpose? Presumably, you have some content you would like to share with the world, and the choice of using the Web as your distribution channel may seem obvious because of its reach and low cost. So why not just create pages with that content and glue them together with embedded links and menus?

The simple answer is that planning pays off. Even if you want to create a straightforward site that explores your passion for peanut varieties or employee pension plans, taking the time to write a business plan will help you organize your thoughts. As Albert Einstein said, "If you can't explain it simply, you don't understand it well enough." At the very least, writing down your reasons for creating the website and what you are attempting to accomplish can serve as the raw content for the site's "About" page.

More important, the exercise of writing down your goals and expectations will provide the foundation for many of the decisions you will have to make as you go through the process. Here are some important considerations:

- ▶ Will this be a content site or a service site?

- ▶ Will the content on the site be static or dynamic?

- ▶ Who will be visiting the website, and why?

- ▶ Is the website intended to generate revenue?

- ▶ How will the website grow in the coming months and years?

The answers to these questions will guide your development approach. It is a choice between building and managing your own website versus using a web service to deliver your content. Each approach has its strengths and weaknesses, and you need to be familiar with the various options for establishing an online presence. Perhaps a Facebook page, Yahoo! store, or Ning site would be a better fit for your needs. These services exist for a reason: to help people get started in online publishing by taking care of the technical details while they concentrate on learning what to do with the content. At the same time, online services limit what you can do on the Web. You are constrained by somebody else's design concepts. Also, your search engine ranking usually is lower because your website is seen as a client of some other organization, not as a publication of its own.

Therefore, this chapter assumes that you have chosen to run your own website. Usually this means having an account with a web-hosting company and registering one or more domain names. Or possibly you have access to a web host through your organization or school. You can run a web server on just about any computer, even a laptop, connected to the Internet.

The next consideration is whether your website will need a content management system to dynamically generate the web pages or whether your concepts can be realized with a structure of hyperlinked files.

CONTENT OR SERVICE SITE?

Perhaps the primary purpose of your site is to provide content to people, without restrictions and without any interaction from visitors. In that case, building and maintaining the site as a collection of HTML files is feasible and, in many ways, a lot simpler. This type of site includes photo galleries, fan sites, restaurant sites, sites covering issues and events, and the websites of many governments. Running a content site is not that much different from offline publishing. It is just easier and cheaper to use bits of data rather than atoms of ink and paper. A content site can connect with other websites and services for supplementary content such as news feeds, map and calendar widgets, and so on, but, basically, it doesn't matter if the visitor is a dog.

On the other hand, if your intention is to interact with your website's visitors, solicit their input, or provide a service to which they may subscribe, you have a service website. This is a critical distinction. Running a site that offers a service or product means that you have many of the same responsibilities (and challenges) as running a business, including production, marketing, sales, and, most important, customer service. Running any kind of business is hard work. It is true that you can run an online business from your kitchen table in your pajamas, but this means that you are only at work from the time you get up in the morning to the time you go to bed at night.

Most websites fall somewhere in between these two poles. A website that primarily delivers content can handle interaction with visitors using email and can carry advertising using third-party ad services and affiliate networks. And a content website can sell products by offloading the payment and fulfillment aspects to third-party services. Running a top-end service website, on the other hand, requires managing a mix of technologies, including databases and network administration.

It is important to know where your planned website sits on this continuum. You need to understand whether your website is an informational content site or an online business to plan for building and launching the website and achieving your goals.

STATIC OR DYNAMIC CONTENT?

You can maintain a public website in one of two ways: as a collection of HTML, CSS, and JavaScript files on a remote server or as data in a content management system (CMS) that generates pages on demand. The former requires the tools to download, edit, and upload files. Typically a web developer maintains a complete copy of a website on a local computer, editing and uploading changes as required. There are many good software applications for managing websites in this manner, from basic HTML text editors to sophisticated integrated development environments (IDEs) that combine FTP, editing, and project management functions in a single software program.

A CMS makes sense if the content has a steady stream of additions, changes, and deletions, with very little need to change the basic structural elements of the HTML documents. A CMS also makes sense if content needs to be searchable or if the same content appears on multiple pages. A web browser is all you need to maintain a CMS-based website, with some occasional tweaking of CSS stylesheets. No HTML coding is necessary until you need a new page type.

Content flow for a website is like cash flow to a business. For any given website, a proper amount of content flow will provide the best return on the time and money you spend creating and managing that content. Too much content flow consumes management resources and may discourage potential visitors who scan through search results, looking for a simple answer. Too little content flow, and a website will die from boredom. Even the robots will get bored if nothing changes. A search engine such as Google's will give a website a higher ranking and visit it more often if it senses fresh content. If you want visitors to bookmark your site or forward your URL to their friends and associates, your site must feature new content on a regular basis that meets or exceeds the expectations of your target audience.

Of course, content is not everything. If two websites offer equivalent content, the site with the better design will win. Better design encompasses a harmonious combination of graphic elements, information architecture, and interactive function. You have much more control over all these design elements when you run your own website than when you use a CMS.

TARGET AUDIENCE

Who will visit this website, and how will they find out about it? This is a marketing question, but it does have technical implications. Search Engine Optimization (SEO) is the practice of making a website friendly to search robots so that your target audience can find it easily. An optimized site knows what its target audience is searching for and is constructed accordingly. Headings, links, images, and even filenames are labeled incorporating keywords that have significance to the target audience.

Other issues depend on the target audience. If the website's content is intended for an international audience, the planning should include the provision of foreign-language translations of key web pages. Other standards may exist, depending on the website's purpose and intended audience. Some published websites may be subject to the requirements of the Americans with Disabilities Act and other national laws.

Perhaps you expect that a significant proportion of the site's visitors will be people using browsers on mobile devices. If so, either the site's layout needs to take into account how those browsers will display the web pages, or the server should do browser detection and provide alternative formatting for less-capable browsers. Twitter is a good example of a website that provides a PC-based browser version at http://www.twitter.com and an alternative version at http://m.twitter.com for mobile users.

MONEY

Money makes the world go 'round. If revenue generation is your website's purpose, your planning should consider the five direct ways in which a website can make money:

- ▶ Selling a product
- ▶ Providing a service to paying subscribers
- ▶ Selling space on your website to advertisers
- ▶ Earning referral fees by directing traffic to affiliates
- ▶ Accepting donations

All of these tasks can occur on the same site, but each technique has implications for the website design and development approach. Money adds another dimension to the planning. Any website that receives money from product sales, paid subscriptions, and donations should have pages explaining the terms of service and your organization's privacy policy. These considerations are less important with advertising sales and affiliate royalties, because those relationships are business-to-business. The question is whether to build the capabilities into your own website or to use third-party services to handle payments, product catalogs, subscribers, and advertisers.

Assuming that the amount of data is enough that it makes sense to keep it in a database, where should that database be? Without going into the data security aspects of that question, there are good arguments for keeping data with third-party services, and there are equally good arguments for maintaining a database on your own server.

You should not keep customer credit card information unless you absolutely have to. It is a burden of trust. A credit card's number and expiration date are all that is needed to make some types of purchases. Many online gaming and adult-content services, for example, don't even require the cardholder's name. Using a payment service means that you never know the customer's complete credit card number and, therefore, have much less liability.

Dozens of reputable payment services on the Web, from Authorize.Net to WebMoney, work with your bank or merchant services company to accept payments and transfer funds. PayPal, which is owned by the online auction firm eBay, is one of the easiest systems to set up and is an initial choice for many online business start-ups. A complete, customized, on-site purchase/payment option, however, should increase sales[1] and lower transaction costs. The payment systems a website uses are one of the factors search engines use to rank websites. Before you select a payment system for your website, check with your bank to see if it has any restrictions or recommendations. You may be able to get a discount from one of its affiliates.

Customer names, email addresses, and other contact information are another matter. If you choose to use a CMS to power the website, it may already be able to manage users or subscribers. If not, you can probably find a plugin that will fit your needs. With an email list you can contact people one-on-one. Managing your own email address list can make it easier to integrate direct and online marketing programs. This means that you can set your privacy policy to reflect your unique relationship with your customers. If you use a third-party service, you must concern yourself with that company's privacy policies, which are subject to change.

THE FUTURE

Many websites are built to satisfy the needs of right now. That is a mistake. Most websites should be built to meet the needs of tomorrow. Whatever the enterprise, its website should be built for expansion and growth. Businesses used to address this matter by buying bigger computers than they needed. Today, however, web hosting plans offer huge amounts of resources for low

---

1. Would you shop at a store if you had to run to the bank across the street, pay, and return with a receipt to get your ice cream?

prices. The challenge now is to choose a website framework that will accommodate your business needs as they evolve over the next few years. Planning for success means being prepared for the possibility that your idea may be even more popular than you ever imagined. It does happen sometimes.

A website built of files provides flexibility, because everything that goes into presenting a page to a visitor is under your direct control and can be changed with simple editing tools. An entire website can physically consist of just a single directory of text and media files. This is a good approach to start with for content-delivery websites. But if the website's prospects depend on carefully managing a larger amount of content and/or customers, storing the content in a general-purpose, searchable database is better than having it embedded in HTML files. If that is the case, it is just a question of choosing the right CMS for your needs. If the content is time-based—recent content has higher value than older material—blogging software such as WordPress or Movable Type may be appropriate. If the website does not have a central organizing principle, using a generalized CMS such as Drupal with plugin components may be the better choice.

The different approaches can be mixed. Most content management systems coexist nicely with static HTML files. Although the arguments for using a CMS are stronger today, it is beyond the scope of this book to explain how to use any of the content management systems to dynamically deliver a website. Because this is a book about HTML, the remainder of this chapter deals with the mechanics of developing a website with HTML, JavaScript, CSS, and media files.

WEBSITES

Or *webspaces*? The terms are almost interchangeable. Both are logical concepts and depend less on where resources are physically located than on how they are intended to be experienced. *Webspace* suggests the image of having a place to put your stuff on the Web, with a home page providing an introduction and navigation. A *website* has the larger sense of being the online presence of a person or organization. It is usually synonymous with a domain name but may have different personalities, in the way that search.twitter.com differs from m.twitter.com, for example.

When planning a website, think about the domain and hostnames it will be known by. If you don't have a domain name for your planned site, think up a few that you can live with, and then register the best one available. Although there is a profusion of new top-level domains such as .biz and .co, it is still best to be a .com.

If you don't know where to register a domain name, I recommend picking a good web hosting company. You can search the Internet for "best web hosting" or "top 10 web hosting companies" to find suggestions. Most of the top web hosting companies also provide domain name registration and management service as part of a hosting plan package and throw in extras such as email and database services. It is very convenient to have a single company manage all three aspects of hosting a website:

▸ **Domain name registration**   Securing the rights to a name, such as example.com

▸ **Domain name service**   Locating the hosts in a domain, such as www.example.com

▸ **Web hosting service**   Providing storage and bandwidth for one or more websites

Essentially, for each website in a domain, the hosting company configures a virtual host with access to a directory of files on one of the company's computers for the HTML, CSS, JavaScript, image, and other files that constitute the site. The hosting company gives authorized users access to this directory using a web-based file manager, FTP programs, and integrated development tools. The web server has access to this directory and is configured to serve requests for that website's pages from its resources. Either that directory or one of its subdirectories is the designated document root of that website. It usually has the name public_html, htdocs, www, or html.

When a new web host is created, either the document root is empty, or it may have a default index file. This file contains the HTML code that is returned when the website's default home page is requested. For example, a request for http://www.example.com/ may return the contents of a file named index.html. The index file that the web hosting company puts in the document root when it initializes the website is generally a holding, "Under Construction" page and is intended to be replaced or preempted by the files you upload to that directory.

The default index page is actually specified in the web server's configuration as a list of filenames. If a file with the first name on the list is not found in the directory, the next filename in the list is searched for. A typical list may look like this:

index.cgi, index.php, index.jsp, index.asp, index.shtml, index.html, index.htm, default.html

Files with an extension of .cgi, .php, .jsp, and .asp generate dynamic web pages. These are typically placed in the list ahead of the static HTML files that have extensions of .shtml, .html, and .htm. If no default index file from the list of names is found in the directory, a web server may be configured to generate an index listing of the files in that directory. This applies to every subdirectory in the website's document root. However, many of the configuration options for a website can be set or overridden on a per-directory basis.

At the most structurally simple level, a website can consist of a single file. All the website's CSS rules and JavaScript code would be placed in style and script elements in this file or referenced from other sites. Likewise, any images or media objects could be referenced from external sites. A website with only one web page can still be quite complex functionally. It can draw content from other web servers using AJAX techniques, can hide or show document elements in response to user actions, and can interact graphically with the user using the HTML5 canvas elements and controls. If the website's index file is an executable file, such as a CGI script or PHP file, the web server runs a program that dynamically generates a page tailored to the user's needs and actions.

Most websites have more than one file. A typical file structure for a website may look something like Example 5.1.

Example 5.1: The file structure of a typical website

```
/
|_cgi-bin                              /* For server-side cgi scripts */
|     |_formmail.cgi
|
|_logs                                 /* Web access logs */
|     |_access_log
|     |_error_log
|
|_public_html                          /* The Document Root directory */
|     |
|     |_about.html                     /* HTML files for web pages */
|     |_contact.html
|     |
|     |_css                            /* Style sheet directory */
|     |     |_layouts.css
|     |     |_styles.css
```

continues

Example 5.1: The file structure of a typical website *(continued)*

```
|
|_images                        /* Directory for images */
|       |_logo.png
|
|_index.html                    /* The default index page */
|
|_scripts                       /* For client-side scripts */
        |_functions.js
        |_jquery.js
```

The file and directory names used in Example 5.1 are commonly used by many web developers. There are no standards for these names. The website would function the same with different names. This is just how many web developers initially structure a website.

The top level of Example 5.1's file structure is a directory containing three subdirectories: cgi-bin, logs, and public_html.

CGI-BIN

This is a designated directory for server-side scripts. Files in this directory, such as formmail.cgi, contain executable code written in a programming language such as Perl, Ruby, or Python. The cgi-bin directory is placed outside the website's document root for security reasons but is aliased into the document root so that it can be referenced in URLs, such as in a form element's action attribute:

```
<form action="/cgi-bin/formmail.cgi" method="post">
```

When a web server receives a request for a file in the cgi-bin directory, it regards that file as an executable program and calls the appropriate compiler or interpreter to run it. Whatever that program writes to the standard output is returned to the browser making the request. When a CGI request comes from a form element like that just shown, the browser also sends the user's input from that form, which the web server makes available to the CGI program as its standard input. formmail.cgi, by the way, is the name of a widely used Perl program for emailing users' form input to site administrators. The original version was written by Matthew M. Wright and has been modified by others over time.

Most web servers are configured so that all executable files must reside in a cgi-bin or similarly aliased directory. The major exceptions are websites that use PHP to dynamically generate web pages. PHP files, which reside in the document root and subdirectories, are mixtures of executable code and HTML that are preprocessed on the web server to generate HTML documents. PHP code is similar to Perl and other CGI languages and, like those languages, has functions for accessing databases and communicating with other servers.

LOGS

A web server keeps data about each incoming request and writes this information to an access log file. The server also writes entries into an error log if any problems are encountered in processing the request. Which items are logged is configurable and can differ from one website to the next, but usually some of the following items are included:

- ▶ The IP address or name of the computer the request came from

- ▶ The username sent with the request if the resource required authorization

- ▶ A time stamp showing the date and time of the request

- ▶ The request string with the filename and the method to use to get it

- ▶ A status code indicating the server's success or failure in processing the request

- ▶ The number of bytes of data returned

- ▶ The referring URL, if any, of the request

- ▶ The name and version of the browser or user agent that made the request

Here is an example from an Apache access log corresponding to the request for the file about.html. The entry would normally be on a single line. I've broken it into two lines to make it easier to see the different parts. The web server successfully processed the GET request (status = 200) and sent back 12,974 bytes of data to the computer at IP address 192.168.0.1:

```
192.168.0.1 -  [08/Nov/2010:19:47:13 -0400]
              "GET /about.html HTTP/1.1" 200 12974
```

A status code in the 400 or 500 range indicates that an error was encountered processing the request. In this case, if error logging is enabled for the website, an entry is also made to the error_log file, indicating what went wrong. This is what a typical error log message looks like when a requested file cannot be found (status = 404):

```
[Thu Nov 08 19:47:14 2010] [error] [client 192.168.0.1]
File does not exist: /var/www/www.example.org/public_ html/favicon.ico
```

This error likely occurred because the file about.html, which was requested a couple of seconds earlier, had a link in the document's head element for a "favorites icon" file named favicon.ico, which does not exist.

Unless you are totally unconcerned about who visits your website or are uncomfortable about big companies tracking your site's traffic patterns, you should sign up for a free Google Analytics account and install its tracking code on all the pages that should be tracked. Blogs and other CMS systems typically include the tracking code in the footer template so that it is called with every page. The tracking report shows the location of visitors, the pages they visited, how much time they spent on the site, and what search terms were used to find your site. Other major search engines also offer free programs for tracking visitors to your website.

PUBLIC_HTML

This is the website's document root. Every website has exactly one document root. htdocs, www, and html are other names commonly used for this directory. In Example 5.1, the document root directory, public_html, contains three HTML files: the default index file for the home page and the (conveniently named) about and contact files.

There is no requirement to have separate subdirectories for images, CSS files, and scripts. They can all reside in the top level of the document root directory. I recommend having subdirectories, because websites tend to grow and will need the organization sooner or later. There is also the golden rule of computer programming: *Leave unto the next developer the kind of website you would appreciate having to work on.*

For the website shown in Example 5.1, the CSS statements are separated into two files. The file named layouts.css has the CSS statements for positioning and establishing floating elements and defining their box properties. The file named styles.css has the CSS for elements' typography and colors. Many web developers put all the CSS into a single stylesheet. However, I have found it useful to have two files, because I typically work with the layouts early in the development process and tinker with the styles near the end of a project.

Likewise, some developers put JavaScript files at the top level of the document root with the HTML files. I like having client-side scripts in their own directory because I can restrict access to that directory, banning robots and people from reading test scripts and other works in progress. If a particular JavaScript function is needed by more than one page on a site, it can go into the functions.js file instead of being replicated in the head sections of each individual page. An example is a function that checks that what the user entered into a form field is a valid email address.

OTHER WEBSITE FILES

A number of other files are commonly found in websites. These files have specific names and relate to various protocols and standards. They include the per-directory access, robots protocol, favorites icon, and XML sitemap files.

.htaccess

This is the per-directory access file. Most websites use this default name instead of naming it something else in the web server's configuration settings. The filename begins with a dot to hide it from other users on the same machine. If this file exists, it contains web server configuration statements that can override the server's global configuration directives and those in effect for the individual virtual web host. The new directives in the .htaccess file affect all activity in the directory it appears in and all subdirectories unless those subdirectories have their own .htaccess files. Although the subject of web server configuration is too involved to go into here in any detail, here are some of the common things that an access file is used for:

- Providing the directives for a password-protected directory
- Redirecting traffic for resources that have been temporarily or permanently relocated
- Enabling and configuring automatic directory listings
- Enabling CGI scripts to be run from the directory

robots.txt

The Robots Exclusion Protocol file provides the means to limit what search robots can look for on a website. The file must be called robots.txt and must be in the top-level document root directory. According to the Robots Exclusion Protocol, robots must check for the file and obey its directives. For example, if a robot wants to visit a web page at the URL http://www.example.com/info/about.html, it must first check for the file http://www.example.com/robots.txt. Suppose the robot finds the file, and it contains these statements:

```
User-agent: *
Disallow: /
```

The robot is done and will not index anything. The first declaration, User-agent: *, means the following directives apply to all robots. The second, Disallow: /, tells the robot that it should not visit any pages on the site, either in the document root or its subdirectories.

There are three important considerations when using robots.txt:

▶ Robots can ignore the file. Bad robots that scan the Web for security holes or harvest email address will pay it no attention.

▶ Robots cannot enter password-protected directories; only authorized user agents can. It is not necessary to disallow robots from protected directories.

▶ The robots.txt file is a publicly readable file. Anyone can see what sections of your server you don't want robots to index.

The robots.txt file is useful in several circumstances:

▶ When a site is under development and doesn't have "real" content yet

▶ When a directory or file has duplicate or backup content

▶ When a directory contains scripts, stylesheets, includes, templates, and so on

▶ When you don't want search engines to read your files

favicon.ico

Microsoft introduced the concept of a favorites icon. "Favorites" is Microsoft's word for bookmarks in Internet Explorer. A favorites icon, or "favicon" for short, is a small square icon associated with a particular website or web page. All modern browsers support favicons in one way or another by displaying them in the browser's address bar, tab labels, and bookmark listings. favicon.ico is the default filename, but another name can be specified in a link element in the document's head section.

sitemap.xml

The XML sitemaps protocol allows a webmaster to inform search engines about website resources that are available for crawling. The sitemap.xml file lists the URLs for a site with additional information about each URL: when it was last updated, how often it changes, and its relative priority in relation to other URLs on the site. Sitemaps are an inclusionary complement to the robots.txt exclusionary protocol that help search engines crawl the Web more intelligently. The major search engine companies—Google, Bing, Ask.com, and Yahoo!—all support the sitemaps protocol.

Sitemaps are particularly beneficial on websites where some areas of the website are not available to the browser interface, or where rich AJAX, Silverlight, or Flash content, not normally processed by search engines, is featured. Sitemaps do not replace the existing crawl-based mechanisms that search engines already use to discover URLs. Using the protocol does not guarantee that web pages will be included in search engine indexes or be ranked better in search results than they otherwise would have been.

The content of a sitemap file for a website consisting of single home page looks something like this:

```
<?xml version='1.0' encoding='UTF-8'?>
<urlset xmlns="http://www.sitemaps.org/schemas/sitemap/0.9"
        xmlns:xsi="http://www.w3.org/2001/XMLSchema-instance"
        xsi:schemaLocation="http://www.sitemaps.org/schemas/sitemap/0.9
        http://www.sitemaps.org/schemas/sitemap/0.9/sitemap.xsd">
        <url>
                <loc>http://example.com/</loc>
                <lastmod>2006-11-18</lastmod>
                <changefreq>daily</changefreq>
                <priority>0.8</priority>
        </url>
</urlset>
```

In addition to the file sitemap.xml, websites can provide a compressed version of the sitemap file for faster processing. A compressed sitemap file will have the name sitemap.xml.gz or sitemap.gz. There are easy-to-use online utilities for creating XML sitemaps. After a sitemap is created and installed on your site, you notify the search engines that the file exists, and you can request a new scan of your website.

ORGANIZATION AND NAVIGATION

Website organization and navigation go hand in hand. A site that is well organized is usually easy to navigate. Pages have names that make sense, and files are organized into directories that logically reflect the website's topic focus. A poorly organized site, on the other hand, is usually difficult to navigate and harder to maintain.

FILES AND DIRECTORIES

Before the introduction of Windows 95, a filename had to be short—no more than eight characters for the name part plus a three-character extension—if you wanted to work with that file on a Windows or IBM operating system. Programmers were comfortable using shorter filenames. They were faster to type and less prone to errors, even if they were more cryptic.

Today, there is no reason to abbreviate or shorten a filename. Because modern HTML editors and development systems keep track of a website's files, you usually have to type in the name only the first time. A filename should be long enough to describe what the file is all about. This will make the robots happier, as well as any programmers who will work on the site in the future. On blogs, where no physical file for a web page exists, the blogging software is often configured to create *permalinks* for post pages by converting the post's title to all lowercase letters and replacing blanks and special characters with dashes. It would not be surprising to find, for example, a URL such as this:

```
http://myblog.com/ten-ways-to-maximize-your-social-media-marketing/
```

Macintosh and Windows operating systems handle filenames with spaces and other special characters nicely. Web servers do not do so well with such characters. In URLs, such characters must be encoded. Avoid using any character in a filename other than uppercase and lowercase letters, digits, periods, dashes, and underscores. Besides using saner and more descriptive filenames, here are some other suggestions for keeping a site organized:

▶ Use all lowercase letters for filenames unless there is a specific reason not to. This will result in better sorting of file listings. Filenames on Windows-based servers are not case-sensitive. This means that a URL such as http://example.org/index.htm will correctly link to the file Index.HTM if it is on a Windows-based server. But the link will break if the website is moved to a UNIX server.

▶ Use consistent filename extensions. All the JPEG images on your site should have the extension .jpg or .jpeg. Pick one and use it for all your JPEG image files. Likewise, use either .html or .htm, but not both, for the HTML files. The same goes for .txt versus .text for text files.

▶ Use subdirectories to organize supporting files such as scripts, stylesheets, and media files. This not only helps keep the files organized as the site grows, but it also makes it easier to back up all your images, for example.

▶ Add version information to the end of a filename if you need to make temporary backup copies of specific files. That is, instead of naming the new version of about.html new_about.html, give it a name like about_new.html.

▶ Use a date stamp for backup copies of files. For example, use about_20100501.html instead of old_about.html or about.bkup.html. Using dates in a year-month-day format will keep them in proper order in date-sorted file listings.

PAGE LAYOUT

On a typical website, most pages share a basic layout consisting of the following:

▶ A header area at the top of the page with the website's name and logo image

▶ A content area, possibly organized into sections and divisions

▶ Sidebars with navigation, advertisements, and other special content

▶ A footer area with address, copyright, and other auxiliary information

The HTML5 specification, in recognizing this as a de facto layout, provides section, header, and footer elements.

Your web pages don't have to follow anyone else's layout. One of my favorite early web pages was a student's project that illustrated the solar system with images of the planets on a black background. The images were scaled proportionally to show their relative sizes and were presented in reverse order from Pluto to Mercury. Each image was in a table cell, with the height of the cell proportional to that planet's distance from the sun.[2] Paging down to the sun (a thick yellow line at the bottom of the page) gave you a true impression of our

---

2. This was before CSS was available, so the student had to use tables to set the distances between the planets.

solar system's size. If printed, the page would have consumed a few thousand sheets of paper! A student today might do a similar project based on the HTML5 canvas element. Imagine swiping your way around the solar system on an iPad or other touch-sensitive computer.

A web page is more than what appears on its surface. It has three-dimensional aspects. Content can be hidden and made to appear using scripting elements and can be layered using CSS positioning. Best of all, a web page can be an interactive platform for deploying widgets and other fun things.

As soon as the basic file structure of a new website is in place, the next step is deciding what should stay the same on every page and what will change. If the website will have different types of pages, you must ask the same question of each page type. A more commonly structured web page with header, footer, and sidebars can have much of that page content coded once and included in each page as it is built.

There are two ways to include common content and markup in web pages: using an offline development environment and using server-side includes. A good development environment uses an HTML editing application with macro functions and defined templates. Pages are edited on a local computer, and authors insert special include tags or commands into the page. These are filled in by the editing program when it publishes the page to the website. Server-side includes are a means of instructing the web server, using commands embedded in the file in the form of special HTML comments, to include other material in the web page before sending it back to the requesting browser. For example:

```
<div id="logo-head">
<!--#include file="logohead.html"-->
</div>
```

The advantage of server-side includes is that if a change is required in one of the common elements, such as adding a new item to the main menu, only the one include file has to be changed. With a client-side development approach, all pages using that template must be republished to the site. However, preprocessing files containing server-side includes uses extra resources on the server. Therefore, many web hosting companies enable this feature only for files that have the special extension .shtml. The use of server-side includes is not as common today as it once was because of the popularity of PHP applications that can do everything server-side includes can do and a lot more. Many web hosting companies enable PHP by default. Check the support pages of your web hosting company, or run a quick test, before deciding to use server-side includes or some other server-side technology.

Often a section of included code is exactly the same on a number of website pages except for just one tiny detail. An example is a main menu with a requirement to highlight the link corresponding to the current page. There is no reason to despair. You can use JavaScript or jQuery after the page loads to fix things.

Let's say you have a menu with three items defined in an unordered list:

```
<ul id="nav">
    <li><a href="index.shtml">Home</a></li>
    <li><a href="about.shtml">About</a></li>
    <li><a href="contact.shtml">Contact</a></li>
</ul>
```

This navigation list is included in every page on your site. You need a way to compare the location of the current page to the values of the href attributes in the list of links. The following two statements create a JavaScript variable, this_page, containing the filename of the current page:

```
last_slash = location.pathname.lastIndexOf('/');
this_page = location.pathname.substr(++last_slash);
```

The first statement finds the location of the last slash in the current page's URL. The second statement extracts from the URL the substring following that last slash.[3] Now you need a jQuery expression that finds the appropriate link in the menu and does something with it. Here is such an expression:

```
$(document).ready(function () {
    var s = '#nav a[href="' + this_page + '"]';
    $(s).addClass('thispage');
});
```

Briefly, this expression calls an anonymous function when the document is ready and the DOM is fully defined. The function selects the anchor element

---

3. To extract the filename without the slash, one must be added to the index of the last slash. This is done with the increment operator (++), because the plus operator (+) in JavaScript means string concatenation. In other words, 2 + 2 = 22 in JavaScript, not 4. This annoying dual use of the plus symbol is the source of many JavaScript bugs.

from the menu whose `href` attribute matches the filename stored in `this_page` and adds a `class` attribute to it with the value `thispage`. That new CSS class can be used to style the `anchor` element differently from the other links as required—to swap foreground and background colors, for example:

```
#nav a { color: blue; background-color: white; }
#nav a.thispage { color: white; background-color: blue; }
```

NAVIGATION

Website navigation can consist of several elements. Most websites have some form of navigation menu—either a menu bar incorporated into the page's header or a list of links in a sidebar. Menu bars should always provide a link back to the website's home page. It is standard practice to link the website's title or logo image in a page's header area to the home page as well. A website with long pages should duplicate the main navigational menu in the footer areas of pages. Websites with many levels of organized content should provide navigation "breadcrumbs," a horizontal list of links providing a path from the current page back to the website's home page.

eBay, the popular auction site, provides a good example of the use of breadcrumbs and other navigational aids. Figure 5.1 shows the top-left portion of an eBay page, which, along with the breadcrumbs, has menu bars and search boxes. eBay's website is, of course, a complicated affair powered by a huge database. Still, eBay has refined its site navigation over the years, and it exemplifies good practices.

Figure 5.1: Navigation items on an eBay page

Breadcrumbs are easy to create. The technique eBay uses is just a simple list of links, with the items displayed inline. The "arrows" separating the "crumbs" are the greater-than character (>) coded with the HTML character entity >. Example 5.2 shows how to duplicate eBay's breadcrumbs with HTML and CSS. Figure 5.2 shows how this appears in a browser.

Example 5.2: HTML and CSS coding for breadcrumbs

```
<!DOCTYPE html>
<html>
<head>
<title>Example 5.2</title>
<style type="text/css">
 ul.bcrumbs li    { display: inline; font: large verdana,sans-serif; }
 ul.bcrumbs li a { text-decoration: none; }
</style>
</head>

<body>

<ul class="bcrumbs">
     <li><a href="/">Home</a> &gt;</li>
     <li><a href="/buy/">Buy</a> &gt;</li>
     <li><a href="/buy/music/">Music</a> &gt;</li>
     <li><a href="/buy/music/cds/">CDs</a> &gt;</li>
     <li><b>Search results</b></li>
</ul>

<hr/>
</body>
</html>
```

Figure 5.2: Breadcrumbs show the way back home

Hypertext links embedded in the content of each page are as important as menus. Although menus are essential in getting visitors to a page with the information they want, links embedded in content allow the site visitors to explore a website in a more unstructured way. Embedded links allow the visitors to follow their own thoughts. Also, robots like embedded links because they add the context information to the current document.

Other forms of navigation can add to a website's usability. These include buttons, drop menus, tabs, and imagemaps. Buttons are useful for links leading to special pages or offerings. Drop menus are handy when you need to present a long list of linked items but don't want to take up too much page real estate. Tabs select sections of different content that occupy the same space. In that respect, tabs are not actually hyperlinks, but a mechanism to bring alternative content sections to the forefront. Imagemaps let you assign links to defined areas of a graphic. All these techniques require a little extra programming, but they are worth it.

Buttons

The HTML button element creates a button. It is most commonly used as a control in forms, but with a little scripting, it can also be used to perform actions anywhere. Buttons can also be defined with the HTML input element when its type attribute is "button". But the input element is self-closing, whereas the button element is a container that allows content with HTML markup.

The button element does not have a default action, so to make it a link, an onclick attribute is needed. The value of the onclick attribute should be a JavaScript expression that sets, for example, the location of the current document. The following code creates a button that, when clicked, takes the visitor to the page about.html:

```
<button onclick="location='about.html';">More Info</button>
```

Example 5.3 defines three buttons. The first uses a variation of the preceding button code. The second button calls a JavaScript function, defined in the page's head section, to pick a random URL. The third button does nothing, because it has a disabled attribute set to "disabled". If that button were enabled, clicking it would close the active page.

Example 5.3: Creating and assigning actions to buttons

```html
<!DOCTYPE html>
<html>
<head>
<title>Example 5.3</title>

<script type="text/javascript">
/* Provide an array of destinations */
  links = [ 'http://yahoo.com',
            'http://google.com',
            'http://bing.com' ];

/* simple function to link to a random URL */
  function goToRandomURL() {
    var x = Math.floor(links.length * (Math.random() % 1));
    location = links[x];
    return;
  }
</script>
</head>

<body style="padding: 36px;">
  <div style="text-align: center;">
    <button id="btn1" onclick="location = this.value;"
            value="about.html">More Info</button>

    <button id="btn2" onclick="goToRandomURL();"
            value="">Random Search Engine</button>

    <button id="btn3" onclick="self.close();"
            disabled="disabled" value="exit.html">Go Away!</button>
  </div>
  ...
</body>
</html>
```

Figure 5.3 shows how the buttons are rendered in a typical browser.

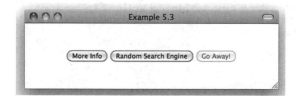

Figure 5.3: Three buttons using JavaScript `onclick` handler attributes

In Example 5.3, the first button is given an `onclick` attribute with the value `location = this.value;` and the URL is set in the value attribute. `this` is a special JavaScript variable that always refers to the document element in question. Putting the URL in an attribute separate from the JavaScript command in the `onclick` attribute makes it easier for other scripting components on the page to read and reset the URL. It also provides a little more information to robots, which are disinclined to scan event handlers and have distaste for JavaScript in general.

The Random Search Engine button works by calling the function `goToRandomURL()`, which uses JavaScript's built-in random-number generator to choose a link from the array of URLs defined just above the function's definition. Using a function in an event-handling attribute allows the same code to be called from anywhere. Although the math in this function looks a bit complicated, it is just an expression for converting the output of the random-number generator, a real number between 0 and 1, to an integer between 0 and the number of items in the array minus 1. (JavaScript arrays start with the index 0.)

The third button's `onclick` attribute contains an expression that closes the active window. `self` is another special JavaScript variable that refers to the current document window. To enable this "Go Away!" button, all that is needed is another button (or any element, for that matter) on the page with an event handler that sets the disabled status to `false`. The JavaScript expression for resetting the button is

```
getElementById('btn3').disabled = false;
```

Why use buttons at all for links if it is possible to use CSS to make an anchor element look and act just like a button? The answer is that a `button` element is generated by the operating system's graphical user interface (GUI) instead of by the browser. It has a built-in set of behaviors that simulate the effect of a physical button. In other words, clicking a button is a more definitive action than clicking a link. Also, buttons can be easily disabled and enabled in response to other page events, as shown by the third button in Figure 5.3.

One last thing about buttons. Like anchor elements, they can contain arbitrary content, including other markup. Unlike anchors, buttons have a defined appearance and behavior determined by the operating system. Depending on which desktop and browser themes the user is using, buttons can look much different than you expect. Therefore, even though any content and markup can be placed inside the button element, it is best not to have too much markup and too many CSS styles there. As with anchor elements, the markup inside a button should not contain any buttons, links, or other elements that respond to mouse or touch actions. The effects of such constructions are unpredictable and will confuse site visitors.

Drop Menus

A drop menu reveals a choice of options when it is clicked. The options stay visible until the mouse or finger is moved outside that element. Drop menus can be created using hidden elements, as described in Example 3.20 in Chapter 3, "Elements of Style," or by using a select element with an event handler, similar to how buttons can be made into links. Like buttons, select elements are rendered by the GUI of the visitor's operating system. They are designed to provide a similar appearance and experience as other applications that run on that user's computer. To use a select element as a menu of links, add an onchange attribute. For example:

```
<select onchange="location = this.options[this.selectedIndex].value;">
    <option value="#">Go to the...</option>
    <option value="about.html">About Page</option>
    <option value="contact.html">Contact Page</option>
</select>
```

This code sets the value attribute of each option element to the destination URL corresponding to that choice. The default for a select element is to show the first option when it is not activated. In this code snippet, the first item serves as a label, and its value attribute is set to the current page. Otherwise, there would be no way to select that first item.

As an alternative to using a select element or CSS drop menu, jQuery provides a nice way to create a drop menu with a hidden element that appears when another element is clicked. Example 5.4 shows how to create a simple drop menu. It still needs CSS to make it look right (see the comments in the code), but using jQuery helps ensure that it will work on most browsers.

Example 5.4: Using jQuery to toggle a hidden menu

```
<!DOCTYPE html>
<html>
<head>
<title>Example 5.4</title>
<script src="http://code.jquery.com/jquery-1.4.2.min.js"></script>
<style type="text/css">
 #state-choice {
    position: relative;        /* to contain the drop element */
 }
 #state-choice h4:hover {
    cursor: pointer;           /* change the pointer on mouseover */
 }
 #states {
    display: none;             /* initial state is hidden */
    position: absolute;
    top: 1.2em;                /* move the links below the heading */
    padding: .5em;
    background-color: white;   /* need to cover of other content */
    border: thin solid;
 }
 #states a {
    display: block;            /* we don't get any breaks around here */
    padding-top: .25em;
    font-size: small;
 }
</style>
</head>

<body>
<div id="state-choice">
    <h4 onclick="$('#states').toggle('slow');">Choose your state</h4>
    <div id="states">
      <a href="award.html">Excited</a>
      <a href="help.html">Confused</a>
      <a href="restart.html">Disappointed</a>
      <a href="loser.html">Angry</a>
    </div>
```

```
    <p>To help us serve you better.</p>
</div>
</body>
</html>
```

Figure 5.4 shows how this code appears in a browser before and after the level-four heading is clicked. The key to making it work is in the jQuery expression assigned to the onclick attribute of the h4 element:

```
$('#states').toggle('slow');
```

The dollar sign ($) beginning the expression is an alias for the jQuery function. The expression instructs the browser to select the element with the id attribute of states. The browser applies a toggle to the element so that, if it is currently hidden, it is displayed, and if it is visible, it disappears when the heading is clicked again. The toggle method takes an optional speed parameter. The strings 'fast' and 'slow' can be used, as well as a number indicating the effect's duration in milliseconds.

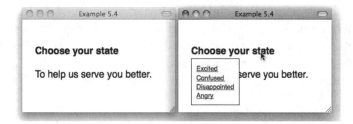

Figure 5.4: A jQuery drop menu

IMAGEMAPS

Every once in a while, the best way to solve a particular navigation problem is graphically. That's why the imagemap exists. If the website's conceptual layout can best be presented as a two-dimensional image, with different areas of the image linked to different pages and resources, an imagemap is appropriate. An internal company website might use a floor plan this way, placing the imagemap on the home page, with possibly a smaller version in a sidebar common to all pages. Imagemaps are also useful when a photograph is featured on a page and parts of the photograph cry out for hyperlinks to external sources of information such as Wikipedia articles or Google search results.

To create an imagemap, use a map element containing one or more area elements. For example:

```
<map name="east-wall">
  <area shape="rect" coords="80,120,200,280"
        href="http://en.wikipedia.org/wiki/Starry_Night"
        alt="Starry Night, Vincent Van Gogh"/>

 <area shape="rect" coords="240,120,400,300"
        href="http://en.wikipedia.org/wiki/Waterlilies"
        alt="Water Lilies, Claude Monet"/>

 <area shape="rect" coords="450,120,574,280"
        href="http://en.wikipedia.org/wiki/The_Bathers_(Cézanne)"
        alt="The Bathers, Paul C&eacute;zanne"/>
</map>
```

The map element can be placed anywhere in the body of the page. It has no displayable content and effectively exists outside the content flow. The coords attributes define the x- and y-coordinates, in pixels, of the top-left and bottom-right corners of each subarea with respect to the top-left corner of the image. Area coordinates can overlap, in which case the first area element that includes the user's click (or finger tap) is the one taken. To use the map, add a usemap attribute to the image element with the map's name:

```
<img src="images/art-museum-wall.jpg"
     alt="Pictures at an exhibition"
     usemap="#east-wall"/>
```

Imagemaps were very popular when first introduced, because they let designers create graphically interesting navigation controls. They fell out of use as designers switched to text styled with CSS, but they may see increasing use again as more location-aware mobile applications are deployed for touch-sensitive devices. Imagemaps do have a few disadvantages:

▶ They are difficult to manage. Both the image and its map must be edited in tandem, usually with different tools.

▶ They provide less information to robots that can't discern the context in which the links appear.

▶ Area shapes other than rectangles do not have good cross-browser support.

TOGGLES AND ACCORDIONS

jQuery methods such as toggle, hide, and show are useful organizational tools for placing hidden content in a page that a visitor can bring into view with a mouse click or finger tap. This keeps pages uncluttered while reducing the number of page loads a visitor must endure to find a specific piece of information. Search engine robots, however, see and index all such hidden content on a page. These techniques are particularly useful for pages with information such as frequently asked questions (FAQ) lists, where the questions are always short text strings and the answers can be anything.

Example 5.5 shows how easy it is to construct a FAQ page with toggled content. The questions and answers are marked up as a definition list, with the questions as the list's terms and the comments as the definition parts. The answers are initially hidden by setting their display property to none. Clicking a question causes the answer to flow in under the question, pushing the remaining content down the page to make room. In Example 5.5, the answer text has been shortened for brevity, but it can include pages' worth of marked-up content, including links and even other toggled content.

Example 5.5: Toggled content using jQuery

```
<!DOCTYPE html>
<html>
<head>
<title>Example 5.5</title>

<style type="text/css">
 #faqs dt { color: #060; font: italic 1.2em sans-serif; margin: 0; }
 #faqs dt:hover { cursor: pointer; color: blue; }
 #faqs dt:before { content: 'Q: '; }
 #faqs dt:first-letter { font-size: 150%; }

 #faqs dd { display: none; margin: .25em auto 1em 2em; }

 p.note { font: small sans-serif; }
</style>
<script src="http://code.jquery.com/jquery-1.4.2.min.js"></script>
<script type="text/javascript">
 function faqShowHide(that) {
```

continues

Example 5.5: Toggled content using jQuery *(continued)*

```
    $(that).toggle('slow');
  }
</script>
</head>

<body style="padding: 18px;">
<h2>Frequently Asked Questions</h2>

<p class="note">Click on a Question to see the answer.
Click again to hide the answer.</p>

<dl id="faqs">
    <dt onclick="faqShowHide('#a1')">
        Why are they always doing road construction work at night?
    </dt>
    <dd id="a1">
     <p>The volume of traffic during the day ... </p>
    </dd>

    <dt onclick="faqShowHide('#a2')">
        Who decides to resurface a particular street?
    </dt>
    <dd id="a2">
     <p>Anyone can request that a particular ... </p>
    </dd>

    <dt onclick="faqShowHide('#a3')">
        How can I find out when construction work will be completed?
    </dt>
    <dd id="a3">
     <p>In order to better inform the public ... </p>
    </dd>
</dl>

</body>
</html>
```

An `onclick` attribute in each question term calls a simple function, `faqShowHide`, with an argument consisting of an id selector for the corresponding answer term. The function consists of a single jQuery expression:

```
$(that).toggle('slow');
```

Passing the `'slow'` argument to the `toggle` method animates the effect. "Slow" is not very slow, lasting only about a second. But it is just enough to provide a visual sense of information revealed without wasting the visitor's time. Unfortunately, this effect cannot be illustrated on paper, so Figure 5.5 shows how the code in Example 5.5 appears with one of the questions toggled open. The text is from the New York City Department of Transportation's website.

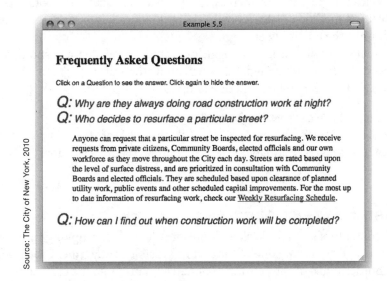

Figure 5.5: A FAQ list using toggled content

The questions in Example 5.5 are styled with a few CSS statements to make it clearer to the site visitor that they are clickable links. Using CSS to prepend a large Q to each question gives it a nice professional finish.

An accordion list is similar to a toggled list in the same sense that a set of radio buttons is similar to a set of checkboxes—only one content section is open at a time. When a different trigger element is clicked, any open element is hidden, and the selected one is revealed. If it is expected that the visitor would close a toggled element before opening another, an accordion saves him that effort. However, if the content elements are related, such that the visitor might want to have more than one revealed at a time, an accordion might be annoying.

To make the FAQ list of Example 5.5 into an accordion list, replace the single expression in the `faqShowHide` function with the following two expressions:

```
$('#faqs dd').slideUp();
$(that).slideDown('slow');
```

This code hides all open dd elements before revealing the selected one. The jQuery methods `slideUp` and `slideDown` are variations of the `hide` and `show` methods, with slightly different animations. The `show` method creates a box whose width and height both increase until it accommodates the content. The `slideDown` method creates a box initially at its full width; only the height expands until the box is big enough.

As a final step, with either the toggle or accordion version, you should provide CSS styles for printed media that will allow the site visitor to print all the questions and answers together. For example:

```
<style type="text/css" media="print">
  #faqs dd { display: block }        /* show all of the answers */
  p.note { visibility: hidden; }     /* hide the instructions   */
</style>
```

TABBED CONTENT SECTIONS

Tabbed content refers to multiple sections of content all occupying the same place on a page, with only one of the sections visible at any time. Labels along the top border (tabs) of the common content area promote the corresponding content section when clicked. In this sense, tabs are not a navigation item but an organizational tool that replaces navigation to distinct pages in a manner that saves the site visitor time. Using tabs provides more content for robots, which can "see" all the sections when they visit the page.

Building a tabbed content section involves HTML, CSS, and JavaScript. In Examples 5.6a, 5.6b, and 5.6c, a tabbed content section is developed without the use of any background images for the tab labels. Figure 5.6, shown in a moment, shows how the tabbed section looks in a browser after the second tab label is clicked. The full listing is rather long, so we will start with the HTML code in Example 5.6a and then move on to the CSS and JavaScript. Not all of the text content is shown in the examples.

Example 5.6a: HTML markup for tabbed content

```
<body>
<h3>The Southern Cook Islands</h3>

<!-- Linked labels for tabbed content -->
<div id="tabs">
    <a href="javascript:void(0);"
       onclick="setTab(this); showTab('#tab1');">Raratonga</a>
    <a href="javascript:void(0);"
       onclick="setTab(this); showTab('#tab2');">Aitutaki</a>
    <a href="javascript:void(0);"
       onclick="setTab(this); showTab('#tab3');">Mangaia</a>
</div>

<!-- tabbed content section -->
<section id="tabbed">

  <!-- First tabbed division -->
  <div id="tab1" class="tabbed-content">
    <img src="images/raratonga.jpg" class="left-float"/>
    Raratonga is the capital and largest of the Cook ... <br/>
    <a href="cook-islands/raratonga.html">Read More</a>
  </div>

<!-- Second tabbed division -->
  <div id="tab2" class="tabbed-content">
    <img src="images/aitutaki.jpg" class="left-float"/>
    Aitutaki is almost an atoll. The barrier reef that ... <br/>
    <a href="cook-islands/aitutaki.html">Read More</a>
  </div>

<!-- Third tabbed division -->
  <div id="tab3" class="tabbed-content">
    <img src="images/mangaia.jpg" class="left-float"/>
```

continues

Example 5.6a: HTML markup for tabbed content *(continued)*

```
    Mangaia is considered the oldest island in the Pacific ... <br/>
    <a href="cook-islands/mangaia.html">Read More</a>
  </div>

</section>
</body>
```

A division with the ID tabs, containing the three tab labels, is followed by the section tabbed, with three divisions corresponding to each of the labels. Each label is an anchor element with an href and onclick attribute. The href attribute of each link contains a JavaScript expression (void(0)) that does nothing. Essentially, it is a link with a null URL. Everything interesting is in the onclick attribute, which calls two JavaScript functions: setTab, to set the active tab, and showTab, to show just the selected tab's content while hiding the other content divisions. Now let's look at the CSS statements in Example 5.6b.

Example 5.6b: CSS layouts and styles for tabbed content

```
<style type="text/css">

#tabs a {                        /* styles for the tab labels */
    text-decoration: none;
    background-color: #eef;
    padding: 4px 8px;
    border: thin solid;          /* round the top corners */
      -moz-border-radius: 7px 7px 0 0;      /* Mozilla: Firefox, Flock */
      -webkit-border-radius: 7px 7px 0 0;   /* WebKit: Chrome, Safari  */
      -khtml-border-radius: 7px 7px 0 0;    /* Opera                   */
    border-radius: 7px 7px 0 0;
}

#tabbed {                        /* set the tabs' containing element */
    display: block;
    position: relative;
    top: auto; left: auto;
}
```

```
#tab1, #tab2, #tab3 {          /* layout of the tab divisions */
   display: none;
   position: absolute;
   margin-top: 2px;            /* tweak to overlay and align the tab */
   width: 85%;
   z-index: -1;
}
div.tabbed-content {           /* styles for the tab divisions */
   background-color: #eef;
   padding: 1em .5em;
   border: thin solid;
}
</style>
```

The CSS for the tab labels is nothing new. The only quirk is in the setting of rounded corners on the tops of the tabs but not the bottoms. These rules:

```
-moz-border-radius: 7px 7px 0 0;       /* Mozilla: Firefox, Flock */
-webkit-border-radius: 7px 7px 0 0;    /* WebKit: Chrome, Safari  */
-khtml-border-radius: 7px 7px 0 0;     /* Opera                   */
```

are for older browser versions that do not yet support the CSS3 border-radius property. Microsoft's Internet Explorer browser versions earlier than IE9 do not support rounded corners. The rest of the code will still work, but the tabs will be square in IE.

The two rules for the "tabbed" section element define it as a relatively positioned block element. A section element must be declared as block in order to work properly in older browsers that do not fully support HTML5. It must be given relative positioning to define it as the containing element for the absolutely positioned child elements (see the section "CSS Positioning" in Chapter 3). Although relatively positioned, the section's location on the page is the same as it would otherwise be, since the offset properties are set to "auto." Without the relative positioning rule, the three content divisions would appear in the top-left corner of the browser's window, covering the level-three heading, instead of within the page content, where we want them to be.

The CSS for the tabbed divisions is in two statements. The first addresses the three divisions by their id attributes to define the layout requirements. The second statement addresses them by their common class attribute and provides the styles. All three divisions are hidden by the rule display: none;. This will be changed for the first division by some JavaScript when the page loads.

Setting the position property to "absolute" frees the three divisions from the content flow, allowing them to find their new common location, with respect to the tabbed section container. A width is given for the division elements as a percentage of the "tabbed" section's width. Otherwise, they would extend to the window's right margin. A negative number for the z-index property allows other content—the bottom border of the labels—to cover these divisions.

The JavaScript code in Example 5.6c defines the two functions setTab and showTab, which are called by the onclick attributes in the tab labels, plus a jQuery statement to initialize the first tab. The JavaScript functions use the jQuery library to make it easy to address the elements using their CSS selectors. The jQuery methods show and hide are perfect for applications like this. The first line of Example 5.6c loads in the jQuery library from Jquery.com's API server. Alternatively, you can download the library and reference it from your own website. Loading it from an external source let's you test the code on your local computer.

Example 5.6c: JavaScript and jQuery functions for tabbed content

```
<script src="http://code.jquery.com/jquery-1.4.2.min.js"></script>
<script type="text/javascript">

// Set the active tab

function setTab(me) {
  $('#tabs a').css('border-bottom-color', 'black'); // reset all
  $(me).css('border-bottom-color',
            $(me).css('background-color'));          // set label
  $(me).blur();                                      // lose your focus
}

// Show the selected division

function showTab(tab) {
  $('#tabbed div').hide();          // hide all divisions
  $(tab).show('slow');              // show active division
}
```

```
// Activate the first tab

$(document).ready( function () {    // wait til the DOM is ready
    showTab('#tab1');               // display the first tabbed area
    setTab($('#tabs a:first'));     // make the first label active
});
</script>
```

The basic idea is to reset all labels or tabs and then set or show the selected one. There are other ways to approach this problem. For example, a global variable can be set by the function that keeps track of which tab is the currently active one. A JavaScript function running in an HTML5-capable browser can set local and session storage items to keep track of the active tab settings in between page visits. The code matters less than the fact that it takes so little of it to achieve the objective.

The setTab function takes as its single argument the anchor element object that called it, which is referred to as me inside the function. The first line of the function resets all the labels by restoring the bottom border. The second line sets the bottom border color of me to its background color, effectively making that line disappear. The blur method, in the third line, removes any highlighting the browser may have added, such as a dotted border, to the tab label when it was clicked.

The showTab function takes the tabbed division's id selector as its argument. The first line hides all the divisions using jQuery's hide method. The second line applies the show method to the selected division. The show method is animated by giving it the 'slow' argument. As with Example 5.5, this provides the visual sense of one section of content replacing another. And, although this pleasing effect cannot be demonstrated on paper, I hope you enjoy the beautiful photograph in Figure 5.6, which was taken by Heidi Cohen and used with her kind permission.

Script elements can go anywhere in an HTML file. Small JavaScript functions, like those used in the preceding example, can be collected into the central script file, functions.js, so that they can be accessed easily in other pages. Script elements can also be placed in the body of an HTML page, making it possible to use variations of these techniques in blog pages and other content management systems.

Figure 5.6: A tabbed content section created with HTML, CSS, and JavaScript

OPENING NEW WINDOWS

When a visitor clicks a link in a page, she expects to go to a new page, which will replace the current page in her browser's current window. However, sometimes we want to break away from the common expectation and open a new window on the subject. The most common case is having links to external sites open in new windows as opposed to the baseline behavior for in-site links. Another case is providing help information on instructional pages, where just enough help is provided in a pop-up window, along with links to other documentation and resources.

For a broad definition, consider a window to be any rectangular screen object that has a title bar and content area. Most windows have other optional properties in common that can be enabled or disabled by both the developer and site visitor. These include the ability to be resized, whether the window can be dragged to other screen locations, and whether scrollbars are enabled. The most trivial window, therefore, is the browser's Alert window, since all it does is present a message along with an OK button to acknowledge that you have seen it. The following code sets an array, message, with messages that are displayed in an alert box when various links are clicked:

```
<script type="text/javascript">
 messages = [
```

```
  'Follow the yellow brick road',
  'Boldly go where no one has gone before',
  'Go to jail. Go directly to jail. Do not pass go'
 ];
</script>
<a href="#" onclick="alert(messages[1]);">Directions</a>
```

The confirm method is similar to alert. It presents a browser alert box with
OK and Cancel buttons. The method returns the value true if the user clicks
OK and false if the user clicks Cancel. This can be used to conditionally follow
a link. For example:

```
<a href="exit.html" onclick="return confirm('Are you Sure?');">Exit</a>
```

There are two ways to open new browser windows: using a target attribute
in an anchor or area element, and using JavaScript's window.open method. The
following anchor element, for example, opens its linked page in a new window
that is a clone of the existing window:

```
<a href="http://outThere.com/" target="_blank">New Adventures</a>
```

The special target attribute value _blank creates an unnamed window.
The other special values are _parent, _top, and _self, to target other windows
depending on their relationship to the window that does the opening. Any
other target value is considered to be a name. If a window already exists with
that name, the new page replaces the document in the named window. Otherwise, a new window with that name is created.

When more control of the opened window's features is needed, the
JavaScript window.open method is used:

```
window.open(URL, name, features);
```

The URL is the location of the document to be loaded in the window. The
name identifies an existing window to open the document in. If it is omitted,
or if no window by that name exists, the document opens in a new window
with that name. For example, this anchor element, when clicked:

```
<a href="#" onclick="window.open('help.html', '',
          'width=450,height=600,scrollbars=1');">help</a>
```

opens a new unnamed 450-by-600-pixel window, loaded with the document
help.html.

The list of features is a string with comma-separated values. There are differences between browsers, but here are the commonly supported features:

`status`	The status bar at the bottom of the window
`toolbar`	The standard browser toolbar, with buttons such as Back and Forward
`location`	The Location entry field where you enter the URL
`menubar`	The window's menu bar
`resizable`	Allows/disallows the user to resize the window
`scrollbars`	Enables the scrollbars if the document is bigger than the window
`height`	Specifies the window's height in pixels (example: `height=350`)
`width`	Specifies the window's width in pixels

`height` and `width` take values in pixels. The other features can be given values of 1 or 0 to enable or disable that feature. The `window.open` method returns a window object that can later be used to manipulate that window. For example, the following HTML creates two buttons—one to open a new window, and another to close it:

```
<button onclick="thatWindow =
   window.open('pop.html', '', 'width=450,height=600');">
   Open that window
</button>
<button onclick="thatWindow.close();">Close that window!</button>
```

By default, a browser shifts focus to the new window, possibly placing it on top of the window that opened it. If you would rather keep the focus on the current window, add `self.focus();` after the open command:

```
<button onclick="
        thatWindow = window.open('pop.html','','width=450,height=600');
        self.focus();">Open that window</button>
```

PAGE HEAD INFORMATION

Now that you have seen some of the interesting things that can go in an HTML document's body, it is time to learn what else is in its head. Here are a few facts about head elements to guide your understanding:

- Head elements are a mixed bag of different tags, many of which do nothing.

- The title element is required. All other head elements are optional.

- Head elements are rarely nested inside each other. Most are self-closing.

- HTML comments can go in the document head. They are always useful.

- The order of elements in the head generally does not matter.

Ordering does matter with style and script elements in that later CSS rules can override earlier ones, and a JavaScript function defined with a given name replaces any earlier defined function that has the same name. But it does not matter if style elements are placed before script elements or vice versa.

META ELEMENTS

The meta element, or tag, represents various kinds of information about a document that cannot be expressed using the title or other elements. The meta element has three different uses, depending on which of the three following attributes is present in the self-closing tag: name, http-equiv, or charset. Only one of these attributes can be present in a meta element.

If either the name or http-equiv attribute is present, the content attribute must also be present. Without content attributes, these meta elements have no reason to exist. The charset attribute specifies the character encoding to apply to the document's data. A document should have only one meta element with a charset attribute. Here's an example:

```
<meta charset="utf-8"/>
```

meta elements with name attributes say things about a document. Each such meta element defines one item of data expressed as a name/value pair using the name and content attributes, respectively. For example:

```
<meta name="author" content="Murasaki Shikibu"/>
```

The following meta tag names are generally recognized by most browsers:

▶ application-name   The name of the application if the web page is one. Only one meta tag with name="application-name" should be in a document.

▶ author   The author of the document's content, not the HTML programmer

▶ generator   The HTML programmer or software, such as CMS, that generated the page

▶ keywords   A list of comma-separated keywords that characterize the content

▶ description   A brief description or summary of the document's content

After the title element, the next most interesting element in a document's head to a robot is the meta tag with the description content. Since this text may be used in search engines' result pages, it should be a clear, concise, and honest statement of the web page's content or concept.

When the name attribute has the value "keywords", the content attribute should contain a comma-separated list of tokens. Each token is a string of characters not containing a comma. Leading and trailing spaces are ignored but spaces and other punctuation within each token are kept. For example, this meta tag has six keyword tokens:

```
<meta name="keywords"
      content="Lincoln, Gettysburg Address, Civil War,
               battle, battlefield, dedication"/>
```

Here are a few points to keep in mind when figuring out what keywords to assign to a page:

▶ **Don't use punctuation.** Most search engines strip such characters when scanning a page's keywords. Few people use punctuation in their searches.

▶ **Major search engines do not place much importance on meta keywords.** Historically, they have not provided any more accurate information about a page than would result from a thorough scan of the actual content.

▸ **Keywords should appear in the body of the page.** Do not add keywords to the meta tag that are synonyms of other keywords if those synonyms are absent from the body content. Search engines may rank your site lower if they think the keywords misrepresent the content.

▸ **Keep the list short.** Over time, you can use the analytical tools provided by Google, Yahoo!, and other search sites to see what keywords people actually used to find your site and adjust your meta tags and content accordingly.

A meta element with the http-equiv attribute must also have a content attribute. The value of the http_equiv attribute is a "pragma" name, essentially an HTTP request option. Most of the pragmas are now handled with other elements. The only remaining pragma of interest is "Refresh," which directs the browser to load or reload a page after some delay. It is useful for pages that reflect up-to-the-second information.

For example, a news organization's front page could include the following markup in the page's head element to make that page automatically reload every 300 seconds (5 minutes):

```
<meta http-equiv="Refresh" content="300"/>
```

To specify that a different page should be loaded in place of the current page, the URL is given in the content, separated from the delay time by a semicolon:

```
<meta http-equiv="Refresh" content="10;url=another_page.html"/>
```

If a meta refresh is used on a page, it should be the only meta refresh in that document. Setting the time delay to 0 effectively creates a redirect. However, if the need to redirect visitors from one page to another is permanent, it is more efficient to use the web server's Redirect directive in the virtual server's configuration section or in a .htaccess file.

LINK ELEMENTS

The link element allows a document to be linked to other resources. The destination of the link element is provided by the href attribute, which must be present and must contain a valid URL. A link element must also have a rel attribute to indicate the type of relationship the link represents. A link element is ignored if either the href or rel attribute is missing.

link elements can be used to import external resources that augment the current document or inform user agents about the relationship that exists between the current document and other documents on the Web. Each link is handled separately. If two link elements have the same rel attribute, they each count as a separate reference or resource. For instance, given two stylesheet links, such as these:

```
<link rel="stylesheet" href="styles1.css" type="text/css"/>
<link rel="stylesheet" href="styles2.css" type="text/css"/>
```

the browser first loads all the CSS rules in styles1.css and then adds all the CSS rules in styles2.css. The normal rules of CSS cascading then apply to the combined stylesheet.

The behavior a browser should follow for links to external resources depends on the rel attribute's value and, in some instances, the value of a type attribute. link elements that provide relationship context for the current document are mostly ignored by browsers but do provide important information to search robots and other interested user agents.

Here are rel values and their href descriptions for resource links:

▶ stylesheet   The URL of a stylesheet that will be imported into the document at that point.

▶ sidebar   The document should be retrieved and loaded into the browser's sidebar, if it has one.

▶ icon   Imports a favorites icon to represent the current document in the browser.

▶ prefetch   Specifies that a resource should be preemptively fetched and cached.

Firefox, Chrome, Safari, and Opera also recognize the rel attribute value "alternate stylesheet", which instructs the browser to present an option to the user to switch stylesheets.

Here are rel values and their href descriptions for relationship links:

▶ alternate   An alternative representation of the current document, such as an RSS feed.

▶ archives   A collection of records that the current document belongs to or might belong to in the future.

- ▶ author   The current document's author's home or profile page.

- ▶ canonical   The official or authoritative URL for the current document.

- ▶ first   Indicates that the current document is part of a series. The href points to the first page in the series.

- ▶ help   A link to help documentation.

- ▶ index   A link to a table of contents or index listing that includes the current document.

- ▶ last   Indicates that the current document is part of a series. The href points to the last page in the series.

- ▶ license   A reference page documenting the licensing terms of a copyright covering the current document.

- ▶ next   The URL of the document that follows the current document in a series.

- ▶ pingback   The address of the pingback server for the current document.

- ▶ prev   The URL of the document that precedes the current document in a series.

- ▶ search   A link to a page for searching through the current document's content and its related pages.

- ▶ tag   The URL is a reference page for a tag that applies to the current document.

- ▶ up   A link to the parent of the current document in a tree-structured collection of pages.

link elements are not required. They are provided primarily to make the Web more knowledgeable about the resources it hosts and as an aid to organizations that deploy custom robots. Here are some additional examples:

```
<link rel="stylesheet" href="/css/style.css" type="text/css"/>
<link rel="alternate" type="application/rss+xml"
      title="example.com RSS Feed" href="http://example.com/feed/"/>
<link rel="pingback" href="http://example.com/xmlrpc.php"/>
<link rel="icon" href="/favicon.ico"/>
<link rel="index" title="example.com" href="http://example.com"/>
<link rel="canonical" href="http://example.com"/>
```

OTHER HEAD ELEMENTS

A few other important head elements need to be discussed. The `title` element (which has already made several appearances in these pages), the `style` element, and the `base` element are described in the following sections along with one of the most useful elements in the document head—the comment.

Comments

The site visitors don't see them, and the robots ignore them, but they will be of enormous help to the next web author or programmer who has to work on the page. Comments can even be placed between the opening `html` and `head` elements. This is a good place to add version, authorship, and update information. It is also a good place to document any dependencies on special resources and provide notes explaining why some coding is different than what would be expected.

The `title` Element

It is easy to understand its purpose: to provide the document's title. There can be only one `title` element in a document, and it is required. The document title can be different from the title of the page established by a level-one heading or other prominent element. This happens when the current page represents only a section of a larger document or when the `title` element combines the general and the specific.

The first and most important guideline for writing good titles is to put the most important words first. The content of the `title` element is used not only for the title of the window that presents the document as a web page in the browser. It is also the label used for tabbed browser windows. These tab labels can get very short if the user has many open at once. The document title also is used for shortcuts, favorites, bookmarks, and sitemaps. Search engine companies pay special attention to the words at the beginning of the title because people naturally search through indexes and catalogs by title in that manner.

It's not necessary to have your domain name in the `title` element of every page on your site. Robots know what site they are scanning, and the page presumably has meta description information and clear page and section headings. Therefore, putting the domain name in the title matters only if this will assist your site's human visitors. You should certainly have the formal name of your organization in the title of the home page, especially if it is not obvious from the domain name. For example, the home page located at http://example.org/ might have this title:

```
<title>The Example Organization</title>
```

and the About page at http://example.org/about.html might have this title:

```
<title>About: Example.Org</title>
```

As a general rule, compose your page titles so that they would make sense as the table of contents entries if your site were transformed into a book.

The style Element

The style element is an important part of the document head and provides one of the three sources of CSS information to the current document. The other two sources of CSS information are stylesheet files imported using link elements and style attributes in the markup of body elements. There is no limit on the number of style elements and linked stylesheets that can appear in the head of a document. All CSS statements are collected, and a "computed" stylesheet is derived according to the rules of the cascade. Specific CSS rules override general rules of the same importance, and later rules override earlier rules of the same specificity.

A CSS style element, or the contents of a stylesheet file, may contain two other types of statements besides those applying style rules to elements: comments and import directives. Comments are enclosed in the character pairs /* */ and generally can appear anywhere in a stylesheet, either between or within CSS statements. They are a very good idea, and you are encouraged to use them liberally. Import directives, which let one stylesheet include the content of another stylesheet file, are discussed in Chapter 3. They always go at the top of a stylesheet before any other statements other than comments and other import directives.

The link element that references a stylesheet can have type and media attributes for selective application of styles in different circumstances. That said, web authors and developers should avoid building complicated stylesheet constructions that depend on the quirks of legacy browsers. The challenge of good web design is to do more with less.

The base Element

The base element can be used to provide a base URL for the hypertext links in a document that use relative addressing. A document should have no more than one base element. A common use of the base element is with test versions of pages on a development server or local PC. If you add a base element such as this:

```
<base href="http://example.net/"/>
```

to the head of a document, links in the body that are coded relative to the current document, such as `<a href="about.html">about</a>`, are resolved as http://example.net/about.html, and not as from the development server, such as http://dev.example.net/about.html.

This applies to all relative URLs in the document, including URLs in `image`, `area`, and `object` elements, as well as any `script` and `link` elements in the document head that appear after the base element. For this reason, care must be taken with the placement of a base element. It is usually placed at the end of the document's head section, and the URLs in any `link` or `script` elements appearing before it are coded using full URLs, unless they too are under development.

The base element can also be used to change the default targeting of links. For example, this element:

```
<base target="_blank"/>
```

instructs the browser to open any links in a new window unless the link (anchor or area element) already has a target attribute with a window name or one of the other special values: `"_self"` or `"_parent"`.

Avoid the use of `base` elements in production websites. They make it more difficult for robots to analyze the site's structure and may hamper the efforts of other developers to maintain the code. There is usually a better approach using web server directives, so check with your local webmaster before adding `base` elements to your documents' heads.

Search Engine Optimization

It is not an understatement to say that the advent of search has changed the Web. For any website that wants to attract visitors, getting the attention of search robots and making it easy for them to index and rank the site is essential. This is the evolving practice of search engine optimization (SEO). You may also consider SEO an art, because the essential goal is to please an audience with interesting concepts and new knowledge. This audience is composed of search robots and other user agents and, like theatergoers, each brings its own tastes and prejudices to a performance. Robot tastes are evolving, and you might be concerned that trying to please all your human and robot visitors is impossible. Fortunately, the major search engine companies document their indexing and ranking protocols and provide tools to measure your website's SEO level.

Pleasing the robots is not enough in itself to earn a high search engine ranking for a website. The search engine ranking of a site for any keyword or phrase is a complex calculation that takes into account the amount of traffic to the site, how well the site's URL is distributed on other high-ranking websites in association with the search term, and the prior history of people using that search term. Increasing search-originated traffic and improving a website's ranking by making it more popular are the art and practice of online marketing. That job is made easier by good SEO practices.

Part of the history that search engines accumulate is a website's *bounce rate*. This is an estimate of the percentage of users who, after clicking a link on a results page for a given search term, do not stay on the selected website long enough to indicate that they have found what they were looking for. You can monitor the bounce rate for any page of a website by signing up for a free Google analytics account and installing its tracking tools, which also improves its estimates. Poor SEO can result in a high bounce rate, because the robots have difficulty identifying the relevant keywords from the noise and may improperly categorize the website.

The Web has numerous guides to good SEO. This is a lively topic of discussion in the blogosphere as well as in books, magazine articles, meetups, and trade shows. But mostly, good SEO starts with writing good HTML. Here are ten basic principles to get you started:

▶ **Use semantic markup** for sections, divisions, headings, paragraphs, blockquotes, lists, and other block elements. If something is a heading, give it heading markup for the robots, and use id, class, and style attributes to make it look right for humans. The following two lines of HTML will look approximately the same to humans:

```
<p><span style="font: 18pt arial;"><b>The Meaning Of Life</b><span></p>
<h1 style="font-family: arial;">The Meaning Of Life</h1>
```

but only the second line is optimized for search engines.

▶ **Write keyword-rich content** containing relevant search phrases as they are most commonly used. Avoid the temptation to use clever metaphors, cultural references, or puns. This technique is overused in magazines, where editorial and advertising copywriters compete to grab readers' attention by offering the unexpected. Consider a feature article titled "Grime and Punishment" about how a small city is sentencing serial parking-law violators to municipal cleanup tasks. This headline might make people smile, but it will only confuse robots. Would anyone looking for information on how cities deal with misdemeanors and minor crime search Google with the phrase "grime and punishment"?

▶ **Use emphasis and strong emphasis** to mark up keywords and searchable phrases in the content. Try not to "bury the lead." That is, if you want a page to rank high for a given set of keywords and phrases, find a way to embed those exact words in the page's opening paragraph—*with emphasis!* If this starts to look too jumbled, reduce the emphasis using CSS. Strongly emphasized text can still be bold, but in a lighter color than normal paragraph text, or a different font:

```
p         { font: normal 1em Arial, Tahoma, sans-serif; color:
#000; }
p strong { font: bold 1em Tahoma, Arial, sans-serif; color: #666;
}
```

▶ **Do not hide important information in images** or other objects that robots cannot scan, such as Flash animations or video. As an exercise, turn off image loading in your browser to see what might be missing from the text. If the page design requires such precisely styled headings and titles that they must be done graphically, use CSS to set the graphic as a background image for a properly coded heading. Then make that heading invisible. For example, instead of a heading that incorporates an image like this:

```
<h2>A Is For
  <img src="images/aardvark.png" alt="Aardvark" height="55"
width="80"/>
</h2>
```

use the image as a background under the complete heading, and make the heading invisible with CSS like the following in a style element or stylesheet file:

```
#aardvark { background: url(aardvark.png) no-repeat right bottom;
            height: 55px; width: 200px; }

#aardvark em { visibility: hidden; }
```

The level-two heading can then be written as follows:

```
<h2 id="aardvark">A Is For <em>Aardvark</em></h2>
```

You may have to adjust the width and padding to match the background to the text, but search robots will see the full heading while humans see the combination of text and image. Use this technique only for special cases and not as a general design technique so that you don't end up editing everything twice.

▶ **Use alternative descriptions for images**. Actually, the alt attribute is required in all images for the page to be considered valid HTML. Search engine robots are very interested in images. If they could see images as we humans do, each image might be worth a thousand words. The robots look first at the value of the image element's alt attribute to try to understand the meaning of an image. But the robots also look at the image's filename and adjacent text for additional context and confirmation of what is in the alt attribute.

▶ **Use descriptive filenames for documents** and media resources where possible. Consider this image element:

```
<img src="images/image_27818.jpg" alt="frank cooking"/>
```

A robot couldn't tell if the image was of a person or a hotdog. It would be better if the file could be renamed and the image element rewritten as follows:

```
<img src="images/frank_smith.jpg" alt="Frank Smith cooking
dinner"/>.
```

If you use good web development tools, you shouldn't have to type filenames more than once. So why not make them longer and more descriptive?

▶ **Label and order menu items with care**. Robots try to identify navigation menus. In so doing, they assume that the order of items in the menu reflects their order of importance to the site visitor. Robots try to match navigation menu items to the titles and major headings of the pages those items are linked to. Make it easy for robots to identify your site's main menu by using the HTML5 nav element and simple lists or menu elements instead of tables, imagemaps, or other complex structures.

▶ **Use title attributes to add descriptions to links** created by anchor and area elements to provide extra information to robots (and people) about the links. title attributes are another place where keywords and phrases can be employed.

Avoid using title attributes to provide generic instructions such as "Click to go to this page." In fact, try to avoid using the word "click" altogether. Your site visitors already know how to use a browser. Also, "tap," "swipe," or "say go" may be a more appropriate instruction than "click" anyway.

Note that you can add title attributes to anchor elements for the robots and suppress them later if they would be annoying to humans. For example, the following jQuery statement:

```
$(document).ready( function () {
  $("#main-menu li a").removeAttr("title");
});
```

inside a script element can be used to remove the title attributes from a navigation menu such as this:

```
<menu id="main-menu">
  <li><a href="index.html" title="Our Home Page">Home</a></li>
  <li><a href="about.html" title="All about Us">About</a></li>
</menu>
```

Because robots do not execute JavaScript, the title attributes will still be there when the robot scans the navigation menu. However, browsers that humans typically use will execute the jQuery statement before the page is fully loaded, and the title attributes will be gone from the links.

▶ **Provide an XML sitemap**, register with search engines, and install their tools. All the major search engines support the XML sitemap protocol, and most of them provide some means of registering your site. Google has "Webmaster Tools," Yahoo! has "Yahoo Site Explorer," and Bing has "Bing Webmaster Central." After registering with these services, you need to verify your site by adding meta tags to the head of your pages containing your keys. These meta tags look something like this for Google, Yahoo!, and Bing, respectively:

```
<meta name="google-site-verification"
      content="7RkWXa9SaHHcPNWx189SReW-ASoOLbUlwIqIInRk5x7"/>


<meta name="y_key" content="761321d5f5e1A5Dd">


<meta name="msvalidate.01"
      content="7B68B3A4A71D530EE81221DFD774282"/>
```

▶ **Use keywords and description meta tags**. List your important keywords
and phrases using a meta keywords tag, and provide accurate, keyword-
rich descriptions using the meta description tag in every web page. Each
page should have exactly one keyword and one description meta tag.

Google says in its documentation that, because of historic patterns of
abuse, it doesn't consider meta keywords to be important sources of
information about a page. However, other search engines and site analysis tools do use the keywords meta tag, so it is a good idea to include
one as long as the information is accurate. Make sure, however, that the
keywords and phrases in the meta keywords element can be found in the
content. Otherwise, a search engine could reduce your site's ranking.

AVOIDING COMMON MISTAKES

When working on websites, doing everything right is a matter of following
well documented standards and good coding practices. But it also requires
you to recognize that a website grows and changes over time. Web authors
and programmers must consider what will likely happen to their work in the
future and avoid some of these common mistakes.

DESIGNING THE PRESENTATION BEFORE THE INFORMATION ARCHITECTURE

This is easy to do because we are conditioned to think visually when asked
to comprehend new information. We even say, "I see!" to indicate our understanding, and we *get the picture* when ideas become *clear* to us. It is difficult to
discuss a proposed website with someone without drawing pictures, and we
cannot draw pictures without making presentation choices. In doing so, our
minds become fixated on that initial visual representation. In comparison,
working with files, flowcharts, and tree diagrams is boring. So it is not surprising that many websites look great but are disorganized in a fundamental way.

As a general guideline, the effort expended on any software development project should consist of three equal parts:

1 Developing the requirements and specifications

2 Writing the code

3 Testing and debugging the software

These are not to be considered three separate phases. Code should be unit-tested and debugged as it is written. Although the requirements generally should be known before code writing begins, often this is not the case. In fact, an empirical law of software engineering states the following:

The requirements of any system are a function of the experience gained in developing and installing the system for its user.

Modern HTML development stresses the importance of separating the semantics of a document from the presentation aspects. Because this is not completely possible in practice, I recommend separating CSS statements into separate files—one stylesheet for the layouts and positioning, and another for the typography, colors, and styles. For any web page that you have to build, first decide on the proper HTML markup for each element and how those elements should be grouped into page divisions and sections. Assign classes and IDs to elements that reflect their roles in the document. Then add CSS to position the page elements to match the layout requirements. Repeat and refine until the page works as expected. Then add the typography and graphic detailing required. Like a well-built car, the design and construction of a web page should start with the engine and power train. Then the controls and instrumentation can be built. The body color and upholstery style should be left for last.

USING OUTDATED TOOLS AND CONSTRUCTION METHODS

If you search Google for "HTML editor" (with the quotes), you will get several million results. If you search for "free HTML editor," you will still get well over a million results. This does not imply that there are millions of editors—only that discussions about HTML editors are intense. Nevertheless, there are certainly hundreds if not thousands of different HTML editors to choose from. How many of these editors are any good? The safe answer is, no more than half of them are better than average.[4]

---

4. This was a favorite joke of my high school statistics teacher: If you define "average" as the median value for a given ranking system, the statement is a tautology.

Some of the more popular HTML and web page editors have been around for many years. Some of these programs have been acquired by other companies with different programming styles and marketing objectives than the original developers. The WYSIWYG HTML editor Dreamweaver is a case in point. It was initially released in 1997 by Macromedia, which was acquired ten years later by Adobe, which bundled Dreamweaver into its Creative Suite product along with Adobe's premiere applications, Photoshop and Illustrator. The software developers at these two companies had different styles of coding, and the result is a mix of legacy and newer code.

Because Adobe Photoshop and Illustrator are de facto standards for graphic design and development (they are routinely listed as requirements in many job offers), Dreamweaver is widely used. However, because of the economics of the shrink-wrapped software business, in which a software upgrade may require operating system updates, which may require hardware upgrades, many developers forgo the hassle and expense and continue to use older versions that do not create optimized or even valid code. But their pages still look great—at least to clients who don't know what to look for under the hood.

NOT VALIDATING THE HTML AND CSS

Let's face it—we all make mistakes. Thankfully, web browsers are very forgiving, and they try to fix most coding errors. But even if our mistakes are ignored and have no effect on the presented page, they are still mistakes and may affect future changes to a page. That is why HTML and CSS validation services exist. The World Wide Web Consortium (W3C) is the organization responsible for drafting the recommendation for HTML standards. It provides an HTML validation service at http://validator.w3.org/. You can find other validation services by doing an Internet search. The W3C's validator is verbose. It finds every missing quote and angle bracket in a page. Input to the validator can either be a page at a public URL, a file uploaded from your local PC, or text entered into the input form.

Validating a web page takes very little time and is essential. After all, because anyone can run any page through a validator, the quality of your work is always open to direct inspection and evaluation. If you use a web page editor with a built-in syntax checker, you can find and fix minor errors as you develop the page. It is not difficult to create error-free web pages.

If you are running a blog, I recommend using a validator before publishing a post or updating a page. The preview can be saved on your local PC for upload into the validator. This will prevent errors in a post that may not be noticeable in the preview from messing up the blog's front page. This can happen, for example, when a link at the end of a post is missing the closing anchor tag (</a>). When reproduced on the front page, the link may extend into the title of the post below it in the listing.

NOT TESTING IN DIFFERENT BROWSERS

Browsers are getting better all the time and are converging on HTML5 as a common standard. But many of the HTML5 specifications for browser behavior are recommendations, not requirements. Also, a wider variety of browsers are in use, across more device types and operating systems, than ever before. Furthermore, browsers are getting bigger and incorporating more features. As a consequence of all this complexity, there are bugs and edge conditions where browser behavior is not well defined. Therefore, there is no way to ensure that your web pages will perform flawlessly without testing them in all the major browsers.

It is human nature to become attached to your favorite tools. When other people encounter problems with your website, it's tempting to blame their poor choice of browser. Avoid falling into this unproductive attitude by making it a point to use different browsers as you work on your website. Testing in Internet Explorer, Firefox, Chrome, Safari, and Opera covers about 98 percent of all browser use, according to data collected on Wikipedia. (Search for "browser share" to find the latest statistics.) Unfortunately, that also means testing on older versions of Internet Explorer. Currently, Internet Explorer, version 6, running on Windows XP, NT, 2000, and earlier versions of Microsoft's operating systems, still accounts for a fifth of all browser usage! This is in spite of the fact that this browser is ten years old and is widely derided for its security issues and lack of support for modern web standards. It is a persistent fact that many people are forced to work with the tools they are given, not the ones they would prefer. Major web service companies such as Google do not provide support for IE6 users of their advanced applications. Whether you choose to support IE6, or any particular browser, is up to you and your regard for your target audience.

Social media provides a solution to the dilemma of too many browsers. You can join a web authors' or developers' community and ask your friends to check out your work in the environments you don't have access to. Make a formal checklist that includes browser name, version, operating system, and device type. If you are doing web work for a client, you will impress that client by presenting the checklist before putting changes into production.

NOT PUTTING IN ENOUGH COMMENTS

Do yourself a big favor and add a lot of comments to your HTML, CSS, and JavaScript code. Use comments within the code to explain the relationship of the markup to the content. Put comments at the beginning of every page to explain the purpose of that page and to provide authorship information and version history. You will thank yourself later, as will anyone else who has to work on the code you left behind after you move on to bigger and better things.

SUMMARY

Here are the important points to remember from this chapter:

- Good websites are the result of good planning. There are many approaches to building a website, and even more tools to help you do it. Spending the time to analyze your requirements will help you choose the best approach to putting your content online.

- A website is essentially a directory of files on a computer running web server software. There are common conventions for naming the subdirectories and files in a website. Some important protocols require the presence of files with specific names.

- Good website organization and good navigation go hand in hand. There are different techniques for providing navigation. Menu bars, drop menus, buttons, imagemaps, and embedded hyperlinks all play a part.

- Content can be hidden on a page and then later revealed in response to a click, tap, or other user action. This provides a way to offer more rich content to search engine robots while avoiding clutter for humans.

- You can add a large variety of information about a page to the head section of an HTML document, including its relationships to other pages on the Web. The head section is also where CSS styles are defined and other resources are associated with the page.

- Search engine optimization is an important part of most website projects. Good SEO starts with the proper use of HTML as a semantic markup language.

Appendix A: HTML5 Quick Reference

T he tables in this appendix list the HTML elements in the HTML5 draft specification, along with a brief description, the applicable content model, and the important attributes for each element. The content model for any element roughly defines what types of content the element may contain.

An asterisk (*) next to the element's name indicates that it is new or significantly changed in HTML5.

Content Model	Description
text	A string of characters containing no HTML markup
phrasing	Text content plus HTML inline elements and comments
flow	Phrasing content plus HTML body elements
empty	The element is not usually written as a container; a self-closing element
metadata	The content consists of HTML head elements and comments about the document
element name	The content depends on the named child element(s)

ROOT ELEMENT

Element	Description	Content Model	Attributes
html	Provides the container for all other HTML markup and content	One *head* followed by one *body* element	

DOCUMENT HEAD ELEMENTS

Element	Description	Content Model	Attributes
head	Provides a container for elements containing information about the document and its relation to other documents and resources	metadata	
title	Provides the title for the document's window	text	none
base	Sets the base URL for any hyperlinks using relative addressing	empty	href, target
link	Provides a URL to a related resource	empty	rel, href
meta	Provides data values relating to the page	empty	name, content, http-equiv
style	Provides a container for CSS statements	CSS statements	media, type
script	Provides a container for client-side executable code, such as JavaScript	code statements	src, type
noscript	Provides content for user agents that do not execute scripts	metadata, flow	

SECTION ELEMENTS

Element	Description	Content Model	Attributes
body	Provides the container for all content elements: HTML markup and content	flow	
section*	Marks a section of a document that can have its own *header* and *footer* elements	flow	
nav*	Marks content containing navigation elements	flow	
article*	Defines a document section that may have its own headings as in a blog index or archive	flow	
aside*	Marks content that is tangential to other information in the document	flow	
header*	Marks content that appears above the main contents of a web page	flow	
footer*	Marks content that appears below the main contents of a web page	flow	
address	Provides information about the document's author	flow	
hgroup*	Groups other elements into a heading section	heading elements	

HEADING ELEMENTS

Element	Description	Content Model	Attributes
h1	Highest-level heading	phrasing	
h2	Second-level heading	phrasing	
h3	Third-level heading	phrasing	
h4	Fourth-level heading	phrasing	
h5	Fifth-level heading	phrasing	
h6	Sixth-level heading	phrasing	

BLOCK ELEMENTS

Element	Description	Content Model	Attributes
div	Marks a division of a page or document section	flow	
p	Represents a paragraph of content	phrasing	
hr	Inserts a horizontal rule	empty	size, width
br	Inserts a line break into the content	empty	clear
pre	Contains preformatted content; white space and line breaks are kept as is	phrasing	
blockquote	Marks a quote from an external source	flow	cite
figure	Provides annotation for figures, photos, diagrams, code listings, and so on	flow	
figcaption	Marks a caption for a *figure* element	phrasing	

LIST ELEMENTS

Element	Description	Content Model	Attributes
ol	Creates an ordered list	*li*	type, start
ul	Creates an unordered list	*li*	type
li	Marks an item of an ordered or unordered list	flow	
dl	Creates a definition list	*dt*, *dd*	
dt	Marks the term part of a definition list item	phrasing	
dd	Marks the definition part of a definition list item	flow	

INLINE ELEMENTS

Element	Description	Content Model	Attributes
a	Creates an anchor that represents either a hypertext link or a link's in-page destination	noninteractive flow	href, name, target
em	Marks contents as emphasized	phrasing	
strong	Marks contents as strongly emphasized	phrasing	
small*	Represents content such as "the fine print"	phrasing	
cite	Marks the title of a referenced work	phrasing	
q	Represents content quoted from another source	phrasing	cite
dfn	Marks the defining instance of a term	phrasing	title
abbr	Represents an abbreviation or acronym	phrasing	title

continues

INLINE ELEMENTS   *(continued)*

Element	Description	Content Model	Attributes
time*	Provides a machine-readable timestamp that is equivalent to the element's content	phrasing	datetime, pubdate
code	Represents a fragment of computer code inline	phrasing	
var	Represents a variable name	phrasing	
samp	Represents sample output of a computer program	phrasing	
kbd	Represents user input to a computer program	phrasing	
sub	Marks the content as a subscript	phrasing	
sup	Marks the content as a superscript	phrasing	
i	Indicates that the content is in an alternative voice or should be italicized but not emphasized	phrasing	
b	Indicates that the content should be in boldface without signifying any special importance	phrasing	
mark*	Indicates a highlight that was added by an editor or author to quoted text	phrasing	
ruby*	Marks content in Asian languages that includes accompanying phonetic or other linguistic info	phrasing, *rt, rp*	
rt*	Marks the text component of a *ruby* element	phrasing	
rp*	Marks the annotation part of a *ruby* element	phrasing	
bdo	Provides bidirectional override for text direction	phrasing	dir

Element	Description	Content Model	Attributes
span	Provides a meaningless inline container	phrasing	
ins	Marks content as inserted by an editing process	phrasing	cite, datetime
del	Marks content as deleted by an editing process	phrasing	cite, datetime

EMBEDDED ELEMENTS

Element	Description	Content Model	Attributes
img	Inserts an inline image into the content	empty	src, width, height, alt, usemap, ismap
iframe	Represents a nested browsing context—one document embedded inside another	flow, HTML document	src, width, height, name, sandbox, seamless
embed	Inserts content from an external source (typically non-HTML from a plugin) into a document	empty	src, width, height, type
object	Represents an external resource, possibly an image or other media type from a plugin	*param*	data, type, width, height, name, form
param	Provides parameters for a plugin invoked by an *object* element	empty	name, value
video*	Inserts a video or movie, possibly with accompanying audio, into the content	*source*	src, width, height, controls, poster, loop, autoplay, preload

continues

EMBEDDED ELEMENTS *(continued)*

Element	Description	Content Model	Attributes
audio*	Provides for the playing of an audio stream	*source*	src, controls, loop, autoplay, preload
source*	Provides the source information for a media element	empty	src, type, media
canvas*	Creates a bitmapped rectangle that scripts can use for interactive manipulation of images and other media objects	transparent	width, height
map	Defines an image map	*area*	name
area	Provides a hyperlink corresponding to an area of an image map	empty	href, alt, coords, shape, target
details*	Provides for additional information that can be exposed by the user agent in response to an event	*summary*, flow	open
summary*	Contains a summary, caption, or legend for its parent's *details* element	phrasing	
command*	Creates a command that the user can invoke	empty	type, icon, label, disabled, checked, radiogroup
menu*	Creates a container for a group of *command* elements	*li*, flow	type, label

TABLE ELEMENTS

Element	Description	Content Model	Attributes
table	Creates a two-dimensional data structure with rows and columns	*caption, colgroup tr, thead, tbody, tfoot*	cellspacing, cellpadding, border, width
tr	Contains a row of table cell elements	*th, td*	
th	Represents a table cell containing heading content	phrasing	width, height, colspan, rowspan
td	Represents a table cell containing data content	flow	width, height, colspan, rowspan
caption	Represents the caption or title of its parent table	flow	
colgroup	Creates a group of one or more table columns	*col*	span
col	Represents one or more columns in a *colgroup* element	empty	span
tbody	Represents a continuous group of table rows containing the body of data in a table	*tr*	
thead	Represents a continuous group of table rows appearing before the table's body element	*tr (th)*	
tfoot	Represents a continuous group of table rows appearing after the table's body element	*tr*	

FORM AND CONTROL ELEMENTS

Element	Description	Content Model	Attributes
form	Creates an area of the page containing fields for user input, grouping those fields for processing	flow	action, method, enctype
fieldset	Marks a section of a form with an optional caption	flow, *legend*	form, disabled
legend	Represents a caption for its containing *fieldset* element	phrasing	
label	Represents a label for a user *input* element or control	phrasing	form, for
input	Creates a user input field in a *form* element	empty	type, value, disabled, size, required, hidden. list
button	Creates a clickable button	phrasing	type, value, disabled
select	Creates either a drop menu for a single option choice or a scrolling, multiple-choice menu	*option*	multiple, size, disabled
option	Provides one choice of its parent *select* element	text	label, value, disabled, selected
optgroup	Groups *option* elements with a common label	*option*	
textarea	Provides a multiline text input field	text	rows, cols, required, disabled, readonly
datalist*	Provides for setting defaults for other *input* elements	*option*	

Element	Description	Content Model	Attributes
keygen*	Marks an RSA encryption key pair	empty	keytype, challenge, disabled
output*	Marks the output of a calculation in a form	phrasing	for, form, name
progress*	Creates a widget that displays the progress of a task or process	phrasing	value, max, form
meter*	Creates a widget that displays a value within a known range	phrasing	value, min, max, low, high, optimum

Legacy Elements

Element	Description	Content Model	Attributes
big	Indicates text that should be rendered bigger than normal text	phrasing	
font	Provides typographic styles	flow	face, size, color
blink	Animates content, making it appear and disappear	phrasing	
center	Centers the content within the containing element	flow	
frameset	Groups a set of window frames, each containing a separate document	*frame*	
frame	Defines a document window that is part of a browser frameset	empty	src, rows, cols
noframes	Provides an alternative document definition for user agents that do not recognize framesets	body content	

continues

LEGACY ELEMENTS *(continued)*

Element	Description	Content Model	Attributes
applet	Provides a container for the execution of a Java applet	flow	code, codebase, width, height
dir	Marks a directory listing	*li*	
strike	Marks text that has been deleted	text, phrasing	

APPENDIX B:
CSS PROPERTIES

The tables in this appendix summarize the CSS properties that can be used to style HTML elements. For each CSS property, the possible values it can be assigned, the default or initial values given to applicable elements, and whether the property's value is inherited by child elements are shown. The tables are separated to indicate groups of complementary properties.

A default value of "ua-dependent" indicates that the value depends on the user agent or browser.

An asterisk (*) next to the property's name indicates that it is a new CSS3 property and may not be supported on all browsers.

EXPLANATION OF VALUES

Value Type	Description
<angle>	A positive or negative *number* between 0 and 360, immediately followed by deg or rad
<color>	A color *name* or *#xxx* or *#xxxxxx* or rgb(*n*, *n*, *n*), where *x* is a hexadecimal digit (0 to 9, a, b, c, d, e, f) and *n* is an *integer* between 0 and 255 or a *percentage*
<integer>	A *number*, without a decimal fraction, including 0, possibly negative

continues

EXPLANATION OF VALUES *(continued)*

Value Type	Description
<length>	A *percentage* or a *number* followed by one of px, em, en, pt, in, mm, cm
<name>	An alphanumeric *string* representing a known object
<number>	A real number, possibly negative, with or without a decimal fraction
<percentage>	A *number* between 0 and 100 followed immediately by the percent sign (%)
<position>	A pair of *numbers* indicating x- and y-coordinates
<rational>	A *number* between 0 and 1
<rectangle>	A pair of *positions* indicating the upper-left and lower-right corners of a rectangle
<string>	A character string, possibly empty
<time>	A *number* immediately followed by s (seconds) or ms (milliseconds)
<url>	*url* followed by a *string* that represents a valid URL in parentheses, such as url(*string*)

CSS PROPERTIES

Property	Values	Default	Inherited
alignment-adjust*	auto | baseline | before-edge | text-before-edge | middle | central | after-edge | text-after-edge | ideographic | alphabetic | hanging | mathematical | <percentage> | <length>	auto	no

Property	Values	Default	Inherited
alignment-baseline*	baseline | use-script | before-edge | text-before-edge | after-edge | text-after-edge | central | middle | ideographic | alphabetic | hanging | mathematical	baseline	no

Property	Values	Default	Inherited
animation*	animation shorthand notation		no
animation-delay*	<time>	0	no
animation-direction*	normal | alternate	normal	no
animation-duration*	<time>	0	no
animation-iteration-count*	infinite | <integer>	1	no
animation-name*	none | IDENT	none	no
animation-play-state*	running | paused	running	no
animation-timing-function*	ease | linear | ease-in | ease-out | ease-in-out | cubic-bezier	ease	no

Property	Values	Default	Inherited
appearance*	normal | <element-name> | inherit	normal	no

Property	Values	Default	Inherited
background	background shorthand notation		no

continues

CSS PROPERTIES *(continued)*

Property	Values	Default	Inherited
background-attachment	scroll | fixed | local	scroll	no
background-break	bounding-box | each-box | continuous	continuous	no
background-clip*	border-box | padding-box	border-box	no
background-color	<color>	transparent	no
background-image	<url> | none	none	no
background-origin*	border-box | padding-box | content-box	padding-box	no
background-position	<percentage> | <length> | left | center | right | top | bottom	0% 0%	no
background-repeat	repeat | repeat-x | repeat-y | no-repeat | space | round	repeat	no
background-size*	<length> | <percentage> | auto	auto	no

Property	Values	Default	Inherited
baseline-shift*	baseline | sub | super | <length> | <percentage>	baseline	no

Property	Values	Default	Inherited
binding*	none | <url>	none	no

Property	Values	Default	Inherited
bookmark-label*	content | <name> | <string>	content	no
bookmark-level*	none | <integer>	none	no
bookmark-target*	self | <url> | <name>	self	no

Property	Values	Default	Inherited
border	border shorthand notation		no
border-bottom	border-bottom shorthand notation		no
border-bottom-color	\<color\>	current *color*	no
border-bottom-left-radius*	\<length\> | \<percentage\>	0	no
border-bottom-right-radius*	\<length\> | \<percentage\>	0	no
border-bottom-style	none | hidden | dotted | dashed | solid | double | groove | ridge | inset | outset	none	no
border-bottom-width	\<length\> | thin | medium | thick	medium	no
border-collapse	collapse | separate | inherit	separate	no
border-color	border-color shorthand notation		no
border-image*	\<url\> | none	none	no
border-left	border-left shorthand notation		no
border-left-color	\<color\>	current *color*	no
border-left-style	none | hidden | dotted | dashed | solid | double | groove | ridge | inset | outset	none	no
border-left-width	\<length\> | thin | medium | thick	medium	no
border-length*	\<length\> | \<percentage\>	auto	no
border-radius*	\<length\> | \<percentage\>	0	no

continues

CSS PROPERTIES *(continued)*

Property	Values	Default	Inherited
border-right	border-right shorthand notation		no
border-right-color	<color>	current *color*	no
border-right-style	none | hidden | dotted | dashed | solid | double | groove | ridge | inset | outset	none	no
border-right-width	<length> | thin | medium | thick	medium	no
border-spacing	<length> | inherit	0	no
border-style	border-style shorthand notation		no
border-top	border-top shorthand notation		no
border-top-color	<color>	current *color*	no
border-top-left-radius*	<length> | <percentage>	0	no
border-top-right-radius*	<length> | <percentage>	0	no
border-top-style	none | hidden | dotted | dashed | solid | double | groove | ridge | inset | outset	none	no
border-top-width	<length> | thin | medium | thick	medium	no
border-width	border-width shorthand notation		no

Property	Values	Default	Inherited
bottom	\<length> | \<percentage> | auto | inherit	auto	no

Property	Values	Default	Inherited
box-align*	start | end | center | baseline | stretch	stretch	no
box-direction*	normal | reverse | inherit	normal	no
box-flex*	\<integer>	0.0	no
box-flex-group*	\<integer>	1	no
box-lines*	single | multiple	single	no
box-ordinal-group*	\<integer>	1	no
box-orient*	horizontal | vertical | inline-axis | block-axis | inherit	inline-axis	no
box-pack*	start | end | center | justify	start	no
box-sizing*	content-box | border-box | inherit	content-box	no

Property	Values	Default	Inherited
caption-side	top | bottom | inherit	top	yes

Property	Values	Default	Inherited
clear	none | left | right | both	none	no

Property	Values	Default	Inherited
clip	auto | inherit | \<rectangle>	auto	no

continues

CSS Properties *(continued)*

Property	Values	Default	Inherited
color	<color> | inherit | transparent	ua-dependent	yes
color-profile*	auto | sRGB | <name> | <url> | inherit	auto	yes

Property	Values	Default	Inherited
columns*	column shorthand notation		no
column-break-after*	auto | always | avoid | left | right | page | column | avoid-page | avoid-column	auto	no
column-break-before*	auto | always | avoid | left | right | page | column | avoid-page | avoid-column	auto	no
column-count*	<integer> | auto	auto	no
column-fill*	auto | balance	balance	no
column-gap*	<length> | normal	normal	no
column-rule*	column-rule shorthand notation		no
column-rule-color*	<color> | transparent	current *color*	no
column-rule-style*	none | hidden | dotted | dashed | solid | double | groove | ridge | inset | outset	medium	no
column-rule-width*	<length> | thin | medium | thick	medium	no
column-span*	1 | all	1	no
column-width*	<length> | auto	auto	no

Property	Values	Default	Inherited
content	<url> | normal | none | inhibit | <string>	normal	no

Property	Values	Default	Inherited
counter-increment	<identifier> | <integer> | none	none	no
counter-reset	<identifier> | <integer> | none	none	no

Property	Values	Default	Inherited
crop*	<rectangle> | auto	auto	no

Property	Values	Default	Inherited
cursor	<url> | <position> | auto | default | none | context-menu | help | pointer | progress | wait | cell | crosshair | text | vertical-text | alias | copy | move | no-drop | not-allowed | e-resize | n-resize | ne-resize | nw-resize | s-resize | se-resize | sw-resize | w-resize | ew-resize | ns-resize | nesw-resize | nwse-resize | col-resize | row-resize | all-scroll | inherit	auto	yes

Property	Values	Default	Inherited
direction	ltr | rtl | inherit	ltr	yes

continues

CSS PROPERTIES *(continued)*

Property	Values	Default	Inherited
display	inline | block | inline-block | list-item | run-in | compact | table | inline-table | table-row-group | table-header-group | table-footer-group | table-row | table-column-group | table-column | table-cell | table-caption | ruby | ruby-base | ruby-text | ruby-base-group | ruby-text-group | *<name>* | none	inline	no

Property	Values	Default	Inherited
dominant-baseline*	auto | use-script | no-change | reset-size | alphabetic | hanging | ideographic | mathematical | central | middle | text-after-edge | text-before-edge	auto	no

Property	Values	Default	Inherited
drop-initial-after-adjust*	central | middle | after-edge | text-after-edge | ideographic | alphabetic | mathematical | <length> | <percentage>	text-after-edge	no

Property	Values	Default	Inherited
drop-initial-after-align*	baseline | use-script | before-edge | text-before-edge | after-edge | text-after-edge | central | middle | ideographic | alphabetic | hanging | mathematical	baseline	no
drop-initial-before-adjust*	central | middle | after-edge | text-after-edge | ideographic | alphabetic | mathematical | <length> | <percentage>	text-before-edge	no
drop-initial-before-align*	baseline | use-script | before-edge | text-before-edge | after-edge | text-after-edge | central | middle | ideographic | alphabetic | hanging | mathematical | caps-height	caps-height	no
drop-initial-size*	auto | <integer> | <length> | <percentage>	auto	no
drop-initial-value*	initial | <integer>	initial	no

Property	Values	Default	Inherited
empty-cells	show | hide | inherit	show	yes

Property	Values	Default	Inherited
fit*	fill | hidden | meet | slice	fill	yes
fit-position*	<percentage> | <length> | top | center | bottom | left | center | right | auto	0% 0%	yes

continues

CSS PROPERTIES *(continued)*

Property	Values	Default	Inherited
float	left | right | none	none	no
float-offset*	<length><length>	0 0	no

Property	Values	Default	Inherited
font	font shorthand notation		yes
font-effect*	emboss | engrave | none | outline | inherit	none	yes
font-emphasize-position*	before | after | inherit	before	yes
font-emphasize-style*	accent | dot | circle | disc | none | inherit	none	yes
font-family	<family-name> | <generic-name> | inherit	ua-dependent	yes
font-size	xx-small | x-small | small | medium | large | x-large | xx-large | larger | smaller | <length> | <percentage> | inherit	medium	yes
font-size-adjust*	<integer> | none | inherit	none	yes
font-smooth*	auto | never | always | <length> | inherit	auto	yes
font-stretch*	normal | wider | narrower | ultra-condensed | extra-condensed | condensed | semi-condensed | semi-expanded | expanded | extra-expanded | ultra-expanded | inherit	normal	yes
font-style	normal | italic | oblique | inherit	normal	yes

Property	Values	Default	Inherited
font-variant	normal | small-caps | inherit	normal	yes
font-weight	normal | bold | bolder | lighter | 100 | 200 | 300 | 400 | 500 | 600 | 700 | 800 | 900 | inherit	normal	yes

Property	Values	Default	Inherited
grid-columns*	\<length> | \<percentage>	none	no
grid-rows*	\<length> | \<percentage>	none	no

Property	Values	Default	Inherited
hanging-punctuation*	none | start | end | end-edge	none	yes

Property	Values	Default	Inherited
height	\<length> | \<percentage> | auto	auto	no

Property	Values	Default	Inherited
hyphenate-after*	\<integer> | auto	auto	yes
hyphenate-before*	\<integer> | auto	auto	yes
hyphenate-character*	\<string> | auto	auto	yes
hyphenate-lines*	\<integer> | no-limit	no-limit	yes
hyphenate-resource*	none | \<url>	none	yes
hyphens*	none | manual | auto	manual	yes

continues

CSS PROPERTIES *(continued)*

Property	Values	Default	Inherited
icon*	<url> | auto	auto	no

Property	Values	Default	Inherited
image-orientation*	<angle> | auto	auto	N/A
image-resolution*	<integer> | normal | auto	normal	yes

Property	Values	Default	Inherited
inline-box-align*	initial | last | <integer>	last	no

Property	Values	Default	Inherited
left	<length> | <percentage> | auto | inherit	auto	no

Property	Values	Default	Inherited
letter-spacing	<length> | inherit	normal	yes

Property	Values	Default	Inherited
line-height	normal | <integer> | <length> | <percentage> | inherit	normal	yes

Property	Values	Default	Inherited
line-stacking*	line-stacking shorthand notation		yes
line-stacking-ruby*	exclude-ruby | include-ruby	exclude-ruby	yes
line-stacking-shift*	consider-shifts | disregard-shifts	consider-shifts	yes

Property	Values	Default	Inherited
line-stacking-strategy*	inline-line-height | block-line-height | max-height | grid-height	line-height	yes

Property	Values	Default	Inherited
list-style	list-style shorthand notation		yes
list-style-image	<url> | none | inherit	none	yes
list-style-position	inside | outside | inherit	outside	yes
list-style-type	disc | circle | square | decimal | decimal-leading-zero | lower-roman | upper-roman | lower-greek | lower-latin | upper-latin | armenian | georgian | lower-alpha | upper-alpha | none | inherit	disc	yes

Property	Values	Default	Inherited
margin	margin shorthand notation	0	no
margin-bottom	<length> | inherit | auto	0	no
margin-left	<length> | inherit | auto	0	no
margin-right	<length> | inherit | auto	0	no
margin-top	<length> | inherit | auto	0	no

Property	Values	Default	Inherited
marquee-direction*	forward | reverse | inherit	forward	yes
marquee-play-count*	<integer> | infinite | inherit	1	no

continues

CSS PROPERTIES *(continued)*

Property	Values	Default	Inherited
marquee-speed*	slow | normal | fast | inherit	normal	no
marquee-style*	scroll | slide | alternate | inherit	scroll	no

Property	Values	Default	Inherited
max-height	\<length> | \<percentage> | inherit | none	none	no
max-width	\<length> | \<percentage> | inherit	none	no
min-height	\<length> | \<percentage> | inherit | none	0	no
min-width	\<length> | \<percentage> | inherit	0	no

Property	Values	Default	Inherited
nav-down*	auto | \<id> | current | root | \<string> | inherit	auto	no
nav-index*	auto | \<integer> | inherit	auto	no
nav-left*	auto | \<id> | current | root | \<string> | inherit	auto	no
nav-right*	auto | \<id> | current | root | \<string> | inherit	auto	no
nav-up*	auto | \<id> | current | root | \<string> | inherit	auto	no

Property	Values	Default	Inherited
opacity*	<rational> | inherit	1	no

Property	Values	Default	Inherited
orphans	<integer> | inherit	2	yes

Property	Values	Default	Inherited
outline	outline shorthand notation		no
outline-color	<color> | invert | inherit	invert	no
outline-offset <length> | inherit		0	
outline-style	none | hidden | dotted | dashed | solid | double | groove | ridge | inset | outset	none	no
outline-width	<length> | thin | medium | thick	medium	no

Property	Values	Default	Inherited
overflow	visible | hidden | scroll | auto | no-display | no-content	visible	no
overflow-style*	auto | scrollbar | panner | move | marquee	auto	yes
overflow-x*	visible | hidden | scroll | auto | no-display | no-content	visible	no
overflow-y*	visible | hidden | scroll | auto | no-display | no-content	visible	no

continues

CSS PROPERTIES *(continued)*

Property	Values	Default	Inherited
padding	padding shorthand notation	0	no
padding-bottom	<length> | inherit	0	no
padding-left	<length> | inherit	0	no
padding-right	<length> | inherit	0	no
padding-top	<length> | inherit	0	no

Property	Values	Default	Inherited
page	page shorthand notation	auto	no
page-break-after	auto | always | avoid | left | right | inherit	auto	no
page-break-before	auto | always | avoid | left | right | inherit	auto	no
page-break-inside	avoid | auto | inherit	auto	no
page-policy*	start | first | last	start	no

Property	Values	Default	Inherited
position	static | relative | absolute | fixed | inherit	static	no

Property	Values	Default	Inherited
punctuation-trim*	none | start | end | adjacent	none	yes

Property	Values	Default	Inherited
quotes	<string> <string> | none | inherit	ua-dependent	yes

Property	Values	Default	Inherited
resize*	none | both | horizontal | vertical | inherit	none	no

Property	Values	Default	Inherited
right	<length> | <percentage> | auto | inherit	auto	no

Property	Values	Default	Inherited
rotation*	<angle> | inherit	0	no
rotation-point*	<position>	50% 50%	no

Property	Values	Default	Inherited
size*	auto | <length><length> | page-size | portrait | landscape	auto	N/A

Property	Values	Default	Inherited
table-layout	auto | fixed | inherit	auto	no

Property	Values	Default	Inherited
target*	target shorthand notation		no
target-name*	current | root | parent | new | modal | <string> | inherit	current	no
target-new*	window | tab | none	window	N/A
target-position*	above | behind | front | back	above	no

continues

CSS PROPERTIES *(continued)*

Property	Values	Default	Inherited
text-align	left | right | center | justify | inherit	left	yes
text-decoration	none | underline | overline | line-through | blink | inherit	none	no
text-emphasis*	none | accent | dot | circle | disc | before | after | inherit	none	yes
text-height*	auto | font-size | text-size | max-size | inherit	auto	yes
text-indent	<length> | <percentage> | hanging	0	yes
text-justify*	auto | inter-word | inter-ideograph | inter-cluster | distribute | kashida | tibetan | inherit	auto	yes
text-outline*	<color> <length> | none	none	yes
text-replace*	<string> | inherit | none	none	yes
text-shadow	<color> <length> | none	none	yes
text-transform	capitalize | uppercase | lowercase | none | inherit	none	yes
text-wrap*	normal | unrestricted | none | suppress	normal	yes

Property	Values	Default	Inherited
top	<length> | <percentage> | auto | inherit	auto	no

Property	Values	Default	Inherited
unicode-bidi	normal | embed | bidi-override | inherit	normal	no

Property	Values	Default	Inherited
vertical-align	<length> | <percentage> | baseline | sub | super | top | text-top | middle | bottom | text-bottom | inherit	baseline	no

Property	Values	Default	Inherited
visibility	visible | hidden | collapse | inherit	visible	yes

Property	Values	Default	Inherited
white-space	normal | nowrap | pre | pre-line | pre-wrap | inherit	normal	yes
white-space-collapse*	preserve | collapse | preserve-breaks | discard	collapse	yes

Property	Values	Default	Inherited
widows	<integer> | inherit	2	yes

Property	Values	Default	Inherited
width	<length> | <percentage> | auto	auto	no

continues

CSS PROPERTIES *(continued)*

Property	Values	Default	Inherited
word-break*	normal | keep-all | loose | break-strict | break-all	normal	yes
word-spacing	normal | <length> | inherit	normal	yes
word-wrap*	normal | break-word | inherit	normal	yes

Property	Values	Default	Inherited
z-index	<integer> | auto | inherit	auto	no

AURAL PROPERTIES

Property	Values	Default	Inherited
cue	cue shorthand notation		no
cue-after	<url> | <integer> | <percentage> | silent | x-soft | soft | medium | loud | x-loud | none | inherit	none	no
cue-before	<url> | <integer> | <percentage> | silent | x-soft | soft | medium | loud | x-loud | none | inherit	none	no

Property	Values	Default	Inherited
elevation	<angle> | below | level | above | higher | lower | inherit	level	yes

Property	Values	Default	Inherited
mark*	mark shorthand notation		no
mark-after*	<string> | inherit	none	no
mark-before*	<string> | inherit	none	no
marks	crop | cross | none | inherit	none	no

Property	Values	Default	Inherited
pause	<time> | <percentage> | inherit	0	no
pause-after	<time> | <percentage> | inherit	0	no
pause-before	<time> | <percentage> | inherit	0	no

Property	Values	Default	Inherited
pitch	<number> | <percentage> | x-low | low | medium | high | x-high | inherit	medium	yes
pitch-range	<number> | <percentage> | inherit	50	yes
play-during	<url> | mix | repeat | auto | none | inherit	auto	no

Property	Values	Default	Inherited
rest*	rest shorthand notation	user agent dependent	no
rest-after*	<time> | none | x-weak | weak | medium | strong | x-strong | inherit	ua-dependent	no
rest-before*	<time> | none | x-weak | weak | medium | strong | x-strong | inherit	ua-dependent	no

continues

Aural Properties *(continued)*

Property	Values	Default	Inherited
richness	<integer> | inherit	50	yes

Property	Values	Default	Inherited
speak	normal | none | spell-out | inherit	normal	yes
speak-header	once | always | inherit	once	yes
speak-numeral	digits | continuous | inherit	continuous	yes
speak-punctuation	code | none | inherit	none	yes
speak-rate	<integer> | x-slow | slow | medium | fast | x-fast | faster | slower | inherit	medium	yes
stress	<integer> | inherit	50	yes

Property	Values	Default	Inherited
voice-balance*	<integer> | left | right | center | leftwards | rightwards | inherit	center	yes
voice-duration*	<time>	ua-dependent	no
voice-family	<name> | male | female | child | inherit	ua-dependent	yes
voice-pitch*	<integer> | <percentage> | x-low | low | high | x-high | inherit	medium	yes
voice-pitch-range*	<integer> | <percentage> | x-low | low | high | x-high | inherit	ua-dependent	yes
voice-rate*	<percentage> | x-slow | slow | medium | fast | x-fast | inherit	ua-dependent	yes

Property	Values	Default	Inherited
voice-stress[*]	strong | moderate | none | reduced | inherit	moderate	yes
voice-volume[*]	<integer> | <percentage> | silent | x-soft | soft | medium | loud | x-loud | inherit	medium	yes
volume	<integer> | <percentage> | silent | x-soft | soft | medium | loud | x-loud | inherit	medium	yes

INDEX

Symbols

$ (dollar sign), 235
~ character
 entity, 36
& (ampersand), 28, 36, 88,
 103
<> (angle brackets), 28, 37
* (asterisk), 119
: (colon), 117, 124
-- (double dash), 35
../ (double-dot)
 shorthand, 87
= (equals sign), 38, 123
! (exclamation point), 118
% (percent sign), 103
+ (plus sign), 103, 123
# (pound sign), 36
? (question mark), 88
; (semicolon), 28, 117
/ (slash), 28, 37
~ (tilde), 36

A

<a> element, 50, 85-86,
 88-90
<abbr> element, 48, 271
absolute positioning, 167
accesskey attribute, 52
accordion lists, 239-240
action attribute (<form>
 element), 100
actions, assigning to
 buttons, 231
<address> element,
 61-67, 269
address blocks, 61-67
<a> element, 271
AJAX (Asynchronous
 JavaScript and
 XML), 16
align attribute, 53
 <image> element, 93
 <table> tag, 80

alignment
 tables, 81-82
 vertical alignment,
  150-152
alternate descriptions, 259
America Online (AOL), 10
& character entity, 37
ampersand (&), 28, 36, 88,
 103
anchors, 50, 85-90
Andreessen, Marc, 7
angle brackets (<>), 28, 37
AOL (America
 Online), 10
Apache, 14
Apple Safari, 183-184
<applet> element, 278
<area> element, 85, 274
Arena, 8
Arial, 129
Arial Black, 129
<article> element, 74, 269

FREE Online Edition

Your purchase of *HTML Manual of Style* includes access to a free online edition for 45 days through the Safari Books Online subscription service. Nearly every Addison-Wesley Professional book is available online through Safari Books Online, along with more than 5,000 other technical books and videos from publishers such as Cisco Press, Exam Cram, IBM Press, O'Reilly, Prentice Hall, Que, and Sams.

SAFARI BOOKS ONLINE allows you to search for a specific answer, cut and paste code, download chapters, and stay current with emerging technologies.

Activate your FREE Online Edition at www.informit.com/safarifree

> **STEP 1:** Enter the coupon code: UUPDKFH.

> **STEP 2:** New Safari users, complete the brief registration form.
> Safari subscribers, just log in.

If you have difficulty registering on Safari or accessing the online edition, please e-mail customer-service@safaribooksonline.com